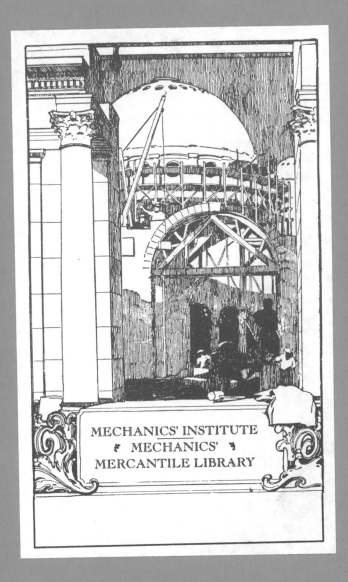

Middle East Illusions

Middle East Illusions

Including *Peace in the Middle East?*
Reflections on Justice and Nationhood

Noam Chomsky

ROWMAN & LITTLEFIELD PUBLISHERS, INC.
Lanham • Boulder • New York • Oxford

ROWMAN & LITTLEFIELD PUBLISHERS, INC.

Published in the United States of America
by Rowman & Littlefield Publishers, Inc.
A Member of the Rowman & Littlefield Publishing Group
4501 Forbes Boulevard, Suite 200, Lanham, Maryland 20706
www.rowmanlittlefield.com

PO Box 317
Oxford
OX2 9RU, UK

Distributed by National Book Network

British Library Cataloguing in Publication Information Available

Library of Congress Cataloging-in-Publication Data

Chomsky, Noam.
  Middle East illusions : including peace in the Middle East?
reflections on justice and nationhood / Noam
Chomsky.
     p. cm.
Includes bibliographical references and index.
  ISBN 0-7425-2699-2
1. Arab-Israeli conflict—1993—Peace. 2. Nationalism—Palestine.
3. Al-Aqsa Intifada, 2000-. 4. United States—Relations—Israel. 5.
Israel—Relations—United States. I. Title.
  DS119.76.C49 2003
  956.04—dc21

                              2002155349

Printed in the United States of America

 ∞™ The paper used in this publication meets the minimum requirements of
American National Standard for Information Sciences—Permanence of Paper for
Printed Library Materials, ANSI/NISO Z39.48-1992.

Contents

Part III: After 9/11: The "War on Terror" Redeclared

Preface

The material that follows focuses primarily on the Israel–Palestine conflict and the crucial U.S. role as it has evolved in the past thirty-five years. The chapters fall into distinct categories. The first five date from the early period, 1968–73, and were originally published in a 1974 book entitled *Peace in the Middle East? Reflections on Justice and Nationhood*. Chapters 6–9 consider similar topics thirty years later, 1997–2002. These chapters look back on what has happened in the intervening years and consider prospects that may lie ahead.

Chapter 5, unlike the others, is concerned not with the Israel–Palestine conflict itself but with its refraction in ideological warfare within the United States. Popular and activist movements of the 1960s aroused great concerns among political, economic, and intellectual elites, which manifested themselves in many ways: among them were warnings of an "excess of democracy" as normally passive sectors of the population were no longer willing to relinquish political and ideological arenas to elites,[1] and efforts by intellectuals to restore a measure of conformity by defaming and discrediting political enemies they blamed for the breakdown of obedience. Chapter 5 reviews some of the ways in which the overwhelming support for Israel after the 1967 war was exploited for such ends, in not particularly attractive ways. There are striking counterparts today in the efforts of those who call themselves "the decent left" to discredit a "radical left" that they despise and fear—and that they largely invent in quite remarkable ways, much as in the earlier stage discussed in chapter 5.[2]

The first nine essays of the book predate the terrorist attacks of 9/11, a date so significant in contemporary history that no further specification need be given. Immediately following the attacks, it was widely assumed that those atrocities, which may have had a greater instant toll than any comparable ones in history, would have far-reaching consequences. That was a reasonable expectation. The target in this case was not Cuba, or Haiti, or Nicaragua, or Lebanon, or Chechnya, or one of the other traditional victims of large-scale state terror extending back over many centuries, but a country of unprecedented power to shape the future. The choices made by its leaders, and tolerated by its citizenry, are sure to have a major impact on what lies ahead, including the travail of the Middle East with its intricate problems and complex strands and roots. It was predictable, and at once predicted, that states everywhere would seize upon 9/11 as a window of opportunity to increase repression and violence in the name of "fighting terror," with the authorization of the reigning superpower. The expectations were quickly fulfilled by Russia in Chechnya, China in its western provinces, Indonesia in Aceh, Israel in the occupied territories, and elsewhere. As also anticipated, states used the opportunity to adopt measures to discipline their own populations, ranging from the dictatorships of Central Asia to more free and democratic societies— sometimes on plausible grounds, often not. The U.S. administration took a stand so extreme as to cause serious rifts even with close allies.[3]

It is not only in the Arab and Muslim worlds that Washington's arrogance and adventurism are regarded as "a menace to itself and to mankind."[4] The desperate drive for war against Iraq, ignoring warnings of possible consequences that could be severe, has only heightened such concerns. There is no historical precedent for such massive popular opposition to a war worldwide even before it is launched. In the United States, one can be misled by poll results, which do not take into account a crucial factor that distinguishes American society from most of the rest of the world: it can hardly escape notice that while Saddam Hussein may be almost universally reviled, it is only in the United States, deluged with propaganda and historically a society immersed in fear, that many people genuinely believe that if we don't stop him today he will kill us tomorrow. The contingency is so remote, except for revenge or deterrence, that CIA and RAND Corporation analysts probably rank it very low among potential threats to be countered. If this unique factor is extricated, attitudes in the United States may well be similar to those in other countries, and even without this necessary corrective, popular opposition to the war is far beyond any comparable case and extends very broadly across the spectrum of opinion.[5]

The final essay, chapter 10, briefly looks into some of the questions raised by the "war on terror" redeclared on September 11 by those in power in Washington today, mostly recycled from the Reagan–Bush I administrations, and following a script that is very familiar to them.

The basic issues discussed in the first four essays remain unresolved and, in my opinion at least, not yet properly addressed. What constituted warnings in the earlier essays now stand all too often as grim reality. For both of the contending national groups, Israeli Jews and Palestinian Arabs, the current circumstances may be the most painful and ominous since the foundation of the State of Israel and the catastrophe suffered by the Palestinians (the *Naqba*) in the aftermath of World War II. Apart from causing death, destruction, and misery throughout the region, the conflict has several times brought the world dangerously close to devastating international conflict. And there is every reason to expect that the same will be true in the future if policies continue on their present course.

The U.S. role remains decisive, as it has been throughout this period. The conventional view holds that Washington has been seeking peace, attempting to resolve contending nationalist demands. That is not false but, rather, virtually meaningless. Everyone seeks peace. The question is: On what terms?

Hussein Agha and Robert Malley (a senior Clinton adminis-tration official concerned with the "peace process") write that "the outlines of a solution have basically been understood for some time now." The basic principle is territorial division on the internationally recognized (pre–June 1967) border, modified so that "Israel would annex a minimal amount of land in the West Bank and in return provide Palestine with the equivalent amount of land from Israel proper."[6] I think their judgment is correct; it has indeed "been understood for some time now" that these are the general contours of a political settlement, if there is to be one. But more should be added.

For twenty-five years, there has been[7] a very broad interna-tional consensus that adopts pretty much the terms that Agha and Malley outline. It modified an earlier consensus expressed in UN Security Council Resolution 242 of November 1967, adopted on U.S. initiative. Official U.S. policy accepted the ba-sic principle of UN 242 that acquisition of territory by force is il-legitimate, and that the territorial settlement should therefore be on the internationally recognized pre–June 1967 borders, with at most "minor and mutual adjustments." At the time, there was no provision for Palestinian rights. We should therefore describe the consensus as strictly *rejectionist*, if we depart from convention and use the term "rejectionist" in a nonracist sense: as applying not solely to those who deny the national rights of Jews but also to those who deny those rights to the indigenous population that was displaced by the Jewish settlers—and in ugly ways, facts that can no longer be denied, as they were through many years of vul-gar propaganda.

The international consensus shifted in the mid-1970s, adopt-ing a nonrejectionist stand for the first time and calling for a Palestinian state in the territories that Israel conquered in 1967—again, with minor and mutual adjustments. The United States, however, retained the rejectionist stand of earlier years, now in virtual international isolation. That has remained true to the present. The "Oslo process" was rejectionist throughout, in-cluding the Camp David 2000 proposals; that is clear as soon as one looks at the projected maps. It should also be understood that when George Bush and Colin Powell now proclaim their "vision" of a Palestinian state—somewhere, some time, with unknown characteristics—they are approaching the level of South Africa forty years ago. And approaching that level from below; the leaders of apartheid South Africa not only had a "vision" of black-run states but went on to establish them, and the "homelands" (Bantustans) they established compare rather favorably with any "vision" that has yet been articulated by authorities in Washington or Israel.

The "minor adjustments" in territorial boundaries have been forcefully and extensively altered over the years by the steady and carefully planned expansion of Israeli settlement in the occupied territories carried out with the critical military, diplomatic, and financial support of the United States. That process continued without change right to the end of the Clinton administration, reaching new heights in the final Clinton–Barak year, and has accelerated since. Agha and Malley write that "the way to get [to the agreed consensus that they describe] has eluded all sides from the start." That is not false, but it leaves out the central reason: Washington has consistently opposed a political settlement on these terms, ever since it vetoed a similar proposal at the UN Security Council in January 1976. That rejectionist stand persisted through the Camp David negotiations and has been intensified since. By now Washington has gone so far as to break with the international consensus even on the crucial issue of the status of Jerusalem. In December 2002, for the first time, Washington voted at the General Assembly in support of Israel's annexation of Jerusalem.[8]

"Jerusalem," furthermore, is an ambiguous and expanding concept; it now includes a significant part of the West Bank, and in the U.S.-backed Israeli interpretation, virtually splits it in two.[9]

A corrected version of the Agha and Malley analysis would be, then, that the outlines of a solution have been understood for a quarter of a century, but "the way to get to it" has been "elusive" because of persistent U.S. opposition. There is good reason to suppose that the relevant Arab states and the Palestinians would accept it (as they did, in much the same form, twenty-five years ago[10]). But the United States continues to back Israel's refusal of a political settlement in these terms. That stance continued through the Clinton years, despite some steps toward accommodation, and has become considerably more extreme since.

The problem, then, is not merely procedural, as Agha and Malley argue but, rather, substantive: until U.S. policy changes, there will be no progress toward the international consensus that has indeed long been understood.

It should be added that the population of the United States, though very poorly informed, has generally agreed with the international consensus (see chapter 9). But on this as on many other matters of considerable significance, policy and public opinion are sharply different.

My opinion in the early years was—and remains—that Israel made a fateful error in rejecting peace in 1971 in favor of expansion, hence confrontation and increasing dependence on the United States. I also continue to believe that during those years, Israel had opportunities to pursue paths far more favorable to all concerned than the two-state settlement that became the international consensus from the mid-1970s—arguably the least bad of the realistic possibilities, at least for the short term. Some reasons are discussed in the early essays that follow. I think they retain their essential validity, even though prospects become more remote as the predictable cycle of violence escalates to the kind of "tribal warfare" that astute observers now perceive and that may drive both societies to destruction.

There are many historical examples of termination and reversal of such processes. Northern Ireland is a recent example; though no utopia and having plenty of difficulties ahead, it is vastly improved over what it was a decade ago. South Africa is another case. Only a few years ago, racial conflict and violent repression seemed to be driving the society to hopeless despair, and while the problems that remain are daunting, they can be approached from a far higher plane than even the more optimistic would have supposed in the very recent past. A much more far-reaching case is Europe. For centuries, Europeans were dedicated to mutual slaughter, on a colossal scale. That ended in 1945, when it came to be understood on all sides that the next time the game is played it will be the last.

In Israel–Palestine, each day's wrenching horror adds new boulders to the walls of hatred, fear, and consuming desire for revenge. But it is never too late to breach those walls. Only the people who suffer the daily pain and anticipate worse tomorrow can seriously undertake this task, but those outside can help substantially to ease the way, though not until they are willing to face honestly their own roles and responsibilities.

Acknowledgments

The introduction and chapters 1–5 were originally published as *Peace in the Middle East? Reflections on Justice and Nationhood*, Pantheon Books, New York, 1974.

Chapter 6 is based on a talk given at Ben Gurion University, Be'er Sheva, Israel, June 8, 1997, at a conference marking thirty years of occupation of the territories conquered in the June 1967 war. First published in *Looking Back at the June 1967 War*, ed. Haim Gordon, Praeger, Westport, Ct., 1999, pp. 3–50.

Chapter 7 is based on the lecture "Prospects for Peace in the Middle East," presented as the First Annual Maryse Mikhail Lecture at the University of Toledo, March 4, 2001.

Chapter 8 originally appeared on ZNet (http://www.zmag.org), October 25, 2000.

An earlier version of chapter 9 was published in the UK under the title "Back in the USA" by *Red Pepper* magazine in May 2002 (http://www.redpepper.org.uk/).

Chapter 10 is based on an article titled "War on Terrorism" published in the Amnesty International quarterly journal *Amnesty Ireland*, issue no. 116, March 2002.

All chapters are reprinted with permission.

Middle East Illusions

Peace in the Middle East?
The 1967 War and the 1970s

Introduction

The struggle that will determine the fate of Israel and the Palestinians takes place simultaneously in three arenas: local, regional, and international. Locally, there is a conflict between two national groups, Israeli Jews and Palestinian Arabs, each claiming rights in a territory of ambiguous boundaries that each regards as its national homeland. Questions of justice and human rights arise primarily in the context of this local conflict. Since 1948, the local conflict has been transformed into a broader regional conflict between Israel and the Arab states, with the Palestinian people generally playing a passive role: victims more than agents. Finally, the region has enormous strategic and economic importance for the great industrial powers. Shortly after the Balfour declaration committing the British government to support the creation of a Jewish national homeland in Palestine, Lord Balfour stated: "I do not care under what system we keep the oil, but I am clear that it is all-important that this oil should be available." Twenty-five years later, Secretary of State Hull emphasized that "there should be full realization of the fact that the oil of Saudi Arabia constitutes one of the world's greatest prizes."[1] During and after World War II, the United States took over the dominant role in controlling these resources, displacing Great Britain, and their value for the industrial societies has never been greater than it is today. We may assume, with fair confidence, that the United States will make every effort to ensure that this great prize will be available, and to the extent possible, under the control of American oil companies.

It has always been clear that if the parties to the local conflict do not reach a stable and peaceful accommodation, then the superpowers will seek to impose a settlement in their own interests, a form of recolonization that only by the merest accident will satisfy the needs and interests of the people directly involved: Israeli Jews and Palestinian Arabs. There is good reason to believe that the primary objective of Egypt and Syria, when they launched the October 1973 attack into territories conquered by Israel in 1967, was to create conditions that would induce the United States to rethink its policies toward the region, and, in its own self-interest, impose a settlement along the lines of UN Security Council Resolution 242 (November 1967) as interpreted in most of the world—that is, with Israel returning to essentially its 1967 borders, a peace treaty among the states of the region, demilitarized zones separating potential combatants, and perhaps a Palestine state in parts of the West Bank and Gaza, subordinated to Jordan and Israel.

It has been suggested that the United States should undertake "the relatively minor adjustment we would be obliged to make in order to get along without Arab oil" and become self-sufficient in energy supplies, so that American policy for the region will be immune to any pressures from the Arab states.[2] Such proposals are virtually irrelevant to the formation of state policy. The problem is not merely access to Middle Eastern oil, but also the profits of major American corporations, not only the giant energy companies, but also others that are looking forward to vast investment opportunities in the Middle East. While the United States might reach self-sufficiency, Europe and Japan, for the foreseeable future, cannot. In one way or another, they will obtain access to the petroleum reserves of the Middle East, vast in quantity and lower in production cost than alternatives currently available. The result could be that U.S. industry, already barely competitive, would be priced out of world markets. The industrial systems of Europe and Japan, with independent resources of energy and raw materials, might surpass the United States in scale and productivity. It is hardly likely that the U.S. government will tolerate such prospects with equanimity.

If the Arab oil producers persist in some form of the current oil politics, then serious conflict is likely within the capitalist world system. The United States will insist on a "united front," which it can control. Its industrial competitors will continue to seek bilateral arrangements with the oil producers or perhaps will also move to coordinated efforts of their own. The real issues are clouded by rhetoric about "greed" and "cowardice." At the heart of the matter, however, are some quite substantial questions: Will the United States and U.S.–based multinational corporations continue to dominate the capitalist world system? Will the major oil companies be able to amass sufficient profits in the final period of petroleum-based energy to ensure their domination of the next phase (coal, nuclear energy)?

In the world of business and finance, there is now much concern that the European states and Japan are making "slow, but apparently inexorable, government inroads into the oil business," and that "national governments are even now beginning to negotiate direct deals with oil-producing countries."[3] "A rush of such deals is under way, with Japan, France, Britain, West Germany, and Italy either having signed, or still negotiating, the sale of arms, factories, and know-how to Iran and Arab states, in exchange for pledges of future oil," a bilateral approach that is "decried by Mr. Simon" (U.S. energy chief).[4] *Business Week* warns that "Americans may be left behind in the stampede for Arab business," quite apart from the "multibillion-dollar U.S. stake in oil," if there is "a backlash of Arab hostility towards the U.S."; "European and Japanese governments and private businessmen are practically falling over each other in a scramble to ingratiate themselves with Arab oil suppliers. . . ."[5] During the October 1973 war, Iraq awarded contracts totaling $260 million to European and Japanese groups, while continuing extensive American projects. It is feared that

European and Japanese competitors may be preferred to U.S. bidders for further development projects.[6] In Egypt and other Arab states, American corporations continued their projects and negotiations through the October 1973 crisis, but the issue remains in doubt throughout the Middle East and North Africa.

The basic issues have been raised with particular clarity in the context of U.S.–Japanese relations. After World War II, the United States permitted Japan to industrialize with few constraints, while maintaining fairly tight control over Japanese energy resources. Well aware of these facts and their implications, the Arab oil producers are offering special inducements to Japan to make bilateral arrangements for Middle East oil. The Saudi Arabian oil minister, Sheikh Ahmed Zaki Yamani, put the matter clearly on a visit to Japan:

> For the time being, the American oil companies are dominating about 70 percent of the oil industry in the whole world. Whether you have an interest in this as Japanese or you don't, this is your decision . . . You do need oil. Oil will be in scarcity very soon, in the coming few years, and therefore you can get much more than the others . . . bilaterally. . . . Now what you will have with us is oil as a quid pro quo for what you give— that's industry and technology.[7]

The Japanese Trade Ministry had already announced plans for extensive technical development projects in Libya, with the possibility of joint ventures in oil exploration. These steps raised

> the possibility of Japan's moving in, in partnership with the Arabs, to occupy the oil-development position long monopolized by the Western majors. Until now Japan has shied away from such a move for fear of offending both the Western majors and the U.S. government.[8]

As Sheikh Yamani pointed out further in Tokyo, there is an implied further cost in bilateral arrangements: "a less close relationship with the U.S.—and especially with the American oil companies."[9] The cost could be serious, not only to Japan, but to U.S.–based corporations and the American government.

The long-range significance of independent European and Japanese initiatives is potentially very great, and there is little doubt that the U.S. government will be concerned to forestall them. The major oil producers, Saudi Arabia and Iran in particular, would doubtless prefer to remain in the American orbit, and can be expected to be cooperative if certain conditions are met. In the case of Saudi Arabia, it is unclear just what these conditions are. King Faisal's pronouncements might be understood as implying a return of Jerusalem to Arab rule and a regional settlement along the lines of the UN resolution. But it is not yet clear what he intends, or how seriously, or whether the United States would be willing to accept such demands. It is, however, most unlikely that the United States will simply tell the Arabs to keep their oil, as Kennan and others recommend. Rather, the United States will move to guarantee its access to, and control over, "one of the world's greatest prizes," insofar as this is possible.

Suppose that the Arab producers persist in the demands they formulated during the October war. Under these conditions, the United States would have several policy options. The most extreme would be invasion, either direct or through a surrogate. This possibility has been discussed, not only on the lunatic fringe, and the Pentagon has been taking no pains to conceal its military exercises in desert regions. Leonard Silk, financial correspondent for the *New York Times*, reported shortly after the October war that Klaus Heiss, Klaus Knorr, and Oskar Morgenstern of Mathematica, Inc., a Princeton research firm, had issued a study done for the Office of Naval Research which expresses their view (Silk's paraphrase) "that the major oil-exporting countries would be vulnerable to military power," though it is "highly unlikely that the industrialized oil-importing states will marshal the will to be tough and to act in unison."[10] There has been no lack of exhortations that the West should marshal the necessary will.

Irving Kristol notes philosophically that "insignificant nations, like insignificant people, can quickly experience delusions of significance . . . smaller nations are not going to behave reasonably—with a decent respect for the interests of others, including the great powers—unless it is costly to them to behave unreasonably." It is our duty to enforce this lesson. "In truth, the days of 'gunboat diplomacy' are never over. . . . Gunboats are as necessary for international order as police cars are for domestic order." Because of "the legalistic-moralistic-'idealistic' mold into which American foreign policy was cast after World War II," we haven't been manning the gunboats as we should (witness our unwillingness to use force in Vietnam). But perhaps this moral flabbiness can be overcome and we can enforce standards of reasonableness on the insignificant nations.[11]

Walter Laqueur, putting it more obliquely, suggests that Middle East oil "could be internationalized, not on behalf of a few oil companies but for the benefit of the rest of mankind." Furthermore, "Egypt could be encouraged to take over the Libyan oilfields." "Internationalzation" is a polite term for invasion, but there should be no moral problem in this, since "all that is at stake is the fate of some desert sheikdoms." Laqueur goes on to suggest that "the internationalization of the Middle Eastern oil resources could be the major test for détente." That is to say, if the Russians do not support us in this humanitarian effort, it will prove that they are not serious about détente.[12] Laqueur's concern "for the benefit of the rest of mankind" does not, for some reason, extend to the natural conclusion that the industrial and agricultural resources of the West should also be internationalized. Nor do I recall that in the past he has urged punishment of the United States for its policies of economic boycott and blockade for many years, or condemned the policies of boycott of Arab labor and production that were a major factor in building a Jewish society in Palestine during the years when he was a journalist there.[13] Presumably the distinction, again, has to do with the relative "significance" of various nations.

Although a policy of direct invasion has its advocates, it is most unlikely, not only because of the inherent dangers and difficulties of execution, but also because there are simpler means available. A less costly and risky alternative would be a return to the Rogers Plan of 1970, which involves the return of Israeli forces to the 1967 boundaries, perhaps with "insubstantial alterations required of mutual security."[14] The basic logic of this proposal, which embodies the main ideas of the UN resolution as outlined earlier, is that the region should be converted into a kind of Latin America, with conservative Arab regimes allied to the United States and Israel embedded into the system.

It seems unlikely that there can be a peace settlement in the region that will leave Israel in control of substantial parts of the occupied territories. A stalemate of this sort might persist for some time, particularly if the Arab oil producers decide that their best interests lie in reconciliation with the United States at the expense of Egyptian and Syrian irredentism and Palestinian demands. But the local and regional conflicts will continue to simmer, and unpredictable developments within the Arab world might cause them to erupt at any moment. The likelihood of military confrontation in the region would remain high, and the international implications would remain threatening, even through periods of temporary stability. Next time, Israeli urban concentrations may not be spared. Even the possibility of a nuclear strike is not small. Sooner or later, it can be expected that the balance of international forces and the array of chance events will be such that Israel will be destroyed, and with it, probably much of the surrounding world. One cannot, of course, predict the course of such affairs with any confidence. But this forecast seems to me, nevertheless, a plausible one if no regional peace settlement is reached.

Under conditions of continued occupation and military con-frontation, the prospects for the Palestinians are dim. They can look forward only to dispersal, suffering, and destruction.

If this analysis is more or less accurate, then the two most likely possibilities for the near future are (1) a stalemate with continued Israeli occupation of territories conquered in 1967, a no-war, no-peace arrangement that carries with it a high probability of eventual destruction for Israeli Jews and Pales-tinian Arabs, and beyond; or (2) an imposed settlement along the lines of the Rogers Plan and the UN resolution of Novem-ber 1967. The latter outcome, while ugly in many respects, might be fairly stable. It would remove the immediate *casus belli* and set the stage for interstate relations that might gradu-ally stabilize. It is likely that the security of Israel would be en-hanced. Israel is as well protected by demilitarized zones on its borders, the reopening of the Suez Canal, the resettlement of Egyptian civilians,[15] and some sort of international guaran-tee, as by thinly defended areas that are a constant provoca-tion. The same is true in the Golan region to the north. It was not considerations of security that motivated Israel to settle and begin to industrialize the Golan Heights (now virtually empty of Arabs, apart from the Druze), or to expel Bedouins from the Rafah region in the south, or expand the borders of Jerusalem, or undertake settlement and investment in the West Bank, the Gaza area, and the Sinai. The annexation pol-icy of the past years is to be explained on other grounds, to which I will return.

While a settlement along the lines of the Rogers Plan and the UN resolution might bring stability, I believe that it will perpetuate conditions that have prevented the realization of the just hopes and highest ideals expressed within each of the warring societies. In a Jewish state, *"klein aber mein,"* there can be no full recognition of basic human rights, and at best, only limited progress toward a just society. Such limitations are inherent in the concept of a Jewish state that also contains non-Jewish citizens. A Palestinian counterpart, founded on bitterness, frustration, and despair and dominated by its neighbors, will be a mirror-image, perhaps even a distorted image. Both will be subject to reactionary forces within and domination from outside. While speculation about such matters is naturally uncertain, still these seem to me reasonable estimates, for reasons to which I will return here and in the essays that follow.

These essays were written in the period 1969–1973, in the belief that Israeli Jews and Palestinian Arabs were pursuing self-destructive and possibly suicidal policies, and that, contrary to generally held assumptions, there were—and remain—alternatives that ought to be considered and that might well contribute to a more satisfactory outcome. These alternatives are by no means original. In fact, they are drawn from one important tendency in pre–World War II Zionism, a tendency which, I believe, acquired new relevance and potential significance after the 1967 war. These alternatives presuppose a willingness on the part of each of the local parties to recognize the essential element of justice in the demands of the other. I have neither the insight nor the presumption to offer a judgment on the respective merits of the counterposed demands and am frankly not overly impressed by the confident assertions I see on the part of others. Each set of demands is just and, in its own terms, compelling. An examination of these just demands suggests, to me at least, that they are not irreconcilable. This remains true under the changed circumstances brought about by the "fourth round" in October 1973.

I am well aware that to Palestinians and Israelis such discussion may seem hopelessly abstract, if not downright immoral. Palestinians may ask how it is possible to compare the rights of the oppressor and the oppressed, the foreign settlers and those whose homes they have taken. Israelis may contend that one cannot balance the simple desire to live in peace in the state established by decision of the United Nations against the demands of those who resort to violence and terror and who threaten the very existence of Israeli society. It is a simple exercise to construct a brief for each side. Some seem to take comfort in this fact, oblivious to the consequences of the positions that they advocate and refusing to comprehend the pleas of their adversaries.

To a Colonel Qaddafi, it seems entirely obvious that the European Jews should return to Europe. There are, after all, many European states, and there is no reason why the people of Palestine, who committed no crime, should be dispossessed by European settlers of the Mosaic persuasion. These should return to the states where hundreds of millions of Europeans already live, leaving the 3 million Palestinians and the "Arab Jews" in their own little slice of territory. To his precise counterparts in the American Jewish community, it seems equally obvious that the Arabs should stay in the Arab countries. There are, after all, many Arab states, and there is no reason why Israeli Jews should be denied their rights by Arabs who happen to regard themselves as Palestinians. The latter should be absorbed into the homeland of more than 100 million Arabs, leaving to the Jews and the Israeli Arabs in their midst the little slice of territory that is all they ask. It is a measure of the bias and irrationality of American opinion that Qaddafi is regarded as a fanatic, whereas his counterparts are considered moderates. It seems to me a plain fact that neither view can be adopted by people with any compassion or sense of justice.

Supporters of the just claims of each contending party who ignore the full complexity of the real situation bear a heavy responsibility. They have reinforced the tendencies of each toward self-destructive policies. Realists who stand above the conflict may note condescendingly that talk of reconciliation is naïve. It is useful to bear in mind analogies—not exact, but nonetheless suggestive—that have been drawn in the essays that follow and elsewhere. Realists of an earlier period understood that it was the highest duty of Germans to massacre Frenchmen and Englishmen, and conversely. There were, to be sure, a few people who failed to comprehend this elementary point. They were regarded with contempt and often bitterly denounced, or—as in the case of Karl Liebknecht and Bertrand Russell—imprisoned so that they would not corrupt others with their strange notion that people could live in peace and work together for social justice. History has a rather different verdict.

In the following remarks, I would like to outline briefly my own perception of the evolving situation, as a basis for the essays that follow.

The Jewish national movement, Zionism, was a product of European "civilization." Palestinian nationalism, as distinct from a more generalized Arab nationalism, was in large measure a product of Zionist success. Between the two World Wars, the local conflict intensified in bitterness and scale as Jewish immigration from Europe increased and the Jewish settlement, the Yishuv, took roots in Western Palestine, bringing economic development and material benefits while often dispossessing Arab peasants through land purchase and boycotting their labor and produce. The motives for the latter policies were complex. In part, they can be traced to chauvinism and an "exclusivist" ideology, but in part they also reflected the dilemmas of socialists who hoped to build an egalitarian society with a Jewish working class, not a society of wealthy Jewish planters exploiting the natives. The Yishuv was thus faced with a profound, never resolved contradiction. The most advanced socialist forms in existence, the germs of a just and egalitarian society, were constructed on lands purchased by the Jewish National Fund and from which Arabs were excluded in principle, lands that were in many instances purchased from absentee landlords with little regard for the peasants who lived and worked on them.

These contradictions did not pass without recognition. One of the earliest settlers wrote in the Hebrew periodical *HaShiloah* in 1907 that Zionism should "avoid a narrow, limited nationalism, which sees no further than itself. . . . Unless we want to deceive ourselves deliberately, we have to admit that we have thrown

people out of their miserable lodgings and taken away their sus-
tenance." Zionism should be based on "justice and law, absolute
equality, and human brotherhood." He was reprimanded for his
"Diaspora way of thinking" and told that "the main thing we
should take into account should be what is good and effective for
ourselves." Commenting on this interchange, Aharon Cohen
observes, "Here we already have in embryo the essence of the debate that was to characterize discussions within the Zionist
movement over the years."[16]

Between the two World Wars, it was possible to imagine a local accommodation throughout Western Palestine—or even
the full territory of the British Mandate—that would be "based
on the fundamental principle that whatever the number of the
two peoples may be, no people shall dominate the other or be
subject to the government of the other," in the formulation of
Nahum Sokolov as he was elected president of the Zionist Organization in 1931.[17] But this admirable principle led to no
constructive programs and met with little response from Palestinians.

Under the impact of the Nazi atrocities, the principle
became—unfortunately, I feel—politically irrelevant. The UN
partition plan of 1947 led to civil war and then to intervention
by armies of the Arab states the day after the Jewish state was
proclaimed on May 14, 1948. In the course of the fighting,
Israel made significant territorial gains. The terms of the local conflict were substantially altered as some 750,000 Palestinians fled or were driven from their homes. An approximately equal number of Jews took their place, about half being
survivors of Hitler's massacres and most of the remainder being "Oriental" Jews who fled or were expelled from the Arab
states. Of the approximately 400 settlements established after
1948, some 350 were on refugee property; about two-thirds
of the cultivated land acquired by Israel had been Palestinian-
owned.[18] Largely acquired by the Jewish National Fund, this
land was exclusively for Jewish use, by law. By 1958, about
250,000 acres of land were expropriated from Palestinians

who remained in Israel.[19] Thousands of Bedouins were expelled.[20]

In 1960, the Knesset (Israeli parliament) enacted the *Basic Law: Israel Lands*, extending to state lands the principles of the Jewish National Fund. According to official figures, 92 percent of the state's surface prior to June 1967 was thereby restricted to Jewish use, in perpetuity. Israeli Arabs were thus excluded by law from 92 percent of the territory of the state.

The "second round," the Israeli–British–French attack on Egypt in 1956, falls within the regional and international arenas of conflict, and the same is true of the 1967 war, which found the superpowers lined up in support of their respective client states.[21] By this time, however, there were the beginnings of an independent Palestinian involvement,[22] and in the aftermath of the 1967 war, Palestinian nationalism became a substantial element in the conflict. The war resulted in Israeli occupation of all of Western Palestine, the Golan Heights, the Sinai, and Sharm al-Sheikh. It also resulted in the flight or expulsion of several hundred thousand Palestinians from villages and refugee camps.

The newly emerging Palestinian organizations suffered a severe setback in 1970–1971 at the hands of the Jordanian army, backed by Israel and the United States. The 1973 war was, once again, primarily a regional conflict between Israel and the Arab states, with the superpowers giving massive aid to their respective clients and finally imposing a cease-fire.[23] Palestinian participation seems to have been marginal, and there is good reason to expect that the Palestinians will remain a minor factor in subsequent negotiations, if they materialize.

From 1970 to October 1973, after the "war of attrition" on the Suez Canal was ended by a cease-fire, Israel seemed firmly in control of the occupied territories. In August 1973, plans were announced for new settlements to these territories in addition to the dozens already established; new towns; expropriation of Arab lands; purchase of land in the occupied areas by the Jewish National Fund. The mayor of Jerusalem called for virtually doubling the jurisdictional area of the city, thus absorbing additional Arab lands. More significant, the governing Labor Party adopted an electoral program for the October elections that amounted to a form of annexation.[24] The leading Israeli newspaper, Ha'aretz, commented on September 4 that "the government gave its approval to [Dayan's] demand to set up settlements and towns within Judea and Samaria [the occupied West Bank] without annexation and without changing its status as an occupied area. . . . Through the initiative of Dayan, it will be possible to take over territories without annexing them and without granting their inhabitants, the Arabs, the rights of citizens in Israel."[25]

The plans went well beyond the West Bank; included were plans for an industrial town on the Golan Heights,[26] projects in the Rafah region near Gaza, and a deep-water port (Yamit) west of the Gaza strip.[27] These plans gave a stamp of approval to the gradual program of de facto annexation that had been under way since the June 1967 war (see chapter 3). The plans reflected the Israeli assessment that their military position was unchallengeable, so that Arab and world opinion could be disregarded.[28]

It is important to bear in mind that this was the electoral program of the governing party, the less expansionist of the two major political groupings. It may be that these programs were a factor in the timing of the October war. They may also play a part in explaining the hostility to Israel on the part of the African states. While, in the United States, this is often described as capitulation to Arab pressure and bribery, the Israeli press has been more realistic. A. Salpeter, writing in Ha'aretz on the decision of Zaire to break relations with Israel, notes: "There is every reason to accept Mobuto's statement that our continued settlement of the territories conquered in 1967 is the main reason for his decision. . . . Changing borders by force of arms is, for reasons peculiar to Africa, received very negatively by African leaders. . . ."[29] The policy of annexation that had been taking shape with increasing clarity contributed to the diplomatic isolation of Israel, a development that poses extreme dangers, as became obvious during the October war. Countries that might have been willing to support Israel against direct aggression, even in the face of the Arab "oil weapon," were unwilling to extend themselves and suffer penalties in support of policies of which they disapproved.

As of September 1973, however, the policy of gradual annexation seemed a short-term success. It was widely believed that Israel might soon approach self-sufficiency in armaments, and Israeli military superiority seemed unchallengeable. General Dayan expressed the prevailing view when he explained to an economic conference in June 1973: "As long as we have Israelis as our soldiers, Americans as our suppliers, the Suez Canal as our military border, and the Arabs as our enemy, we should be alright."[30] Other generals gave more grandiose predictions (see chapter 4). The commander of the Israeli air force stated in July 1972 that Israeli air superiority over Egypt was increasing and "that, in effect, the Israelis had 'cracked' the Soviet–Egyptian missile defense system along the Canal."[31] Kimche, whose analysis draws heavily on Israeli government sources, concludes that this Israeli military supremacy was a major factor in leading Brezhnev to apprise Nixon in May 1972 "of the Soviet intention to disengage from the Egyptian–Israeli conflict." It partially explains, he contends, Soviet willingness to accept—he believes, to initiate—the expulsion of Soviet advisers from Egypt in July 1972.

By this time, the Russians had "decided to seek an accommodation with the United States in the Middle East and the Mediterranean at the price of abandoning the Soviet positions in Egypt and the military confrontation with Israel." What is more, Russia feared "the possible emergence of a new and powerful Middle Eastern alliance based on the two stronger military powers in the area—Israel and Iran." Israeli experts also expressed confidence in their growing industrial and technological superiority, and this confidence was shared by independent analysts.[32]

The U.S. government had every reason to regard its policy of tacit support for the Israeli occupation as successful. During the 1967–1973 period, the United States gave diplomatic support as well as substantial economic and military aid to Israel and Jordan, as well as to Iran, Saudi Arabia, and the Gulf oil producers. Given the basic goals of American policy, outlined above, there was little reason to be dissatisfied with the status quo. From 1967 to October 1973, support for Israeli occupation of the territories was consistent with the general objectives of American policy and, of course, with the domestic needs of American administrations as well. A major threat to American interests is radical Arab nationalism. The oil producers and the United States had, and still have, a common interest in blocking any such force, and thus tacitly accepted the arrangements resulting from the 1967 war, rhetoric aside. In 1970–1971, this joint policy achieved a notable success when the Palestinian guerrilla movements were decimated.[33] At that time, U.S. government policy was vacillating between two options: the Rogers Plan and tacit support for permanent Israeli occupation. After the "war of attrition" and the crushing of the Palestinians, the Rogers Plan was dropped.

Considering the situation shortly before the October 1973 war, Kimche writes that "the decisive development" of the past fifty years is that "Israel had become the major military factor in the Middle East"; it could "strike at will with only the tacit approval of the United States government" and had thus become "indispensable to the United States," which was immobilized by the achievement of parity between the superpowers.[34] Israeli spokesmen expressed themselves in similar terms (see chapter 4). The belief that Israel might become the "watchdog" for the West[35] was by no means novel. It can be traced at least to Vladimir Jabotinsky's argument during World War I that "in the Middle East, nationalism will spread among indigenous populations; only the stable support of a nation that is foreign in culture and social forms from the other peoples in the region can serve as a prop for the British forces in this region."[36]

At one time, these were the views of reactionary extremists. By 1973, however, they had become the common coin of leading political and military figures—a most unhappy development.[37]

Some of those who shared the assessment of Israeli military and economic predominance nevertheless opposed annexation because of the "demographic problem." The latter phrase is used to refer to the problem posed by the existence of Arabs in a Jewish state. With a large and rapidly growing Arab population, the Jewish state, it was feared, could not achieve the "social cohesion" necessary for security, quite apart from other unpleasant internal consequences.[38] On these grounds, some Israeli doves rejected the policy of gradual annexation and suggested that there be an "autonomous Palestinian entity" with open borders to Jordan so that commercial relations could be maintained and so that those Palestinians "who will be unemployed may, eventually, emigrate to the oil-producing states of the Persian Gulf."[39]

Given the commitment to a Jewish state and the belief in Israeli military and economic supremacy, it is not surprising that there was no serious political challenge to the policy of incorporation of the occupied territories. Even some Israelis who were opposed to these policies felt that they were forced on Israel by the refusal of the Arab states to negotiate.[40] Implicit in this judgment is the belief that no Israeli initiative toward the Palestinians could provide the basis for security and regional peace. In fact, for many Israelis the question does not even arise. They simply adopt the position of Minister of Information Israel Galili: "We do not consider the Arabs of the land an ethnic group nor a people with a distinct nationalistic character." As Prime Minister Golda Meir put it:

It was not as though there was a Palestinian people in Palestine considering itself as a Palestinian people and we came and threw them out and took their country away from them. They did not exist.[41]

On this assumption, the Palestinians "are not a party to the conflict between Israel and the Arab states," as an Israeli court ruled in 1969. Foreign Minister Abba Eban, supposedly a dove, can thus insist that the Palestinians "have no role to play" in any peace settlement.[42]

This is a convenient position for Israelis to assume, since once it is adopted, moral issues vanish. In the context of a regional conflict with the Arab states, Israel's moral position is strong—apart from the issue of the occupied territories, and problems here could be attributed to the Arab refusal to negotiate. The problem of the Palestinians, on the other hand, is difficult to face honestly and openly. Better to put it out of mind, as is commonly done in the United States as well. This is particularly easy when the Palestinians turn to terrorism as a last resort, to impress their existence on popular consciousness. Then it is easy to dismiss them as a collection of gangsters. Nagging doubts can be put to rest by propaganda about the flight of the refugees as a "tactical maneuver" on orders from the Arab armies.[43] Partisans of national movements have never found any difficulty in believing what has to be believed, regardless of the facts.

Much has been made in the West of the refusal of the Arab states to settle the regional conflict through direct negotiation with Israel, but it has less often been noted that Israel has not only refused categorically to negotiate with the Palestinians—and still does—but has even officially denied their existence as a national entity. In the United States, even the use of the word "Palestinians" has called forth angry denunciations. Perhaps one could expect nothing else. Israel is a state like any other; Zionism is a national movement like any other. As for the explanation, perhaps it is enough to quote Jon Kimche's observation on what he calls "this curious Israeli refusal to consider the Palestinian solution": "It was as if the assertion of a Jewish nation required the rejection of the existence of a Palestinian nation."[44]

Certainly, this is a view that has been expressed on the extreme right. Menachem Begin once warned a Kibbutz audience of the danger inherent in recognizing a Palestinian people. Asked about this, he responded:

> My friend, take care. When you recognize the concept of "Palestine," you demolish your right to live in Ein Hahoresh. If this is Palestine and not the Land of Israel, then you are conquerors and not tillers of the land. You are invaders. If this is Palestine, then it belongs to a people who lived here before you came. Only if it is the Land of Israel do you have a right to live in Ein Hahoresh and in Deganiyah B. If it is not your country, your fatherland, the country of your ancestors and of your sons, then what are you doing here? You came to another people's homeland, as they claim, you expelled them and you have taken their land. . . .[45]

Since the Six-Day War of June 1967, such views have been expressed quite openly by advocates of direct annexation of the occupied territories, eliciting some sharp controversy in the Israeli press. The controversy renews, in contemporary terms, the debate over the essential meaning of Zionism discussed earlier (cf. p. 14). Clearly, this "curious Israeli refusal to consider the Palestinian solution" must be overcome if Israel is to adapt itself to the settlement that is likely to be imposed by the United States, or if initiatives are to develop within Israeli society that might lead to other, and I believe preferable, alternatives.

During the period 1967–1973, there were opportunities for a local accommodation that could have insulated Israel–Palestine from regional conflicts and perhaps—though this is more doubtful—from the machinations of the great powers. Had there been a local settlement, it is highly unlikely that the Arab states could have mobilized their populations for renewed military conflict, even if they had wanted to. Nor could they have achieved anything like the same diplomatic successes, even with the "oil weapon." But the preconditions, mentioned earlier, were never realized or even approached, on either side.

There have been groups in Israel that sought a way out of the impasse through recognition of Palestinian rights. The principles of Siah (Israeli New Left), approved by the Third National Conference in July 1972, begin with the statement that "Eretz Yisrael/Palestine is the territorial basis for the self-determination of two peoples," Jews and Palestinian Arabs, and call for a settlement on the basis of the June 4, 1967, borders with mutual recognition of two independent states and of the right in principle for Jews and Arabs to choose their homes within this region. But such groups and such programs were never able to challenge state policy so long as it seemed successful.

The intransigence of the Israeli government and the public in general on this issue was reinforced by the solid support it received in the United States, where a kind of hysteria almost made discussion impossible.[46] The predictable result was that the opportunities for a local settlement were lost, and the stage was set for the inevitable regional war. What came as a surprise was not the war itself, but rather its timing and the relative success achieved by Arab armies. Israel's General Sharon, now the hero of the 1973 Sinai campaign and a leader of the political right, states that "in a general way" the war came as no surprise: "It was obvious to me since the Six-Day War that if we do not reach some sort of solution with Egypt, there will ultimately be no escape from a new round" because of the "difficult situation" in which the Egyptians were placed, even though the situation remained satisfactory for the other three major actors: Israel, the United States, and the Soviet Union.[47] Thus it was not surprising that Egypt and Syria undertook "to conquer a part of the territories that Israel conquered in the Six-Day War," so as to achieve the primary political objective of "breaking the diplomatic deadlock."[48]

The annexation policy was not openly adopted and proclaimed. Rather, Israeli policy simply drifted in that direction. (Some of the early stages are described in chapter 3.) It was only in August 1973, with the adoption of the Galili Protocols, that the governing party gave the policy a more or less official form. The argument, throughout, has been security. But a review of the facts suggests that the annexation policy is to be explained on other grounds. Consider, for example, the Sinai where Israel is most likely to agree to some kind of compromise settlement. The Sinai brings Israel a net income of some $400 million a year, an amount equivalent to about one-third of its export earnings, while Israeli occupation deprives Egypt of about $600 million a year.[49] Prospects for the future are bright, particularly if Dayan's plans for the deep-water port of Yamit are implemented. Apart from economic considerations, which are not insubstantial, the settlement and integration of "Judea and Samaria" (the occupied West Bank) are motivated by mystical attachments to the "historic land of Israel," invoked in official and other pronouncements (cf. pp. 95–96). In the October 1973 war, Israeli settlements in the Golan Heights proved to be a liability from a military point of view, but Israel is nevertheless planning to double Jewish settlement there and to construct a new urban center.[50] A forced settlement along the lines of the UN resolution would be inconsistent with all such programs, but the issue is not primarily one of Israeli security.

Somewhat related conclusions have been drawn by Israeli doves. Professor Jacob Talmon has repeatedly deplored the fact that Israeli policy has been based

> on the assumption that we will be able to act as we wish, up to full annexation, while ignoring the opinions of other countries. In other words, we will have the power and opportunity to dictate our will to the whole world.[51]

In many articles, he has explained the fallacy in these assumptions and pointed to their grim consequences, an exercise in rationality that has earned him little applause on the part of partisans of annexation (cf. p. 146). Others have commented on the racist arrogance that led Israelis to believe that Arabs would never be able to contest Israeli force.[52] One of the most outspoken critics of the annexation policy, Reserve General Mattityahu Peled, outlined the three "myths" that led to the

near-disaster in October 1973. The first myth was that Arabs
were incompetent cowards who would never be capable of initiating an attack. The second was that Israeli air superiority
guaranteed instant victory in the unlikely event of an Arab
attack.

> The third myth, probably the biggest, was the tendency to
> believe—with an incredible arrogance that showed through in
> every domain—that we could force the Palestinians, all the
> Arabs and the whole world to accept a territorial status quo for
> the next 30 or 40 years. After all, weren't we superior, infallible,
> unbeatable? And didn't we have Washington in our pocket
> thanks to a powerful Zionist lobby in the United States? Weren't
> we containing the Soviet Union and the communist bloc? What
> did it matter that Africa, Asia, and the Third World were hostile
> to us, since Mr. Nixon's veto at the United Nations had suc-
> ceeded in taking the stuffing out of their anti-Israeli resolutions?
> In short, General Dayan and his cronies thought we were the
> undisputed masters of the Middle East and of history.[53]

It cannot be stressed too often that American Zionists who have
supported these delusions and, with their cries of anti-Semitism
and other hysterical abuse,[54] quite successfully suppressed any
discussion of the dangers and alternatives, bear a measure of responsibility for the events of October 1973, a very close call for
the State of Israel. Furthermore, the lesson has not been learned,
as will be seen in chapter 5.

General Peled has explained over and over again that the new
1967 boundaries did not increase the security of Israel; quite the
contrary, demilitarized zones might leave Israel in a better position from a strictly military point of view. Those who make a
fetish of security, he argues, have been concerned "not with Israel's security but with her territorial dimensions."[55]

Although the intended message is quite different, some Israelis who tend toward the "activist" end of the spectrum on the
issue of boundaries and security make essentially the same point.
Michael Bar-Zohar rejects the argument of the doves that settle-

ments on the Golan Heights served no useful security purpose (and, in fact, were an impediment to Israeli military operations there):

> However, it is incorrect to maintain that the purpose of the set-tlements on the Golan Heights was for security. The Golan Heights settlements had hardly any security function to fulfill, just as no such function was to be attached to Kiryat Arba (in Hebron) or to the projected town of Yamit. The Golan settle-ments were of a purely political character. The purpose was to create facts in the area, to establish roots in a region we regarded as vital and to demonstrate our firm purpose not to retreat from that area. . . . Settlements on the Golan Heights were also in-tended to determine facts, which will be difficult to alter when the time comes. Under pressure, one can move a line on a map, one can move army units stationed in empty terrain—but it is far more difficult to uproot settlements and people who have struck roots in the land. That was the purpose of the Golan settlements—and not any notion of establishing a buffer of border-settlers. . . .[56]

Bar-Zohar does not go on to make the further observation that considerations of security have regularly been used to disguise the post-1967 policy of "creating facts" in the occupied areas, nor does he explore the purposes of the latter policy, perhaps because they are clear enough. Like many others, he argues that the October 1973 war demonstrated that Israel must retain the occupied territories, for if that war had been launched from the 1967 borders, the fighting would have taken place within settled areas. Putting aside the fact that Israel is intent on set-tling the occupied areas, this argument would be a rational re-sponse only to the proposal that the situation should revert to that of 1967. It does not even begin to deal with the actual pro-posal of the doves: that the occupied territories be demilita-rized. Then no surprise attack can be launched from the 1967 borders, and there is no substance to the fears expressed by Bar-Zohar and others or to their arguments about "strategic depth."

If the Sinai were demilitarized, the Israeli army would have ample foreknowledge of any Egyptian penetration of this buffer
zone and, as Peled and others have pointed out, would be in an
advantageous position to counter it, as in 1967. Nor would
there be any shelling of Israeli settlements from a demilitarized
Golan Heights;[57] nor would Tel Aviv be in artillery range if the
West Bank were demilitarized. By scrupulously avoiding the actual proposals of those who oppose continued "creeping annexation," the "activists" tacitly concede the accuracy of the
assessment that security is being invoked simply as a disguise
for territorial ambitions.

There is much loose talk about "security guarantees" that con-
fuses these issues further. Thus it is claimed, correctly, that superpower guarantees are unreliable and that it is impossible to
count on the United Nations. Therefore, it is urged, Israel must
be in a position to guarantee its own security.[58] But in this world,
Israel will never be in a position to guarantee its own security, no
matter what its borders may be and no matter how massive its armaments. Guarantees of security do not exist. In the long run, Israel's security rests on relations with its neighbors. The policy of
annexation rules out long-term security as unobtainable and thus
virtually guarantees further military conflict and the ultimate destruction of a state that can lose only once. The annexation
policy also maximizes the short-term threat, by stimulating irredentist forces in the surrounding states and gaining them international support. The short-term threat was regarded as slight in
the past few years—mistakenly, as the October war revealed. It is
easy to plead "security" to disguise very different motivations.[59]

In the essays that follow and elsewhere, I have argued that socialist binationalism offers the best long-range hope for a just
peace in the region. Surely this conclusion is debatable, but not,
so far as I can see, on grounds of security. A local accommodation between Israeli Jews and Palestinian Arabs would enhance
the security of both. The barrier, within Israel, has not been the
problem of security, but rather commitment to a Jewish state.
Palestinians and their supporters also offered no acceptable basis

for discussion and accommodation, with rare exceptions. In no case was the issue one of security.

It has been widely and, I think plausibly, speculated that the October war and subsequent events will gradually impel the United States to resurrect the Rogers Plan in some form (see chapter 4). There is every reason to expect that Egypt, Jordan, and Saudi Arabia will acquiesce (cf. note 14), whatever their longer-term goals may be. There will be extremely difficult problems, such as the status of Jerusalem, but one can at least imagine ways in which they might be resolved under super-power pressure. The Palestinian leadership, which is in any event powerless, seems to have reluctantly acceded to this pro-gram, apparently under Russian pressure.[60] Russian goals in the region seem to remain limited, and the Soviet Union continues to support the UN Security Council Resolution 242, with its likely consequence that Egypt will return to the American orbit along with Saudi Arabia and the Gulf oil producers. The crucial short-term question is whether Israel will submit to U.S. pres-sure and reverse the policies of the past few years. This would be a bitter pill, but Israel has successively cut off its options and now has little room to maneuver if the United States follows what seems a likely course of action, perhaps after the next stalemate collapses.

American moves in this direction would constitute a return to past policies. In 1953, Dulles suspended economic aid to Israel to compel it to end its project for unilateral diversion of Jordan water, and in 1956, Eisenhower compelled Israel to withdraw from the Sinai after the joint Israeli–French–British aggression against Egypt. A return to past policies would provoke a bitter political conflict in the United States. Since the crushing Israeli military victory of June 1967, American public opinion has been overwhelmingly sympathetic to Israel and its policy of de facto annexation. I return to this matter in chapter 5.

A forced settlement along the lines of Resolution 242 would enable Egypt and Saudi Arabia to revert to their preferred role as American client states; and Israel would remain the major military force in the region, with substantial arms production[61] and advanced industrial development. As such, it would remain a valued ally for the United States, which will continue to rely on Israeli and Iranian power to offset Russian influence and disruptive Arab forces. An Iranian diplomatic source explains that "without Israeli power in the Middle East, the Shah feels that the Arabs would be difficult to control and the Russians would very much gain an upper hand in the entire area."[62] Value judgments aside, there is plausibility to Senator Henry Jackson's observation that Iran, Israel, and Saudi Arabia "have served to inhibit and contain those irresponsible and radical elements in certain Arab states . . . who, were they free to do so, would pose a grave threat indeed to our principal sources of petroleum," and that "the Saudis understand . . . that Israel and Iran play a vital stabilizing role."[63] Like the United States, Saudi Arabia fears Russian influence, revolutionary movements in the peninsula (where Iran is already heavily engaged in counterinsurgency), the leftist regime of South Yemen, and future Qaddafis. It is likely to accept a powerful Israel, with more limited ambitions, within an American-based alliance. The same is true of Egypt. Even if the United States were to impose a variant of the Rogers Plan, this would in no sense be interpretable, as some have argued, as "abandonment of Israel."[64]

Such a plan, if implemented, may lead to the reconstitution of what has been called "the triangle of 'gendarmes' consisting of Riyadh, Teheran, and Tel Aviv."[65] The internal disputes that will persist have their value for the imperial powers, which need Arab oil, but which must also find a way to reverse the flow of Western currencies to the Arab treasuries.[66] As has often been observed, "one very substantial way of doing this is to sell arms."[67] Iran is arming itself to the teeth, obviously with the intention of dominating the Persian Gulf. The oil boycott had barely been put into effect when it was reported that the U.S. air force and navy were "involved in an extensive program to strengthen the defenses of Saudi Arabia . . . with fighter planes, radar, and military advice," and with the sale of thirty Phantoms in the offing.[68] There is no contradiction here. The central concern of U.S. policy is that Saudi Arabia remain a loyal ally and that it be dependent on the United States for armaments and economic development. A certain tension in the region may even be conducive to the projected imperial settlement.

Russia requires Western currencies if it is to pursue its policies of détente, and can therefore be expected to try to maintain a major role in providing armaments to the Arab states, as will the European powers.[69] The gradual conversion of Israel into a military arsenal can be expected to continue under such an arrangement. About one-quarter of the Israeli work force is reported to be employed in armaments production, which already constitutes a major export industry and may soon become the major source of foreign exchange.[70] The interests of ruling groups and the imperial powers converge on the creation of a network of hostile states, jointly committed to repression of radical nationalism. Not a pretty picture, but a plausible projection, I am afraid. One might add that a system of balkanization under the American aegis, while perhaps fairly stable, nevertheless contains explosive forces that might erupt into a major war.

If the emerging system includes a Palestinian state, there is every likelihood that it will be under the domination of Israel and Jordan, which will continue to pursue parallel policies as American allies. Since 1967, Israel has come to rely heavily on an Arab proletariat imported by day from the occupied territories. Shortly before the October war, the Israeli minister of commerce and industry, former army chief of staff Haim Bar-Lev, stated that Israel and the territories would remain "a single economic unit" under any political solution that might arise.[71] There can be no objection in principle to economic integration of Israeli and Palestinian societies—on the contrary, it would be most desirable under conditions of political parity and relative economic and social equality. But it is evident from the context of Bar-Lev's remarks and from the presupposed social and economic conditions that the "single economic unit" is to be controlled by Israel and Israeli capital. The same concept was expressed in the Galili Protocols. Israeli reliance on transient Arab labor from the "Palestinian state" might well continue under the kind of settlement that seems now to be under consideration, along with other forms of economic integration and Israeli investment. The Palestinian state is likely to be a kind of Bantustan, a reservoir of cheap labor, thus overcoming the fears of Israeli liberals that annexation would erode the Jewish character of the state, while perpetuating conditions of economic dependence.

Under any arrangement that can be imagined for the near future, Israel will remain a Jewish state—that is, a state based on the principle of discrimination. There is no other way for a state with non-Jewish citizens to remain a Jewish state, as all but the most irrational must concede. Very likely, the policies of expropriation, expulsion, establishment of pure Jewish settlement areas, exclusion of Arabs from state lands, and repression of independent political activity that challenges the basic exclusivist ideology will all continue (see chapters 3 and 5). It is hard, even under the best of circumstances, to see how conditions might be otherwise.

Israel will continue to be a state where "the moment the magic word security is uttered, the wheels of the machine of Justice slow down . . . even when these security reasons cannot convince a reasonable man," as in the case of the uprooted people of the villages of Biram and Ikrit, "illegally evicted from their homes."[72] This exploitation of "security reasons" will persist alongside high levels of justice and democracy (by world standards) for the privileged majority. Israel will be a garrison state, surrounded by hostile neighbors, though probably more secure than before, since further regional wars will no longer be inevitable. It will also, quite likely, remain a state with a strong element of religious coercion. Jacob Talmon has observed:

In Israel today, the Rabbinate is rapidly developing into a firmly institutionalized Church imposing an exacting discipline on its members and facing the general body of laymen as a distinct power. This is not a religious development, but, ironically enough, the outcome of the emergence of the State. The latter has given birth and legitimacy to an established Church.[73]

He also points out that none of this has roots in Jewish tradition. The theocratic elements in Israeli society, without parallel in the industrial world, are often explained in terms of the problems of coalition politics, but the reasons seem to me to lie deeper. Such a development is not very surprising in a society in which some basis must be established—in ideology, cultural attitude, and law—to distinguish the privileged majority from the non-Jewish citizens.

For similar reasons, one can expect the Palestinian state, if it comes into being, to develop on the same model. The Palestinian movement is sometimes described in the West as a movement of revolutionary socialists, but this is far from an accurate characterization.[74] Radical and libertarian elements in the movement will not have a bright future in a Palestinian state dominated by its neighbors, with discriminatory structures that may even be exaggerated in reaction to hopelessness and subordination.

In this way, history will perhaps realize the worst fears of early Zionist leaders, such men as Arthur Ruppin, who was in charge of colonization in the 1920s and who warned just fifty years ago that "a Jewish state of one million or even a few million (after fifty years!) will be nothing but a new Montenegro or Lithuania." He warned that Zionism must no longer pursue Herzl's "diplomatic and imperialist approach" and must recognize that "Herzl's concept of a Jewish state was possible only because he ignored the presence of the Arabs."[75] He was not alone in this view. Berl Katznelson, addressing a Mapai conference in 1931, said:

... I do not wish to see the realization of Zionism in the form of the new Polish state with Arabs in the position of the Jews

and the Jews in the position of Poles, the ruling people. For me
this would be the complete perversion of the Zionist ideal. . . .[76]

Our generation has been witness to the fact that nations aspir-
ing to freedom who threw off the yoke of subjugation rushed to
place this yoke on the shoulder of others. Over the generations in
which we were persecuted and exiled and slaughtered, we learned
not only the pain of exile and subjugation, but also contempt for
tyranny. Was that only a case of sour grapes? Are we now nurtur-
ing the dream of slaves who wish to reign?[77]

It seems to me not impossible that after the experience of
building and living in new Montenegros and Lithuanias, Jews
and Arabs may turn to a better way, one which has always been
a possibility. It will be based on the fundamental principle, already cited, "that whatever the number of the two peoples may
be, no people shall dominate the other or be subject to the government of the other." Each people will have the right to participate in self-governing national institutions. Any individual will
be free to live where he wants, to be free from religious control,
to define himself as a Jew, an Arab, or something else, and to live
accordingly. People will be united by bonds other than their
identification as Jews or Arabs (or lack of any such identification). This society, in the former Palestine, should permit all
Palestinians the right of return, along with Jews who wish to find
their place in this national homeland. All oppressive or discriminatory structures should be dismantled, and discriminatory practices should be condemned rather than reinforced. The society
will not be a Jewish state or an Arab state, but rather a democratic multinational society.

Many schemes can be imagined that would conform to such
general principles as these. To cite just one—not the only one:

The regime in Palestine must at all times assure both the Jews
and the Arabs the possibility of unhampered development and
full national independence, so as to rule out any domination by
Arabs of Jews, or by Jews of Arabs. The regime must foster the
rapprochement, accord, and cooperation of the Jewish people

and the Arabs in Palestine . . . [which will be] . . . a federal state, comprising an alliance of cantons (autonomous districts), some with Jews in the majority, and some with Arabs; national autonomy of each people, with exclusive authority in matters of education, culture, and language; matters of religion: under the control of autonomous religious congregations, organized as free statutory bodies; the highest body of the state: the federal council, consisting of two houses—(a) one representing nationalities in which Jews and Arabs will have equal representation, and (b) one in which representatives of the cantons will participate in proportion to their respective populations. Any federal law and any change in the federal constitution can be enacted only with the agreement of both houses.

This was not the suggestion of an idle visionary or utopian dreamer remote from the social and political struggle, but of David Ben-Gurion, in an internal party discussion in October 1930.[78] There are those who argue that such proposals were put forth hypocritically, as a tactic at a particular moment. I think that the circumstances and manner in which these proposals were made, and an analysis of the social conditions at the time, support a different interpretation. I think that the proposals of Ben-Gurion, Pinhas Rutenberg,[79] and others reflected a commitment to justice and a clear understanding of what a new Lithuania or Montenegro would become. These proposals, I think, were the honest expression of men who did not want to be the Poles in a new Poland in which the Arabs would be the Jews. It should be recalled, in particular, that these were years of class struggle as well as "nation building" in Palestine. In opposing the Revisionist demand for a Jewish state in the 1930s, Ben-Gurion, a labor leader as well as a spokesman for Jewish nationalism, was also expressing a very different conception of what kind of society the new Palestine was to be (see chapter 1).

There was, to be sure, a significant change in the positions taken by Ben-Gurion and others through this period. In 1931, speaking before the Seventeenth Zionist Congress, Ben-Gurion stated:

We declare before world opinion, before the workers' movement, and before the Arab world, that we shall not agree, either now or in the future, to the rule of one national group over
the other. Nor do we accept the idea of a Jewish state, which
would eventually mean Jewish domination of Arabs in Palestine.[80]

And before the Royal Commission in 1937, he testified as
follows:

If Palestine were uninhabited we might have asked for a Jewish
state, for then it would not harm anyone else. But there are other
residents in Palestine, and just as we do not wish to be at the
mercy of others, they too have the right not to be at the mercy of
the Jews.[81]

In 1940–1941, an Arab member of the Jerusalem Municipal
Council, Adil Jabr, after consultation with Palestinian and other
Arab leaders, drafted a proposal for a binational Palestine based
on full equality within a broader federation of autonomous
states.[82] The proposal was presented to Ben-Gurion by Chaim
Kalvarisky, a long-time advocate of Jewish–Arab cooperation.
According to Kalvarisky, Ben-Gurion rebuffed the offer with
"unrestrained anger," describing it as "an abomination" and refusing to deal with the document at all. Cohen comments:

The bottleneck was Jabr's fourth proposal suggesting a binational Palestine, based on parity in government. Ben-Gurion's
unwillingness to agree to parity (which he had ostensibly favored since 1931), and not the oft-heard complaint that "there
is no one to talk to in the Arab camp," was the real obstacle on
the way to accord.

Jabr's own reaction to the negative response on the part of
Moshe Shertok (later Sharett) when the proposal was offered
was, according to Kalvarisky, that "as long as talk on accord is
vague, the Jews would be found to be very agreeable to accord
and peace, but when matters progressed to the stage of concrete

proposals they will put all kinds of obstacles in your path and cause its failure." The event lends support to the argument that the socialist binationalism of centrists such as Ben-Gurion was merely rhetorical. Intervening events provide, I believe, a more plausible explanation: the complex internal strife in Palestine in 1936–1939 (see chapter 1), World War II, and the realization of the meaning of Nazi success for the Jewish communities in Europe.

Whether driven by events or drawn by opportunity, the centrist socialists in the Zionist movement had abandoned any interest in a solution based on political parity by the early 1940s, and the Revisionist demands became the official position of the Zionist movement. Opposition to a Jewish state continued in the left wing of the Histadrut (the Jewish labor movement) and among intellectuals such as Judah Magnes, Martin Buber, and others who formed the Ihud. There were many reasons why earlier plans for a political solution based on the principle of equality and nondomination failed. It is not necessary to relive that history, though it is important to understand it. It seems to me that at this moment it is important for such alternatives to be considered and debated, and furthermore to be implemented by Jews and Arabs who will be repelled by the imperial settlement and will seek a more decent life.

If this comes about, it will be as part of a broader movement struggling for social justice. There must be a basis for cooperation. It will take place only among people who find that they are united by bonds that transcend their nationalist associations. If there is to be a return to the Zionist principle of 1931, that "whatever the number of the two peoples may be, no people shall dominate the other or be subject to the government of the other," it will only be within the context of an effort to create a socialist society. Within Israel, this will mean a return to the egalitarian ideals and libertarian social structures of the Yishuv. It will mean a return, under the new conditions of an advanced industrial society, to the principle expressed by the Jewish labor movement in 1924, that "the main and most reliable means of strengthening friendship, peace, and mutual understanding between the Jewish people and the Arab people is . . . the accord, alliance, and joint effort of Jewish and Arab workers in town and country."[83] Socialist binationalism is a possibility; binationalism without domination is otherwise an empty formula.

These essays are motivated by a conviction that some form of socialist binationalism offers the best hope for reconciling the just and compelling demands of the two parties to the local conflict in the former Palestine and that, however dim the prospects may seem, it is important to keep that hope alive until such time as popular movements within Israeli and Palestinian society, supported by an international socialist movement that does not now exist, will undertake to make such a hope a reality.

I HAVE INTRODUCED no changes of substance in editing the essays for publication here. Each one attempts an assessment of the situation existing at the time of writing. Any such assessment is always hazardous and involves a fair amount of speculation. I therefore cited the best sources I could find and gave what seemed to me, at the time, the most reasonable evaluation of existing conditions. Changing events have led to a reassessment in a number of respects, and there can be little doubt that this will continue to be the case. But the basic argument remains.

A few final remarks on the origin of the essays. Chapter 1 is based on a talk given at MIT in a general forum organized by Arab students in March 1969. It appeared in *Liberation*, November 1969, and in Herbert Mason, ed., *Reflections on the Middle East Crisis* (Mouton, The Hague, 1970). Chapter 2 was an invited talk before the Third Annual Convention of the Association of Arab-American University Graduates, held in Evanston, Illinois, October 29–November 1, 1970. As noted in the introductory remarks, I did not keep to the assigned title, retained here. The text appeared in Abdeen Jabara and Janice Terry, eds., *The Arab World: From Nationalism to Revolution* (Medina University Press, Wilmette, Illinois, 1971). Chapter 3 is in two parts. The first part is the approximate text of a talk given at Holy Cross College, Worcester, Massachusetts, in February 1971, in a symposium on the Middle East. The second part was added in June 1972. The two parts appeared in the *Holy Cross Quarterly*, Summer 1972. Chapter 4 was written in October 1973, immediately after the cease-fire went into effect, and appeared in *Ramparts*, January 1974. Chapter 5 has a different focus. It is concerned with attitudes toward the Arab–Israeli conflict in the United States and the curious ways in which the peace movement and the American left have been brought into this issue. It was written in January 1974, as was this introduction.

Nationalism and Conflict in Palestine

These remarks are based on a talk delivered at a forum of the Arab Club of MIT. I am grateful to many Arab and Israeli students for their helpful comments and criticism. From many conversations with them, I feel that they are much closer to one another, in their fundamental aspirations, than they sometimes realize. It is this belief that encourages me to speculate about what may appear to be some rather distant prospects for reconciliation and cooperative effort. There can be few things more sad than the sight of young people who are, perhaps, fated to kill one another because they cannot escape the grip of fetishism and mistrust.

Before discussing the crisis in the Middle East, I would like to mention three other matters. The first has to do with my personal background and involvement in this issue. Secondly, I would like to mention reservations I feel about discussing this topic on a public platform. And finally, I want to stress several factors that limit the significance of anything I have to say. Ordinarily, these matters might be out of place, but in this case I think they are appropriate. They may help the reader to place these comments in a proper context and to take them as they are intended.

To begin with some personal background: I grew up with a deep interest in the revival of Hebrew culture associated with the settlement of Palestine. I found myself on the fringes of the left wing of the Zionist youth movement, never joining because of

certain political disagreements, but enormously attracted, emotionally and intellectually, by what I saw as a dramatic effort to
create, out of the wreckage of European civilization, some form
of libertarian socialism in the Middle East. My sympathies were
with those opposed to a Jewish state and concerned with Arab–
Jewish cooperation, those who saw the primary issue not as
a conflict of Arab and Jewish rights, but in very different terms:
as a conflict between a potentially free, collective form of social
organization as embodied in the Kibbutz and other socialist institutions on the one hand, and, on the other, the autocratic
forms of modern social organization, either capitalist or state capitalist, or state socialist on the Soviet model.

In 1947, with the UN partition agreement, this point of view
became unrealistic, or at least unrelated to the actual drift of
events. Prior to that time it was perhaps not entirely unrealistic.
And again, I think, today this may be a realistic prospect, perhaps
the only hope for the Jewish and Arab inhabitants of the old
Palestine.

I should say, at the outset, that my views have not changed
very much since that time. I think that a socialist binationalist
position was correct then, and remains so today. Implicit in this
judgment are certain factual assumptions regarding the prospects
for Arab–Jewish cooperation based on an interpretation of interests along other than national lines. These assumptions are not
solidly grounded and are surely open to challenge, as is the implicit value judgment concerning the desirability of a socialist binational community as compared to a subdivision of Palestine
into separate Arab and Jewish states or the establishment of a
single Jewish or Arab state in the whole region that would preserve no form of communal autonomy. These are the questions
that I would like to explore, quite tentatively, and subject to
reservations that I will mention.

Returning to my personal experience, the partition plan
seemed to me at best a dubious move, and perhaps a catastrophic
error. Of course, I shared the general dismay over the subsequent
violence and the forceable transfer of populations. A few years

later I spent several very happy months working in a Kibbutz and for several years thought very seriously about returning permanently. Some of my closest friends, including several who have had a significant influence on my own thinking over the years, now live in Kibbutzim or elsewhere in Israel, and I retain close connections that are quite separate from any political judgments and attitudes. I mention all of this to make clear that I inevitably view the continuing conflict from a very specific point of view, colored by these personal relationships. Perhaps this personal history distorts my perspective. In any event, it should be understood by the reader.

Let me turn next to certain reservations that I have about discussing the topic at all. These reservations would be less strong in an Israeli context, where my point of view might at least be a reasonable topic for discussion, though it would not be widely shared, I presume. The American context is quite different. In general, the spectrum of political thinking in the United States is skewed sharply to the right as compared with the other Western democracies, of which Israel is essentially one. Interacting with the narrow conservatism that dominates American opinion is an ideological commitment to a perverse kind of "pragmatism" (as its adherents like to call it). This translates into practice as a system of techniques for enforcing the stability of an American-dominated world system within which national societies are to be managed by the rich in cooperation with a "meritocratic elite" that serves the dominant social institutions, the corporations, and the national state that is closely linked to them in its top personnel and conception of the "national interest." In this highly ideological country, where political commitments often border on the fanatic, the question of cooperation in the common interest can barely be raised without serious miscomprehension. Specifically, there is little likelihood of a useful discussion of the possibilities for Arab–Jewish cooperation to build a socialist Palestinian society when the terms are set by the conservative coercive "pragmatism" of American opinion.

It is, furthermore, characteristic of American ethnic minorities that they tend to support the right-wing forces in the national societies to which they often retain a cultural or economic
connection. The American Jewish community is no exception.
The American Zionist movement has always been a conservative
force within world Zionism, and tended toward maximalist and
strong nationalist programs at a time when this was by no means
typical of the Palestinian settlement itself. To cite just one case,
the Zionist Organization of America was, I believe, the first organized segment of world Zionism to formulate as an official doctrine "that Palestine be established as a Jewish commonwealth"
and to condemn any program that denies these "fundamental
principles," even the program of the politically rather conservative Ihud group in Palestine, which was specifically repudiated
(October 1942).[1] At the Basel Congress of the World Zionist Organization in 1946, the first after the war, Chaim Weizmann was
impelled to condemn the nationalist extremism of the American
delegation.[2] Today, it seems to me that this general conservatism
and nationalist extremism are harmful to the long-range interests
of the people of Israel as well as to the search for a just peace; in
any event, they have helped create an atmosphere in the United
States in which discussion and exploration of the basic issues is
at best quite difficult.

An Israeli writer like Amos Oz, for whom the abandonment
of the Jewish state "is a concession we could not make and shall
never be able to make," can nevertheless appreciate the absolute validity of the right of the Palestinian Arabs to national
self-determination in Palestine: "This is our country; it is their
country. Right clashes with right. 'To be a free people in our
own land' is a right that is universally valid, or not valid at all."
He sees the conflict as a tragedy, "a clash between total justice
and total justice. . . . We are here—because we can exist
nowhere but here as a nation, as a Jewish state. The Arabs are
here—because Palestine is the homeland of the Palestinians,
just as Iraq is the homeland of the Iraqis and Holland the
homeland of the Dutch." The Jews have no objective justifica-

tion other than "the right of one who is drowning and grasps the only plank he can." The Palestinian Arabs understand the meaning of Zionism only too well, he says; they regard themselves "as the despoiled owners of the whole country, with some reluctantly accepting the situation and some not accepting it at all."[3] Similarly, General Moshe Dayan speaks quite clearly of the justice of the Arab position: "It is not true that the Arabs hate the Jews for personal, religious, or racial reasons. They consider us—and justly, from their point of view—as Westerners, foreigners, invaders who have seized an Arab country to turn it into a Jewish state."[4] Speaking at the funeral of a murdered friend, just before the Sinai campaign of 1967, Dayan said: "We must beware of blaming the murderers. Who are we to reproach them for hating us? Colonists who transform into a Jewish homeland the territory they have lived in for generations."[5] In a pro-Zionist Israeli journal, a senior official of the government of Israel can propose that formal sovereignty should be ceded to a binational Palestinian Union ("a constitutional monarchy headed by the present ruler of the Kingdom of Jordan," "a union of Jewish and Arab settlement areas, each of which will be guaranteed autonomy in matters of culture, education, religion, and welfare").[6]

I mention these examples, which can be multiplied, to illustrate a significant difference between the Israeli and the American Jewish communities. In the latter, there is little willingness to face the fact that the Palestinian Arabs have suffered a monstrous historical injustice, whatever one may think of the competing claims. Until this is recognized, discussion of the Middle East crisis cannot even begin. Amos Oz introduces his essay by deploring the fact that "anyone who stands up and speaks out in these days risks being stoned in the market place and being accused of Jewish self-hate or of betraying the nation or desecrating the memory of the fallen." To the American Jewish community, these words apply quite accurately, more so than to Israel, so far as I can determine. This is most unfortunate. Political hysteria benefits no one. The barriers that have been raised to any serious discussion of the issues will only diminish what meager possibilities may exist for peaceful reconciliation.

Finally, I want to emphasize that I approach these questions with no particular expert knowledge or even intimate contact, nothing more than what I have just described. Nor do I have any specific policy recommendations in which I, at least, would place much confidence. Specifically, I doubt very much that any American initiatives are likely to be helpful. As to initiatives by the American government or other great powers—these might well prove disastrous.

With all of these reservations, I feel that the problem must still be faced, and with a sense of considerable urgency. The reasons for this sense of urgency are put very well by Uri Avneri, in one of the most important of the recent books on the Middle East crisis:

An uneasy cease-fire prevails along the frozen fronts of the recent war, a cease-fire fraught with dangers, broken by intermittent shots. The armies confronting each other across the cease-fire lines are arming quickly. A new war is assumed by all of them as a virtual certainty, with only the exact timing still in doubt. But the next war, or the one after it, will be quite different from the recent one, so different, in fact, that the Blitzkrieg of June 1967, will look, in comparison, like a humanitarian exercise.

Nuclear weapons, missiles of all types, are nearing the Semitic scene. Their advent is inevitable. If the vicious circle is not broken, and broken soon, it will lead, with the preordained certainty of a Greek tragedy, toward a holocaust that will bury Tel Aviv and Cairo, Damascus and Jerusalem.

Semitic suicide is the only alternative to Semitic peace.

A different kind of tragedy is brewing in Palestine itself. If no just solution is found soon, the guerilla war of organizations like al-Fatah will start a vicious circle of its own, a steep spiral of terror and counter-terror, killing and retaliation, sabotage and mass deportation, which will bring undreamt-of miseries to the Palestinian people. It will poison the atmosphere and generate a nightmare that will make peace impossible in our lifetime, turning Israel into an armed and beleaguered camp forever, bringing the Arab march toward progress to a complete standstill, and perhaps spelling the end of the Palestinian–Arab people as a nation—the very people for whose freedom al-Fatah fights in vain.

Cease-fire—this is not a passive imperative. In order to cease fire, acts of peace must be done. Peace must be waged—actively, imaginatively, incessantly. In the words of the psalmist: "Seek peace and pursue it." The search can be passive—the pursuit cannot.[7]

General Dayan speaks with equal realism, in the remarks from which I have already quoted: "As long as we have to fulfill our aims against the will of the Arabs, we shall be forced to live in a permanent state of war."

I do not see any way in which Americans can contribute to the active pursuit of peace. That is a matter for the people of the former Palestine themselves. But it is conceivable that Americans might make some contribution to the passive search for peace, by providing channels of communication, by broadening the scope of discussion and exploring basic issues in ways that are not easily open to those who see their lives as immediately threatened. It cannot be said that anything serious has been done to realize these possibilities.

I suspect that the major contribution that can be made in the United States, or outside the Palestine area, is more indirect. The situation in the Middle East, as elsewhere, might be very different if there were an international left with a strong base in the United States that could provide an alternative framework for thinking and action[8]—an alternative, that is, to the system of national states which, under the circumstances of the world today, leads to massacre and repression for the weak and probable suicide for the strong. I am thinking of an international movement that could challenge the destructive concept of "national interest," which in practice means the interests of the ruling groups of the various societies of the world and which creates insoluble conflicts over issues that in no way reflect the needs and aspirations of the people of these societies, an international left that could represent humane ideals in the face of the powerful institutions, state and private, that dominate national policy and determine the course of international affairs.

In the specific case of the Palestine problem, such a new framework, I think, is desperately needed, and I can imagine no source from which it might derive other than a revitalized international movement that would stand for the ideals of brotherhood, cooperation, democracy, social and economic development guided by intrinsic, historically evolving needs— ideals that do belong to the left, or would if it existed in any serious form. Perhaps the most significant contribution that can be made to reconciliation in Palestine by those not directly involved is to work for the creation of an international movement guided by these ideals and committed to a struggle for them, often in opposition to the national states, the national and international private empires, and the elites that govern them.

It is perfectly possible to construct an "Arab case" and a "Jewish case," each having a high degree of plausibility and persuasiveness, each quite simple in its essentials. The Arab case is based on the premise that the great powers imposed a European migration, a national home for the Jews, and finally a Jewish state, in cynical disregard of the wishes of the overwhelming majority of the population,[9] innocent of any charge. The result: hundreds of thousands of Arab refugees in exile, while the "law of return" of the Jewish state confers citizenship, automatically, on any Jew who chooses to settle in their former homes. The Zionist case relies on the aspirations of a people who suffered two millennia of exile and savage persecution culminating in the most fantastic outburst of collective insanity in human history, on the natural belief that a normal human existence will be possible only in a national home in the land to which they had never lost their ties, and on the extraordinary creativity and courage of those who made the desert bloom. The conflict between these opposing claims was recognized from the start. Arthur Balfour put the matter clearly, as he saw it, in a memorandum of 1919:

... in Palestine we do not propose even to go through the form of consulting the wishes of the present inhabitants of the country, though the American [King–Crane] Commission has been going through the form of asking what they are. The four great powers are committed to Zionism and Zionism, be it right or wrong, good or bad, is rooted in age-long tradition, in present needs, in future hopes, of far profounder import than the desires and prejudices of the 700,000 Arabs who now inhabit that ancient land.[10]

The Arabs of Palestine may be pardoned for not sharing this sense of the priorities.

Not only can the Arab and Jewish case be formulated with power and persuasiveness; furthermore, each can be plausibly raised level of a demand for survival, hence in a sense an absolute demand. To the Israelis, the 1948 war is "the war of liberation." To the Arabs, it is "the war of conquest." Each side sees itself as a genuine national liberation movement. Each is the authentic Vietcong. Formulated within the framework of national survival, these competing claims lead inevitably to an irresoluble conflict. To such a conflict there can be no just solution. Force will prevail. Peace with justice is excluded from the start. Not surprisingly, the image of a crusader state is invoked by men of the most divergent views: Arnold Toynbee, Gamal Abdel Nasser, Yitzhak Rabin, and many others.

The likely evolution of the conflict should be particularly evident to the Israelis, given the Jewish historical experience. The exile of the Palestinian Arabs is taking on some of the characteristics of the Jewish Diaspora. There are similarities between the emerging national movement of the Palestinian Arabs in exile and the Zionist movement itself. In "an open letter to the occupiers of my homeland," a Palestinian refugee writes these words:

Theodore Herzl once said the Jews must go to Palestine because it was "a land without people for a people without land." I cry, I sorrow, for that land was mine. I am people, the Palestinians are

people, and you who have suffered such persecutions, have forced
us to pick up your ancient cry: "*NEXT YEAR, JERUSALEM.*"[11]

It is unlikely that the sentiments expressed in this letter will diminish in intensity. Rather, it is reasonable to expect that each
Israeli victory will strengthen the forces of Palestinian Arab nationalism. Whatever agreements may be reached between Israel
and the Arab states—and any agreements seem, for the moment,
quite unlikely—these forces will no doubt persist. Israel is incapable of conquering the Arab hinterland, it is partially dependent on Western support (a weak reed, at best), and it can lose
only once. The prospects are not attractive.

Many Israeli spokesmen believe that the terrorism of the
Arab movements (from the Arab point of view, the resistance
to the occupying forces) can easily be contained, that it is an
unpleasantness on the order of traffic accidents. I am in no position to judge, but it is far from certain. Eric Rouleau cites an
Israeli spokesman who told him "that the commandos had
considerably improved their equipment, technique, and fighting spirit." He cites a statement by Moshe Dayan that it is
wrong to think of the fedayeen only as criminals, that in fact
they are "inspired by a patriotism and idealism that should not
be underestimated."[12] There are reports indicating growing
sympathy for the fedayeen in the occupied territories,[13] where
an Israeli journalist describes the attitude of the Arabs as now
ranging "from passive dislike to open hatred."[14] Some knowledgeable Israeli observers sense, furthermore, that "growing
numbers of Israeli Arabs, torn between conflicting loyalties,
are being drawn into the unrest," noting correctly that this development is "more alarming from Israel's point of view" than
the terrorism itself.[15] Yet it appears an inevitable development.
Under the existing conditions, the Palestinian Arabs will inevitably be regarded as a potential fifth column and treated as
second-class citizens.[16] It would be most remarkable if they did
not react, ultimately, in such a way as to fulfill these fears. Furthermore, it is unimaginable that these fears will abate, so long

as the threat of extermination remains. The likely consequences are all too clear.

Israel asks only peace, normal relations with its neighbors, and its continued existence as a state. But when the Arab–Israel conflict is posed in the terms of national conflict, it is quite unlikely that these aims can be achieved. Israel can hardly hope to make peace on its terms with the Arab states for the simple reason that these terms do not make provision for the rights of the Arabs of Palestine, now largely in exile or under military occupation, as they see their rights. The Palestinian Arabs are increasingly becoming an organized force, certain to press their demands in conflict with the Arab states and with Israel as well. This force cannot be overlooked, nor can its claims be lightly dismissed. The major consequence of the Six-Day War may prove to be the consolidation of the Palestinian Arabs, for the first time, as a serious political and paramilitary force. If so, then the framework of national conflict is indeed a prescription for Semitic suicide.

Eric Rouleau speaks of "the classical chain reaction—occupation, resistance, repression, more resistance." There are other links in this chain. The Israeli journalist Victor Cygielman writes: "One thing is sure, terrorism will not succeed in wrecking Israel, but it may succeed in ruining Israeli democracy."[17] He is speaking of the demoralizing effect of "such measures of collective punishment as the blowing up of houses, administrative arrests and deportation to Jordan," and he comments that "the arrest of several citizens of Taibe and Haifa [i.e., within the territory of Israel itself] on the charge of having tried to establish *El Fatah* cells on Israeli soil, may show a developing trend." Other Israeli intellectuals have voiced similar fears.

Still other dangers are pointed out by the Israeli Middle East expert Shimon Shamir:

> Perhaps the highest price that Israel might have to pay for a prolonged political domination of the Palestinian Arab society would be in the field from which Israel derives its strength—the spirit of its citizen-army. It can be doubted whether a society

whose institutions have been engaged for a long time in frustrat-
ing the political demands of a large Arab population could again
manifest the same spirit of absolute solidarity, of fighting with
one's back to the wall, of raging resistance to threats of extermination.[18]

In part, this "high price" is a consequence of the occupation. But
the occupation is unlikely to be abandoned until security is guaranteed, and there is no way for security to be guaranteed within
the framework accepted by both sides.

It is natural to think that security can be achieved only
through strength and through the use of force against a threatening opponent. Perhaps so. But those who adopt this course
must at least be clear about the likely dynamics of the process to
which they are contributing: occupation, resistance, repression,
more resistance, more repression, erosion of democracy, internal
quandaries and demoralization, further polarization and extremism on both sides, and ultimately—one shrinks from the obvious
conclusions. It is not evident that security is to be achieved
through the use of force.

There is some historical experience on which we can draw. My
impression—I stress again the limitations of my knowledge—
is that by and large, the effect of coercion and force is to create
a strong, vigorous, often irrational opponent, committed to the
destruction of those who wield this force. There is an exception,
of course, namely, when the opponent can be physically
crushed.

It seems clear that the current exercise of force is having just
this effect. Terroristic attacks on civilians simply consolidate
Israeli opinion and drive the population into the hands of
those who advocate the reliance on force. If this process does
succeed in destroying Israeli democracy and turning Israel into
a police state, the Palestinian Arabs will have gained very little thereby. Similarly, collective punishment, razing of houses
and villages, detention, and exile, surely have the effect of
strengthening the hands of those in the Palestinian Arab

movement who see the physical destruction of Israeli society as the only solution.

In the past, I think that much the same was true. Prior to 1948, the Jewish community in Palestine in general tried to avoid the use of force and coercion and to refrain from a policy of reprisal in response to physical attacks and terror. The policy of *Havlagah*—restraint—in the late 1930s was not only a moral achievement of the highest order, but was also, it seems, reasonably effective as a tactic. There were groups in the Jewish settlement that did believe in the resort to terror against the Mandatory authorities and reprisals against the Arab revolt (itself largely directed against the Mandatory—"a furious but futile revolt against Great Britain"[19]). These were the groups of the extreme right—chauvinist, anti-Arab, antilabor, with their social roots among the Zionist bourgeoisie and the associations of private farmers. Tensions between these groups and the Socialist–Zionist settlers "erupted in a miniature Jewish civil war early in the 1940s."[20]

As to the policy of anti-Arab reprisal, instead of my trying to assess its effects, let me simply present the words of the political arm of the terrorist organizations:

> Out of the humiliated souls of Palestine Jewry, the Irgun Tsevai Leumi (National Military Organization) was born. It was created by a few dynamic spirits within the national youth and was inspired by Jabotinsky's untiring propaganda for Jewish self-defense—propaganda that for years had been stigmatized by official Jewish leaders as "Fascist," "militarist," and "reactionary."[21] In September, 1937, the Irgun struck. During the first week of that month, the Arabs killed three Jews. The Irgun executed thirteen Arabs for the crime. In panic-stricken fury, the Arabs derailed a train, ambushed one Jewish bus and bombed another—claiming the lives of fourteen more Jews. For two months, Arab terrorism flamed again with murderous violence.[22]

Evidently, a great tribute to the effectiveness of the reprisal policy. The document goes on to explain how the Irgun "avenged the murder of every Jew," while "the flustered Jewish Agency publicly denounced the actions of the Irgun 'which (it said) are marring the moral record of Palestine Jewry, hampering the political struggle and undermining security.'" The accuracy of the charge is illustrated by the continuing account of Irgun actions— for example, of how the Irgun fearlessly invaded Arab settlements on the occasion of an Arab parade celebrating the 1939 White Paper, "transform[ing] the day of victory into a day of mourning," and so on.

It was semifascist elements such as these that were largely responsible for the reprisals, which had the effects just indicated. The same, I believe, was largely true at the time of the partition agreement. Let me quote a report from the *Bulletin* of the Council on Jewish–Arab Cooperation, a group that emphasized "the possibilities for independent political action by workers as a class, as contrasted to reliance on decisions of any of the big powers":

> The role of the Jewish terrorist bands (Irgun Zvai Leumi and the Stern group) in the recent fighting can be seen from a listing of their activities. Dec. 7—they threw a bomb into the Arab market place in Haifa. Dec. 11—they bombed Arab buses in Haifa and Jerusalem, killing and wounding many, and shot two Arabs in Jerusalem. Dec. 12—bombings and shootings in Haifa, nearby Tireh, Gaza, Hebron and other cities, killing many Arabs. Dec. 13—Irgun agents bombed Arab buses, killing 16 and wounding at least 67 Arabs. Jewish terrorists carried out a series of assaults on Dec. 15, attacking Arab buses, Arab pedestrians and random personnel of the Transjordan Frontier Force.

> These actions began precisely at the time when it appeared to newspaper correspondents and to the *Bulletin* correspondents in Palestine that Arab attacks were subsiding, or when, after enduring much hardship from Arab terrorist dominance, Arabs took initiative to effect formal understandings with Jewish neighbors against all armed terrorists. At no time did the Jewish terrorists even claim to be attacking the Mufti's bands or to be making any

differentiation among Arabs. The special attention to Haifa, a workers' city where the Arabs had committed almost no attacks, indicates the intention to arouse Arab workers to anti-Jewish reprisals.[23]

During these and following months, Arab terrorists, both Palestinian and infiltrated, were responsible for widespread murder and destruction, giving substance to the statements of men like Azzam Pasha, secretary general of the Arab League, who announced "a war of extermination and a momentous massacre which will be spoken of like the Mongolian massacre and the Crusades."[24]

One cannot fail to note, throughout this period, the similarities of intent on the part of the terrorists on both sides, and still more strikingly, the impact of each in strengthening the influence of the other and increasing the general polarization and drift toward irresoluble national conflict. Perhaps the conflict was unavoidable. In any event, the policy of terror and reprisal made a major contribution to intensifying it and embittering relations among people who must cooperate, ultimately, if they are to survive in some decent fashion.

Reprisals have a certain logic within the framework of national conflict. One who sees a national conflict between all Arabs and all Jews might well argue that any terrorist act by any Arab or Jew can properly be the occasion for a reprisal against any Jew or Arab. In this way, the terror continues on its upward spiral, and the use of force is given new legitimacy within each of the polarizing societies.

Even from a narrow point of view, one can raise the factual question of the actual effects of the reprisal policy. I have already noted two occasions when its effect on security was at best dubious. Let me turn to a third, a few years later. I quote from Nadav Safran, a well-known Harvard Middle Eastern scholar with pro-Israel sympathies. Commenting on the Israeli attack on the Gaza strip in 1955, the first major reprisal against Arab-held territory by the Israeli army, he has this to say:

The Egyptian authorities tended at first merely to wink at infiltration undertaken for all sorts of purposes from the Gaza strip under their control. But after a murderous Israeli retaliatory raid on
Gaza in February 1955, the Egyptian government responded defi-
antly by launching a deliberate raiding campaign from Gaza and
Jordan. . . . Israeli retaliatory attacks only increased the defiance
of the Egyptian authorities and the murderousness of the raids,
until finally Israel took advantage of a favorable conjuncture to
launch an all-out invasion of Sinai and the Gaza strip in October
1956.[25]

Once again, the policy of forceful reprisal had rather dubious
consequences, from the point of view of security. Safran goes on
to say that since the 1956 war the border has been quiet (prior to
the Six-Day War), so that the 1956 attack was a success from the
Israeli point of view, as he sees it. But Safran's analysis—which is
highly professional and informative—suffers from a fundamental
defect typical of the "realist" political science of which his work
is a good example. He disregards the people of Palestine and considers only the relations among national states and the interplay
among them at the level of coercive force. This choice of framework, which is quite explicit, is appropriate for the study of some
aspects of the problem, but one who focuses on "the manipulation of various forms of coercion in the service of policy, and of
policy in the service of enhancing the means of coercion"
(Safran) will no doubt miss a great deal. Safran, by virtually eliminating from consideration the Arab population of Palestine, seriously underestimates the rise of Palestinian Arab nationalism.
In particular, he fails to see the significance of the rise of al-Fatah, which many observers believe to be a genuine expression—
the first—of the national consciousness of the masses of Palestinian Arabs.[26]

The moderate Lebanese journalist Ghassan Tueini described
"the formation of *Fatah* [as] the single most significant event in
the Arab World for 50 years."[27] There is a fair amount of evidence that this represents the thinking of many Palestinian intellectuals, who might agree with a teacher in East Jerusalem that

the "Palestinians had to take matters into their own hands," that they have captured "the imagination of the Arab masses . . . thanks to the Israeli policy of retaliation as well as a strenuous effort on their part."[28] The explicit goal of al-Fatah is to involve the masses in struggle, now that they have recognized the futility of looking to the Arab states for salvation. "In our view, any liberation activity that does not try to involve the masses properly is doomed to failure, since it ignores the most important element influencing the struggle."[29] It is clearly recognized that this may draw the Arab countries into war. The prospect is welcomed, even if the result is a defeat, which will lead to an extended occupation and further opportunities for growth of the liberation movement. In the article just quoted, Nasr (see note 28) continues: "No Arab–Israeli settlement (even one sponsored by Nasser) is worth the paper it is written on without fedayeen agreement." This seems plausible, given the growth of al-Fatah as an expression of Palestinian Arab national consciousness.

If these assessments are accurate, as the information available to me suggests, then Safran's analysis of the interstate conflict is of only marginal relevance.

Returning to the matter of force and security, Safran argues that though the 1955 reprisal and subsequent retaliatory attacks increased the Egyptian support for terrorism, nevertheless after the 1956 war the level of violence subsided. However, from another point of view that takes in a somewhat longer time span, the 1956 war contributed significantly to violent confrontation. The 1956 war apparently provided the immediate impulse for the formation of al-Fatah, and, as just noted, this counts as a rather questionable gain from the point of view of Israeli security. According to Chaliand (see note 26), until 1961 the organization was occupied with establishing the nucleus of a political organization among the Palestinian intelligentsia, and then for several years proceeded to develop a paramilitary organization. Its first casualty was suffered at the hands of a Jordanian soldier in 1965, and until the Six-Day War it was strictly controlled by the Arab states. The catastrophic defeat of June 1967 left a political and

military vacuum that was quickly filled by al-Fatah, now relatively free from the constraints formerly imposed and solidly
based in the Palestinian population.

Most observers agree that the Israeli retaliatory attack on
Karama in March 1968 "marked a turning point in the evolution
of the Palestine armed resistance movement."[30] It enormously increased the strength and prestige of al-Fatah (which claimed a
victory and was believed, whatever the facts may be) among the
Arab masses and, as a result, with the Arab states, which, no
doubt reluctantly, are forced to grant to the Palestinian resistance
considerable latitude. The organization now claims to be unable
to absorb the volunteers flocking to it.[31]

As I have already noted, some Israeli commentators concede
that the movement exhibits considerable élan and vitality,
though few regard it as a true military threat. Ehud Yaari (see
note 29) is probably fairly representative of informed Israeli opinion when he writes:

> Even its most vigorous critics cannot deny Al-Fatah its character
> as an ideological movement, as well as an active military organi-
> zation. The skeleton of the new theory has already been set up;
> only actual experience can show whether it will put on flesh and
> blood. The fundamental difference between the wave of terror
> that preceded the Sinai Campaign in 1956 and the wave that has
> been growing since 1965 lies in the fact that in contrast to the
> murderous groups acting for revenge or profit, Israel now faces a
> terrorist organization with a specific political theory; terror one of
> a number of elements.

In short, it seems accurate to say that Israel now faces a liberation
movement modeling itself consciously on others that have
proven successful. Many differences can be noted. However, still
taking the narrow view of Israeli security, the evolution from
predatory bands to a conscious mass-based liberation movement
hardly counts as a success for the policy of security through force.

Israeli retaliation is seen by al-Fatah leadership as a major
weapon in their arsenal. The Fatah leader Yasser Arafat says:

Thank for God for Dayan. He provides the daily proof of the expansionist nature of Zionism. . . . After the 1967 defeat, Arab
opinion, broken and dispirited, was ready to conclude peace at
any price. If Israel, after its lightning victory, had proclaimed
that it has no expansionist aims, and withdrawn its troops from
the conquered territories, while continuing to occupy certain
strategic points necessary to its security, the affair would have
been easily settled with the countries that were the victims of
the aggression.[32]

Other Fatah spokesmen have expressed similar views. One,
quoted by Hudson (see note 31), advocates violence because it
"forces the Israelis to retaliate desperately and indiscriminately
against the surrounding Arab countries, but in so doing Israel
only diminishes its reputation in the international community
and forces the Arab governments into even greater solidarity
with the Palestinians," who will themselves, it is expected, be
drawn into resistance in reaction to the harsh reprisals in the occupied areas or the neighboring countries.

How accurate this analysis may be I am in no position to
judge. I suspect that it is fairly realistic. It relies on factors often
overlooked by the "realist" analysts who think only in terms of
national states that monopolize the instruments of coercion and
use them to achieve the "national interest" as conceived by their
respective elites. What is overlooked is the dynamics of a popular national movement. With all differences that have so often
been stressed, there still remains an analogy to Vietnam, where
American force, applied on an enormous and horrifying scale, led
to a tremendous upsurge of Vietcong strength.[33] In this respect,
the situation in Palestine may be similar. A story has it that
Dayan once advised that the Israeli military study the American
policy in Vietnam carefully, and then do just the opposite. This
advice is difficult to follow for an occupying power, operating
within the framework of national conflict.

It seems to me that something like the foregoing is what is suggested by the history of the past years. The policy of reprisal,
widely shunned by the socialist masses in Palestine in earlier

years, has, not surprisingly, become national policy with the establishment of the state. As noted, it has a certain logic within the framework of national conflict. It is the logic of despair and ultimate disaster.

One might argue that it is rather cheap, from 5,000 miles away, to urge the advantages of a policy of conciliation in preference to the harsh tactic of repression and reprisal (or a combination of the carrot and the stick). How else are we to defend ourselves from the terrorist attacks? Or, from the other side, how are we to liberate our homeland except through violent resistance? Each reproach is legitimate, in its own terms. Still, certain questions must be faced: What are the actual consequences of violence, on either side? Is there an alternative to the framework of national conflict, the relentless pursuit of "national interest" through force?

With regard to the first question, I can only repeat that each side seems to be to be locked into a suicidal policy. Israel cannot hope to achieve peace on its terms by force. Rather, it will simply build the forces that will lead to its eventual destruction by force, or to a permanent garrison state, or, perhaps, to some form of colonization of the area by the great powers to enforce their form of stability—not too unlikely if nuclear weapons and missiles enter the picture.[34] Unless it achieves a settlement with the Palestinian Arabs, or crushes them by force, Israel will no doubt be unable to reach any meaningful agreement with Egypt or the other Arab states. There will be a constant temptation to undertake pre-emptive strikes, which, if successful, will simply reconstitute the original conflict at a higher level of hostility and enhance the power of those who demand a military solution. For Egypt, an acceptable long-term strategy may be "to reduce the margin of Israel's military superiority to the point when Israel can no longer win battles except at great human cost."[35] The internal effects in Israel might be such as to destroy whatever was of lasting human value in the Zionist ideal. Perhaps it is appropriate to recall the warning of Ahad Ha-am, quoted by Moshe Smilansky in expressing his opposition to the Biltmore Program (see note 1):

In the days of the House of Herod, Palestine was a Jewish State. Such a Jewish State would be poison for our nation and drag it down into the dust. Our small State would never attain a political power worthy of the name, for it would be but a football between its neighbors, and but exist by diplomatic chicanery and constant submission to whoever was dominant at the time. Thus we should become a small and low people in spiritual servitude, looking with envy towards the mighty fist.[36]

Parallel comments apply with respect to the Arab states and the Arab liberation movements. There is no possibility that the Jewish population of Israel will give up its cultural autonomy, or freely leave, or abandon a high degree of self-government. Any plan of liberation that aims at these goals will lead to one or another form of massacre, or perhaps to recolonization by the great powers. In this case, too, whatever is of lasting human value in the movement for Arab liberation can hardly survive such policies, and will be submerged in reaction and authoritarianism.

Within the framework of "national interest," of the conflict of "Jewish rights" and "Arab rights," the problem cannot be resolved in terms that satisfy the just aspirations of the people of what was once Palestine.

In principle, there is a very different framework of thinking within which the problem of Palestine can be formulated. How realistic it is, I am not competent to judge—though I might add that I am not too impressed by the "realism" of contemporary ideologists, including many who masquerade as political scientists, historians, or revolutionaries. The alternative is ridiculously simple, and therefore no doubt terribly naïve. It draws from one part of the historical experience and the expressed ideals of the Zionist and Arab nationalist movements, from currents that can barely be perceived today, after two decades of intermittent war, but that are nonetheless quite real.

The alternative to the framework of national states, national conflict, and national interest, is cooperation among people who have common interests that are not expressible in national terms, that in general assume class lines. Such alternatives are open to those who believe that the common interest of the great masses of people in Palestine—and everywhere—is the construction of a world of democratic communities in which political institutions, as well as the commercial and industrial system as a whole, are under direct popular control, and the resources of modern civilization are directed to the satisfaction of human needs and libertarian values. There is little reason to suppose that these interests are served by a Jewish state, any more than they are served by the states of the Arab world. Feeling this way, I read with some slight degree of optimism such statements as this by a spokesman for one of the Palestinian Arab organizations:

> It is not enough simply to wear khaki and shoot to have a revolution, and the Palestinian youth are not giving their lives just to restore the oppressive rule of landlords and big businessmen in Palestine.[37]

Such comments bring to mind the position of the Left Front of Histadrut, which won 20 percent of the vote in the August 1944 elections, on a platform that included this statement:

> The Left Front will fight for the construction of Palestine as a joint homeland for the Jewish people returning to its land and for the masses of the Arab people who dwell in it; for setting up of a state form for Palestine in the spirit of the brotherhood of peoples, nondomination, and national fraternity—in accordance with the national, social, and political interests of the two peoples, and looking forward to the creation of a socialist Palestine.[38]

A social revolution that would be democratic and socialist, that would move both Arab and Jewish society in these directions, would serve the vital interest of the great majority of the people in Palestine, as elsewhere. At least, this is my personal belief, and a belief that was surely a driving force behind the Jewish settlement of Palestine in the first place. It is quite true, I believe, that "Zionism, being the outcome partly of Jewish and partly of non-Jewish enlightenment, and being also a secular reaction to Jewish assimilation . . . conceived the Jewish national revival more in terms of the realisation of a harmonious 'just society' than in terms of the realisation of Jewish political independence."[39] Or, to be more exact, this was a major element in the prewar settlement.

This tendency is given little emphasis in the predominantly political and military histories. It is presented and analyzed in such works as the Esco Foundation study (see note 1), or in Aharon Cohen's massive study of Jewish–Arab cooperation and conflict (see note 19), with its extensive documentation of efforts—abortive, but not hopeless—to create a binational Palestinian community in which the vital interests and just goals of Jews and Arabs might be met. The problem, as he formulates it, has always been this: "how to weave together concrete interests and high aspirations, to create the conditions for cooperative and compatible efforts, to exploit the given objective possibilities and to strengthen the forces working to advance the common good, both material and spiritual." The greatest obstacle has been "the failure to understand the true significance of this task, narrowness of vision and insufficient effort." As Cohen correctly observes: "In the absence of the intellectual and moral courage to face this failure honestly, there is no hope of repairing that which demands repair . . . no hope of breaking out of the magic circle: an increase in the Jewish constructive effort in Israel, an increase in its strength—and along with it, an increase in the dangers that threaten all of these achievements. . . ."

This is, I believe, the proper standpoint from which to approach the problems of today, as it was a generation ago. Then it represented, I think it is fair to say, a significant position in the Palestinian Jewish community—a matter to which I will return. Ben-Gurion once wrote that only an insane person could attribute to Zionism the wish to force any of the Arab community from their homes: "Zionism has not come to inherit its place or to build on its ruins. . . . We have no right to harm a single Arab child, even if with this we could achieve all that we wish."[40] It can never be too late to try to recapture this vision.

A movement to create a democratic, socialist Palestine—optimally, integrated into a broader federation—that preserves some degree of communal autonomy and national self-government is not beyond the bounds of possibility. It might build on what, to my mind, is the outstanding contribution of the Zionist movement to modern history—the cooperatives, which have proven to be an outstanding social and economic success and point the way to the future, if there is to be a future for the human race. The long-standing position of the left wing of the Kibbutz movement was "that the kibbutz was not simply a form of settlement but a way of life, the raison d'être of Zionism."[41] One of the consequences of the partition—to my mind, an extremely unfortunate one—has been the relative decline in importance of the collectives within Israel. Perhaps this trend could be reversed if the national struggle were to be transcended by a movement for social reconstruction of a revitalized Arab–Jewish left. Admittedly, the possibilities seem slight. But there are some historical precedents that are hopeful. One thinks at once of Yugoslavia, where in the course of a successful social revolution, "the old conflict-provoking ethnic ties (Serb, Croat, and so forth) give some evidence of being less 'irrational' and less binding, with more individuals thereby willing to think of themselves quite simply as individuals operating within a broad Yugoslav context."[42]

If the Arab and the Israeli left are to develop a common program, each will have to extricate itself from a broader national movement in which the goals of social reconstruction are subordinated to the demand for national self-determination. One can imagine a variety of possibilities for binational federation, with parity between partially autonomous communities. A common political and social struggle might take the place of national conflict—as meaningless, ultimately, as it was to those who slaughtered one another for the glory of the nation at Verdun.

National ties are strong, and any steps toward cooperation must build upon them. True cooperation can only be for common goals, and between equals. In this respect, the formation of al-Fatah might prove to be a significant step toward peaceful reconciliation. A shattered, fragmented society cannot come to terms with a well-organized, technologically advanced counterpart. The Israeli left can lose nothing, and can perhaps gain a great deal, by trying to relate itself in some way to the newly consolidating Palestinian Arab community, particularly its left-wing elements. To do so, it will have to see the other side of the coin (as Aharon Cohen has put it on several occasions) and offer a positive and meaningful program for cooperation, even one with long-range and perhaps still distant goals. Given the present constellation of forces, it is reasonably clear that the initiative must come from this source. It is not for me to suggest concrete steps—in fact, the bare beginnings perhaps already exist.[43] To extend them and build upon them should be the major preoccupation of those concerned to create the conditions for a just peace.

Might there be any Arab response to such initiatives? From the information available to me, it seems that there might very well be a response. Consider, for example, the following remarks in a recent editorial in the official organ of the Arab Socialist Union, the only functioning political organization in Egypt.[44]

. . . the new society [in Palestine] must be open to all Jews, Moslems, and Christians without exclusiveness or discrimination between first and second-class citizens; and this non-racist nature of the new state must impose its implications and principles, by necessity, on its constitution and laws, and on the rights and duties of the citizens. . . . [This strategy] must be crystallized into a "dynamic organization" that will strengthen all Arabs and Jews antagonistic to imperialism, Zionism, and all forms of racism on the local and international levels. . . . In my opinion, the first step in building this front, which will completely change the balance of power, is the joint responsibility of the Palestinian Resistance on the one hand, and of the Jewish local and world masses antagonistic to imperialism and Zionism, on the other. This front, by undertaking such a progressive program, which represents the will for liberation from imperialism and racism, will not be serving the interest of the Arab and Jewish masses . . . alone, but will serve humanity's movement in advancing towards a new world free of colonialism, imperialism and aggression, and free of the dangers of a total destructive war which is the situation in the Middle East today, one of the world's most explosive regions.

The editorial is said to be "the fruits of a positive discussion which I had the opportunity to conduct at consecutive meetings with a number of the leaders of Fatah and the Popular Front in addition to some Arab friends among revolutionaries and intellectuals." Fatah statements repeatedly call for "the destruction of the Zionist and racist structures [of the state of Israel and the establishment of a] secular and democratic Palestine reaching from the Mediterranean to Jordan"[45] (I presume this means including Jordan).

Y. Harkabi, who quotes a number of statements of this sort (see note 26), observes that "the Arabs' objective of destroying the state of Israel (what may be called a 'politicide') drives them to genocide," since Zionism is not only a political regime or a superstructure of sorts, but is embodied in a *society*." This is a possible, but not an absolutely necessary, interpretation of such proposals.[46] The Israeli left might well give a different interpretation, first, to the aspirations of Zionism, and correspondingly, to the intention of these statements. By so doing, it may help to give substance and reality to a more sympathetic and constructive interpretation.

The goal of a democratic socialist community with equal rights for all citizens and the goal of "a federative framework with the Kingdom of Jordan and the Palestinian people, based on cooperation in the fields of security and economics"[47] do not, on the face of it, appear to be incompatible. There may, then, be room for fruitful and perhaps eventually cooperative effort between the Arab and the Israeli left. I suspect that the fundamental stumbling block to any agreement will prove to be the Israeli "law of return," which Ben-Gurion has described as "the peculiar sign that singles out the State of Israel and fixes its central mission, the Zionist–Jewish mission . . . the foundation scroll of the rights of the Jewish people in Israel."[48] It is primarily by virtue of this law that Israel is a "Jewish State." It is hard to imagine that the Arabs of Palestine will consent to a law which, in effect, prevents them from returning to their homes on the theory that the Jews of the world have a more pressing need and a greater right to settle in this land. I have seen no sign that any substantial segment of Israeli opinion is willing to consider the abandonment of the principle embodied in the "law of the return."[49]

It seems to me that the situation of today is more like that of 1947 than of any intervening period. Furthermore, there have been twenty years of experience from which, perhaps, something has been learned. Both international and domestic factors are more conducive to a peaceful resolution of the conflict than has been the case for some time.

As to the international situation, the possibilities of great power conflict are quite real, and insofar as their leaders are rational, neither of the great powers can conceivably fail to fear such a conflict.[50] It is also possible that the great powers have learned that even in their narrow self-interest, attempts to organize the Middle East within an imperial system are not likely to be successful. Dulles's Baghdad Pact led to the Nasser–USSR arms deal, which significantly increased the flow of weapons and the level of tension in the Middle East. Attempts to intervene in Syria, Lebanon, and Jordan in 1957–1958 ranged from the ludicrous to near-disaster. Safran describes them as "the final failure in the succession of unsuccessful British, British–American, and American attempts since the end of World War II to organize the Middle East heartland in the frame of the Western alliance system."[51] The Soviet attempt to intervene, for example in Iraq, was no less of a catastrophe.[52] Perhaps, then, the great powers might be willing to keep hands off, even to permit some form of genuine socialist development in the Middle East outside of the

framework of competing imperialisms, if it has substantial domestic roots.

A sensible American policy would encourage Israel to break
free of Western influence. Out of a felt need to rely on the Western powers, Israel has been unable to support anticolonial forces
in North Africa and the Middle East—for example, the Algerian
FLN. Such a policy must, naturally, be harmful to the development of decent relations with the Arab countries and their peoples. A different Western policy might, in principle, permit options that would, no doubt, be more congenial to much of the
Israeli population itself. It might also, in principle, include the
kind of economic assistance that actually contributes to development—in this case, to help close the economic and social gap between Arab and Jewish populations, a prerequisite to any real cooperation. The chances that such a policy will be undertaken are
no doubt slight.

Far more important are the domestic factors, no longer what
they were twenty years ago. In 1947, the Palestinian Jewish community was traumatized by the Holocaust. It was aware that no
world power would be willing to lift a finger to save the miserable
remnants of European Jewry, no more than they were at the international conferences of Evian in 1938 or Bermuda in 1943.
Furthermore, it was psychologically impossible to contemplate
the resettlement of these tortured victims in a new diaspora. The
Palestinian Jewish settlement acted accordingly and did succeed
in settling 300,000 Jewish refugees in a Jewish state, but at a fear-
ful cost. An approximately equal number of Jewish refugees
reached Israel after having been expelled from the Arab countries in the wake of the 1948 war, and hundreds of thousands of
Arab refugees fled, or were driven from their homes in the new
State of Israel. For those Arabs who remained, living standards
have no doubt improved, but there is much evidence that many
were dispossessed of homes, land, and property, and deprived of
the right of free political organization.[53]

Today the situation is very different. The Nazi massacre,
though unforgettable in its horror, no longer determines the

choice of action. Rather, it is the living death of the refugee camps and the steady drift toward further misery yet to come that set the terms for policy.

From the perspective of twenty years, I think we can see the extent to which the war jarred the Zionist movement into a new and somewhat different course, which might still be modified without an abandonment of its fundamental aims. The concept of a Jewish state is not so deeply rooted in the history of the Jewish settlement of Palestine as one might be led to believe, judging by the temperament that has prevailed in recent years. I have already mentioned that the first official formulation of the demand for a Jewish state was in 1942, when the war was under way and the center of World Zionism had shifted to the United States. After an extensive analysis, the Esco Foundation report concluded: "It is not too much to say that the position of the Zionist leadership from the Twelfth Carlsbad Congress in 1921 [the first to convene after the Balfour declaration] to the Twenty-First Congress in Geneva in 1939 was strongly tinctured with bi-nationalism."[54] At the Congress of 1931, Weizmann insisted that security could be achieved only by establishing friendly relations with the Arabs of Palestine on the basis "of complete parity without regard to the numerical strength of either people."[55] Ben-Gurion spoke in similar terms in testifying before the Peel Commission in 1937.[56] Even Jabotinsky insisted only that "the Jewish point of view should always prevail" in a state that had "that measure of self-government which for instance the State of Nebraska possesses,"[57] and his nationalist extremism caused him to leave the Zionist organization several years later. Many others—Kalvarisky, Arlosoroff,[58] Magnes, Smilansky—labored incessantly to establish a dialogue with Palestine Arabs that would lead to Arab–Jewish cooperation within a binational framework.

Their efforts were not so unsuccessful as is often claimed.[59] In the early 1920s several Arab peasant parties called for Arab–Jewish cooperation against exploiters, and in Haifa, largely a working-class city, the former Arab mayor (who had been removed by the British) was a member of an upper-class Muslim

society that spoke of the need for Arab–Jewish cooperation.[60] A
number of conferences of Jews and Arabs took place, some that
appeared to offer some promise, though no serious efforts were
made by official bodies to carry matters further. There were joint
strikes and demonstrations of Arab and Jewish workers until
1947, and among agricultural communities there was undoubtedly much friendly contact, persisting beyond the establishment
of the state.

Many of the Arabs who attempted to maintain friendly relations were assassinated, as were some who combatted the politics
of the Arab leadership. One example, just prior to the partition
agreement, was the case of the Arab labor leader Sami Taha, who
was murdered after an attempt to form an Arab "workers' party,"
free from the control of the Arab Higher Committee.[61] He had
called for a democratic Palestinian state in which Jews and Arabs
would have equal rights. He was a supporter of Musa al-Alami,
who had been involved in earlier discussions with Weizmann and
others and was regarded as a spokesman for the rights of Arab
workers and peasants.[62] It seems fair to say that there was an un-
written unholy alliance of sorts among the Jewish and Arab
right-wing terrorist organizations and segments of the British
forces, all engaged in terroristic attacks that polarized the two societies and killed a number of those who attempted reconciliation (see note 20).

Perhaps the most significant case was that of Fawzi al-
Husseini, who was assassinated in November 1946. He was the
nephew of the Mufti, Haj Amin al-Husseini. He had taken part
in the 1929 riots and had been imprisoned by the British during
the 1936–1939 revolt. Later, he became convinced of the necessity for Arab–Jewish cooperation, and just a few weeks before he
was killed, he signed an agreement in the name of a new organization, Falastin al-Jadida (New Palestine), with the League for
Arab–Jewish Rapprochement that had been founded in 1939 and
was headed by Kalvarisky. The document expressed the desire of
each organization "to support the activities of [the other] and to
assist it in all possible ways to make them a success."[63]

In the months before his death, he had spoken widely in support of such a view. Some of his remarks deserve fuller quotation:

> There is a way for understanding and agreement between the two nations, despite the many stumbling blocks in this path. Agreement is a necessity for the development of the country and the liberation of the two nations. The conditions of agreement—the principle of non-domination of one nation over the other and the establishment of a bi-national state on the basis of political parity and full cooperative effort between the two nations in economic, social and cultural domains. Immigration is a political problem and within the framework of general agreement it will not be difficult to solve this problem on the basis of the absorptive capacity of the land. The agreement between the two nations must receive international authorization by the UN, which must guarantee to the Arabs that the bi-national independent Palestine will join a federation with the neighboring Arab states.

These principles were written into the agreement between the League and Falastin al-Jadida.

At a meeting of Jews and Arabs at the home of Kalvarisky in Jerusalem, Fawzi al-Husseini lauded Kalvarisky's long-term efforts in the cause of Arab–Jewish cooperation, noted their partial success, and announced his intention to undertake similar efforts among the Arab population. He expressed his belief that, despite the support of the Mandatory authorities for the Arab leadership of Jamal al-Husseini and the Mufti, his efforts would meet with success if they received moral, organizational, and political support from the Jewish community and if cooperative efforts showed concrete results.

These efforts did receive a hopeful response in the Arab community, according to Cohen, but were cut short by Fawzi al-Husseini's assassination. The mood of World Zionism is indicated by the reaction at the Zionist Congress in Basel, when a spokesman for Hashomer Hatzair, Y. Chazan, spoke of the murder. According to the report in *Davar*: "Laughter and hilarity were caused by the story (of Chazan) about one Arab, a Zionist sympathizer, who was killed in Jerusalem because he believed in Jewish–Arab agreement and favored immigration. From the Revisionist rows someone commented: 'So this one Arab was killed, and now no one remains.'"

Such people as Chaim Kalvarisky and Fawzi al-Husseini existed. Many of them paid with their lives for the efforts to bring about reconciliation and peace. Because the support for them was insufficient, many, many more have been killed and maimed and driven from their homes, to empty, wasted lives, to hatred and torment. And the story has not yet come to an end.

I should like to conclude these remarks with an excerpt from an editorial statement in the *Bulletin* for Jewish–Arab cooperation in January 1948, just at the outbreak of the Twenty-Year War. I think that these words were appropriate then, and that they are again appropriate today:

> A major obstacle to bringing about peace in Palestine is the prevailing view that most Jews have of what they want from the Arabs. *What they would essentially prefer is that the Arabs be passive in respect to the Jews.* They want the Arabs not to object to Jewish immigration and construction, not to be too closely involved in the Jewish economy, and currently not to attack Jews or to harbor the attackers. In return, the Arabs would get economic benefits from the neighboring Jewish economy, would be gradually modernized economically and politically, and would on their part not be attacked by the Jews. *The weakness of this view is that people are not passive.* They may appear passive in that they accept the controls and ideas of relatively static upper classes. But when economic and social changes take place about them, they react to them. When the Arab upper class tries to direct the population into anti-Jewish attitudes, the Jewish workers cannot counter this by asking the Arab population not to react at all and to leave the Jews alone. They can only offer the Arabs an alternative way of reacting, one more useful to the Arab peasants and workers.

The only practicable alternative to war is therefore not peace but cooperation. In a long-range political sense, we can say that the only alternative to a war between nations is not a static peace . . . but a war between classes, between ruled and ruler, of the Jewish and Arab worker and peasant against the two upper classes, against the fascist parties of both nations, and the British or other outside interests that want to control the area.

These remarks, I repeat, were made in early 1948. They have a certain relevance to the situation of today. In particular, I think it is important to consider the idea that the only practicable alternative to war is not peace but cooperation—the active pursuit of peace—and that cooperation cannot exist in the abstract, but must be directed to the satisfaction of real human needs. In the Middle East, as elsewhere, these needs can be perceived as they are reflected—caricatured, I believe—in terms of "national interest." This way, it seems to me, lies tragedy and bitterness. Other ways are open, and they might provide a way to a better life, not only in Palestine, but in every part of this tragic and strife-torn world.

2

A Radical Perspective

L et me begin by entering a disclaimer. What I have to say will not be particularly radical. I will be satisfied if it is somewhat realistic and more or less humane. There may be, some day, a program of action in the Middle East that is both radical and realistic. However, it seems to me that that day is still remote.

I would like to distinguish very clearly between predictions and recommendations. A plausible analysis of the present situation leads, I am afraid, to unpleasant conclusions. I frankly expect them but do not recommend them. It is possible to recommend more attractive alternatives. It may even be possible to work toward them. One can only be skeptical, however, as to whether such efforts will succeed.

The participants in the Palestine tragedy of the past half-century perceive it as a national conflict: Jews against Arabs. To such a conflict—or better, to a conflict so perceived—there is no solution except through force.

This conclusion is, of course, not unique to the Arab–Israeli conflict. Rather, it is typical of national conflicts. Consider the Franco–German conflict in World War I. Those who spoke out against that meaningless slaughter were regarded as traitors. When Karl Liebknecht opposed war credits, he was denounced as a lunatic, a fanatic. These traitors and lunatics were right, of course. Both sides were following a losing strategy. Again, this is typical of national conflicts, which rarely serve the interests of those who are slaughtering or threatening one another.

In the present case, I think that each side is pursuing a losing strategy. Israel is, at the moment, the more powerful military force by a large margin. It is capable of striking far more
serious blows. The fate of the city of Suez is a sufficient example. According to recent reports, Israel is the only Middle Eastern power possessing medium-range surface-to-surface missiles
that can be fitted with conventional or nuclear warheads.
From inside Israel they could reach Cairo and Alexandria. It
seems likely that Israel is on the verge of producing nuclear
weapons and may, in fact, already be doing so.[1] Israel has been
hoping that, by exercising military force, it can bring the Arab
states to the negotiating table on its terms and can get them to
suppress the Palestine guerrilla movement. Such plans are not
likely to succeed. The Israeli scholar Y. L. Talmon writes that
"Israel may be able to win and win and go on winning till its
last breath, win itself to death. . . . After every victory, [it faces]
more difficult, more complicated problems. . . . The abyss of
mutual hatred will deepen and the desires for vengeance will
mount."[2] Though Israel has military superiority, it cannot administer a crushing blow. Such a capability might well lead to
Russian intervention, destruction of Israel, and perhaps a nuclear war.

For example, those Israelis who believe that the way to
achieve security is through military strength were pleased
when the United States supplied Israel with Phantom jets,
which the Israeli air force used in deep-penetration bombing
raids on Egyptian targets. The result was a Russian intervention that reestablished the earlier military "balance" at a much
higher level of force and potential danger. In general, each
military success simply reconstitutes the struggle at a higher
level of bitterness and hostility, a higher level of military force
(compare 1948, 1956, 1967, and 1970), a higher level of potential danger to all concerned. From the Israeli point of view,
this is a losing strategy. Israel can win every conflict but the
last. Sooner or later, it is likely that at some moment the international situation will be unfavorable. That moment, if it

arrives, will be the end of Israel, though the catastrophe will probably be far greater in scale.

Even in the short run, it is a losing strategy. Israeli democracy can hardly survive with 1 million Arabs in the occupied territories who cannot become citizens with equal rights because Israel insists on a dominant Jewish majority. The army will plausibly argue that the territories cannot be abandoned for reasons of security. Present Israeli policy speaks of secure and guaranteed borders. Everyone knows, of course, that there is no such thing as a guarantee of security. If Israel were to write the peace treaty itself and everyone were to sign on the dotted line, this would not guarantee security. The result is a hopeless impasse.

Furthermore, Israel is forced to be increasingly dependent on the world powers, in particular, the United States. It is common these days to hear Israel described as a tool of Western imperialism. As a description this is not accurate, but as a prediction it may well be so. From the point of view of American imperial interests, such dependence will be welcomed for many reasons. Let me mention one that is rarely considered. The United States has a great need for an international enemy so that the population can be effectively mobilized, as in the past quarter-century, to support the use of American power throughout the world and the development of a form of highly militarized, highly centralized state capitalism at home. These policies naturally carry a severe social cost and require an acquiescent, passive, frightened population. Now that the Cold War consensus is eroding, American militarists welcome the threat to Israel. The Joseph Alsops, with supreme cynicism, eagerly exploit the danger to Israel and argue that only the American martial spirit and American military power are capable of saving Israel from Russian-supported genocide. This campaign has been successful, even in drawing left-liberal support.

The Arabs are also following a losing strategy. Egypt, for example, has taken terrific punishment because of Israeli air superiority, and there is no reason to doubt that this will continue. It is likely that the technological gap will increase rather than decline. Similarly, the Palestinian movement cannot succeed in its present form. Israel is not Algeria. Its inhabitants will not be driven out or freely leave or abandon a high degree of self-government. Any policy directed to these ends will lead to continued destruction, to a strengthening of the reactionary and repressive forces on all sides, and perhaps to a form of recolonization by the great powers—in any event, to increasing dependence on the imperial powers, which have their own interests in maintaining such dependence.

The tragic irony is that each side, in fighting for national independence, is losing it in the course of the struggle. Since 1947, arms expenditures alone have surpassed $25 billion and are increasing. This in itself is a kind of recolonization, which may be followed by more direct forms. All of this can only be described as an enormous tragedy for the people of the Middle East. One recalls a warning of Rosa Luxemburg: "In the era of rampaging imperialism, there can be no more national wars. [The assertion of] national interests can only serve as a means of deception, of betraying the working masses of people to their deadly enemy, imperialism."

The situation of the Palestinian Arabs is at the heart of the Arab–Israeli impasse. Their problems, their demands, their rights and prospects have not been seriously discussed in the West and are cynically disregarded. In fact, the Palestinians are at best an annoyance and an embarrassment to every powerful group in the Middle East and to the great powers as well. I think it is no exaggeration to say that all of the national states directly involved in the area are united in the hope, open or secret, that the Palestinians will somehow quietly disappear. Correspondingly, their efforts not to disappear as a political or social force lead them into conflict with the great powers and most of the Middle Eastern states. It is not surprising, therefore, that their national movement, or at least some elements in it, seems to be moving in a revolutionary direction. The development of this movement, which is a matter of enormous significance for the future of the Middle East, will also very largely determine the possibilities for a just peace.

It is difficult to be optimistic when considering the possibilities for a just peace in the Middle East. Peace and justice, though surely interlinked, are very different. At least we know what we mean when we speak of peace. When we speak of justice, matters are not so simple. There are, as I have noted, apparently just demands of conflicting national groups, demands that appear to be quite incompatible. But it is, nevertheless, surely true that the search for justice transcends national lines; some would argue that it requires abolishing and overcoming national divisions. For the left, in particular, the problem of justice is inextricably linked to the problem of radical social transformation in every existing society. For this reason alone—it is not the only one—the left has been deeply concerned with the evolution of the Palestinian movements.

The Palestinians have suffered a severe historical injustice in that they have been deprived of a substantial part of their traditional home. I believe that this much, at least, can be conceded by any reasonable person. This injustice is—if we are to be honest—irreversible, except through means that are impossible to execute, given the present realities. Even if such means were practical and realistic, they would be intolerable to civilized opinion. The Palestinian groups that have consolidated in the past few years argue that this injustice could be rectified by the establishment of a democratic secular state in all of Palestine. However, they frankly acknowledge—in fact, insist—that this would require elimination of the "political, military, social, syndical, and cultural institutions" of Israel. I am quoting here from the May 6, 1970 program of the Unified Command of the Palestinian Resistance Movement, which included all the Palestinian organizations. The same program enunciates the principle that no basic change in Israeli institutions can be achieved by forces within Israel so that the elimination of these institutions must be achieved through armed struggle.

I am not concerned here with the legitimacy of this position, but rather with its implications. Given the assumptions, the conclusions no doubt follow. Furthermore, acceptance of the conclusions as the basis for action guarantees that the major assumption will remain true—that is, all elements of Israeli society will be unified in opposing the armed struggle against its institutions. Therefore, no basic change in Israeli institutions will be carried out by forces within Israel acting in concert with Palestinians with similar aims. The further consequences are those I have already mentioned. Specifically, the struggle will be a suicidal one for the Palestinians, who have already suffered miserably. Even if, contrary to fact, the means proposed could succeed—I repeat and emphasize, even if, *contrary to fact*, these means could succeed—they would involve the destruction by force of a unified society, its people, and its institutions—a consequence intolerable to civilized opinion on the left or elsewhere. In my opinion, no one who has any concern for the Palestinians would urge such a course upon them.

George Habash has recently described a disagreement in the Palestinian movement as to whether the principal concern should be the struggle over Israel or whether the movement should concentrate first on overthrowing the reactionary Arab governments which have indirectly prevented the liberation of Palestine. It is possible that events may have resolved this disagreement and that the strategy of the left—devotion of more energy to overthrowing the reactionary Arab governments—may predominate. This will be an extremely difficult course; as I noted earlier, one can expect virtually unanimous opposition from the established states of the region, as well as from the great imperialist powers—in particular, the United States and the Soviet Union. Nevertheless, there are some possibilities of success, perhaps along the Vietnamese model, though one should not push the analogy too far.

Suppose that the first stage of the struggle succeeds, as it may, and a revolutionary government is established in Amman or, perhaps, elsewhere. Then what is proposed is the slogan "an Arab

Hanoi in Amman." But consider the implications. If what is suggested is that the revolutionary regime of Jordan will be a rear
base for a popular resistance in the occupied territories, then the
slogan is, arguably, appropriate in principle, though one may
question its realism. But if it suggests that the Arab Hanoi will be
a rear base for the liberation of what is now Israel, then the analogy is wholly inappropriate. It would be appropriate only if one
accepted the American government's propaganda line that the
war in South Vietnam was exported from the North. For, apart
from any judgment of right or wrong, the fact is that the Jewish
population of Israel would be unified in opposing this armed
struggle. It would, therefore, in no sense be a war of liberation on
the Vietnamese model, but rather a war between states that are
legitimate in that they receive the overwhelming support of their
own populations, as the American government likes to pretend
is the situation in Indochina.

I note with interest that a recent statement of the Democratic
Front (PDFLP) quotes approvingly the following statement attributed to Lenin: "The victorious proletariat cannot impose any
'happiness' on any foreign people without bringing to an end its
own victory." The observation is correct. A society must carry
out its own revolution, achieve its own "happiness." Revolutionary struggles cannot be exported. They must be indigenous.

It is widely assumed on all sides that a program of social
change implemented by Arabs and Israelis acting in concert is
impossible. The statement I quoted from the program of the Palestinian Resistance Movement was to that effect. If the assumption
is correct, there are only two alternatives. The first is a continu-
ation of the national struggle between Jews and Palestinian
Arabs, both sides being locked into the losing strategy that I have
already discussed. This will lead either to the physical destruction of the Palestinians or to a much wider—probably nuclear—
war, with unpredictable consequences. No serious person will
succumb to romantic illusions about these matters. It is difficult
and dangerous to speak of inevitability in history, but such an
outcome is surely of very high probability. In particular, it is a

grave, even suicidal error to believe that the situation is in the relevant respects analogous to Vietnam or even to Algeria.

The only other alternative, granted that the assumption is correct, is the establishment of a Palestinian state in the currently occupied areas. Certain groups in Israel and, recently, in the U.S. government have spoken of such a solution. If such a state were under Israeli military protection (that is, occupation), it would be little other than a kind of Bantustan. I suspect that only extreme pressure from the great powers could lead Israel to accept a truly independent Palestinian state. If this is the end of the matter, the result will be a balkanization of the Levant—an ugly, though conceivably stable, system of small, hostile, suspicious, irredentist societies, very possibly reactionary and repressive as well.

Must we accept the judgment that there is no possibility of a program of social change implemented by indigenous forces in both societies? One can only speculate. However, I think it is premature to accept the counsel of defeat and despair that holds this to be out of the question. What might be the character of such a program, and to whom might it be directed? National states can do very little other than what they are now doing. Such a program could be undertaken only by those in both societies with an interest in some framework other than national conflict. Such groups exist, but they cannot function or gain credibility so long as the fear of "the national enemy" remains paramount within the framework of national conflict.

There may, however, be a different framework. The Jews and the Arabs of the former Palestine claim national rights to the same territory. Each national group demands, with justice, the right of self-government and cultural autonomy. In principle, these demands could be reconciled within a federal framework, perhaps in the form of two federated republics with parity, a guarantee of a high degree of autonomy combined with significant economic integration, highly permeable boundaries, and an ending of all legal ties to outside elements (the world Jewish community and Pan-Arab ties), though, of course, cultural and social connections could remain. Such a program would involve the abandonment of some degree of independence; one must compare it, however, with the abandonment of independence that is an inevitable consequence of national conflict. It would involve an element of risk—how can we trust our adversary?—but this must be compared with the risks inherent in national conflict. There is, of course, no such thing as a riskless policy.

The primary and most crucial difficulty, however, is the absence of a common program. There is, or should be, a common goal: the creation of a democratic, free, socialist society. For the great mass of the population in the Middle East, as elsewhere, this is the natural and proper goal, much as it may be subordinated in the national conflict. Such a program might, in principle, create a common bond between Arab and Jewish left-wing popular forces. One can only hope that sharp national boundaries will crumble as the struggle for a new society takes precedence on an international scale. But it is certain that no such goal can be achieved, or even imagined, if the means proposed is armed struggle by one society against another. It is certain that if any such goal is to be achieved, it will be through the joint efforts of indigenous mass movements in the several societies of the Middle East. To repeat the phrase attributed to Lenin by the PDFLP: "The victorious proletariat cannot impose any 'happiness' on any foreign people without bringing to an end its own victory."

An editorial statement in the Israeli journal *New Outlook* proposed that "binationalism could . . . be a banner or a long-range program on which Jews and Arabs could unite and which could make them readier to yield the short-range concessions that more immediate agreements will demand." In part, I agree with the statement. I do not agree with the implicit assumption that the "concessions" away from separate and opposing nationalisms are unwelcome, though perhaps necessary. And I think that binationalism alone, without a program of social reconstruction that can bring Jews and Arabs together in a common cause, will not be a meaningful "banner or a long-range program." But the general point is correct. It would be quite important for left-wing groups within each of the warring national societies to formulate a long-range program that would meet the basic demands of the other and would provide a basis for some degree of common effort. I have suggested that this is not impossible. Such a long-range program must, first of all, mitigate the fear that social destruction—destruction of independent institutions—will be a consequence of relaxing the military confrontation. It should also aim to overcome the paralyzing and destructive tendency of people to identify themselves solely, or primarily, as Jews or as Arabs rather than as participants in a common effort—perhaps still remote—to achieve social justice, freedom, and brotherhood—those old-fashioned ideals that are within reach and can be achieved if only the will is there.

For those of us who are removed from the immediate struggle, it is important to try to open channels through which the goals and aspirations of the people of the Middle East can be expressed and to try to respond to these expressions with an attitude that is both sympathetic and critical. There has been far too much hysteria over this issue; although it would be wrong and inhuman to deny the strong emotions it evokes, it is irresponsible to yield to these emotions and to fail to consider consequences, prospects, and costs. Far too much is at stake.

Reflections on a National Conflict

I

The present crisis in the Middle East encompasses a range of issues and conflicts. There is a potential conflict between the two great imperial powers. There is, in a sense, a kind of recolonization of the region as the small states lose their independence to their temporary protectors and allies and squander their limited resources in what may be an endless struggle. Israel and the surrounding states are in a state of war. There are tensions, which in 1970 erupted into a bloody war, between Palestinian Arabs and the largely Bedouin forces of Hussein. There are conflicts among the Arab states, in particular, a long-standing rivalry—in a sense, it goes back to the biblical period—between Egypt and Iraq.

But overshadowing all of these is the conflict between two nations that claim the right of national self-determination in the same territory, which each regards as its historic homeland. The conflict is military, to be sure, but it has a moral dimension as well. The fact is that each of these competing claims is just in its own terms. Furthermore, each claim is in a sense "absolute"—a demand for survival. If this root conflict is not resolved with some semblance of justice, then the other conflicts will continue to simmer, and occasionally explode, and will continue to threaten a catastrophe that may dwarf the repeated tragedies of the past few years. The experience with the Rogers Plan is an example. It excluded the Palestinian Arabs, and in this sense was unjust. This injustice should be rectified. If it is not,

there are likely to be further bitter consequences, such as the hijack-
ings and the Jordanian civil wars.

I read not too long ago a formulation of this root problem by
Daniel Amit, an Israeli scientist at Brandeis University, that seems
to me to put the matter well. He writes:

> As far as the Palestinians are concerned the origin of the conflict
> is the establishment of a Jewish society and eventually of the
> State of Israel in Palestine. They consider it a totally immoral act
> which resulted in the destruction of their society. This claim is to
> my mind beyond argument. The extenuating circumstance,
> namely, that European society has become an intolerable place
> for Jews to live in, can help to defend the moral motivations be-
> hind Zionism but cannot shed any doubt on the Palestinian moral
> grievance. It can also be used to promote understanding between
> two groups with a history full of suffering.
>
> On the other hand, the destruction of the Israeli society as a
> way to correct that moral injustice is blatantly immoral. Such
> a program in no way follows from the recognition of the griev-
> ance of the Palestinians. What does, however, follow is the
> recognition of the following principle:
> Palestinian Arabs and Israelis have equal rights in the whole
> territory of Mandate Palestine.

This principle he suggests as a "moral point of reference," which implies no specific practical steps, but which might serve as a framework
for the adjudication of claims and the outline of a long-range program.

In fact, none of the parties in the conflict has accepted this principle, or any meaningful "moral point of reference" that might provide
the framework for a just solution. Neither Israel nor any of the Palestinian organizations has unequivocally recognized the national rights
of its opponent in this conflict. Neither has recognized unequivocally
the right of the other to national self-determination, to independent
national institutions, political, social, and cultural, that express the
character of their national life as they choose to develop it.

There have been, in the past few years, some moves on each
side toward recognition of the fundamental right of the other.

Thus on the Israeli side, Golda Meir, who before had denied the very existence of the Palestinians, revised this position in October 1970 in an important, though, I believe, still unsatisfactory statement. Fatah made some explicit public declarations (November 1969–January 1970), stating in clear terms their acceptance of the right of all present Israelis to remain in the secular state that they envision in Palestine, though this move remains (1) ambiguous, since it appears to be in contradiction to the Palestinian covenant which they still accept, and (2) unacceptable, since it is not coupled with a recognition of the right of Israelis to national self-determination, with the institutions that express this national right.

It is not surprising that such tentative moves meet with cold rejection and hostility on the other side. For one thing, they remain ambiguous and unsatisfactory. For another, it is simpler and more comforting in a situation of conflict to regard one's opponent as the very incarnation of evil. Thus as far as I can discover, there was no mention within Israel of the Fatah declarations, apart from one inexplicit allusion by Arab specialist Shimon Shamir, and American Jews continue to deny their existence, though a more rational approach would be to welcome such moves, while rejecting them as still unsatisfactory and questioning them as ambiguous. Similarly, there has, to my knowledge, been no departure in the Palestine Liberation Organization from its uncompromising insistence on the destruction of Israeli institutions, a program which is as intolerable from a moral point of view as it is suicidal from the point of view of political and military realities.

In fact, each side insists that whatever apparent moves toward conciliation are made by the other are "for external consumption only"—deceitful propaganda that conceals the essential aim of domination or destruction. Those who wish can find statements and declarations to support this conclusion. One recalls the statements of Azzam Pasha and Ahmed Shuqeiry calling for the physical destruction of the Jews. And it is claimed—no doubt correctly—that the Arab press has contained statements implying that the conciliatory gestures are for propaganda purposes.

There is, in fact, quite an industry devoted to seeking out horrendous statements from the Arab press that express—allegedly—
the true intentions of the Arabs, concealed beneath their occasionally conciliatory rhetoric. Similarly—and this is something that one
forgets too easily—it would be possible to make a case that Israel is
concealing its true objectives and that Israelis are speaking with one
voice within, another without. Suppose, for example, that one was
bent on proving that Israel is a racist state committed to genocide
and indefinite expansion. He might proceed to "prove" this claim by
citing, for example, a statement in the journal of the Israeli Army
Rabbinate (*Machanaim*, April 1969), in which one "Shraga Gafni"
cites biblical authority for driving the "Canaanite peoples" from the
land of Israel. He explains that "not every enemy deserves peace."
Specifically:

> As to the Arabs—the element that now resides in the land but is
> foreign in its essence to the land and its promise—their sentence
> must be that of all previous foreign elements. Our wars with them
> have been inevitable, just as in the days of the conquest of our
> possessions in antiquity, our wars with the people who ruled our
> land for their own benefit were inevitable. . . . In the case of en-
> emies who, in the nature of their being, have only one single goal,
> to destroy you, there is no remedy but for them to be destroyed.
> This was the judgment of Amalek.

For details of the judgment of Amalek, see 1 Samuel 15.

The advocate of this position might take note of the fact that the
Israeli government did not at first support the Jewish settlement of
Hebron in the occupied West Bank, but soon committed £6 million
(Israeli) for dwellings for Hebron settlers. Furthermore, General
Dayan writes that for one hundred years the Jewish people have
been carrying out a process "of colonization to enlarge the borders
here—let there not be a Jew to claim that this process is over. Let
there not be a Jew to say that we are nearing the end of the road."[1]
And Yosef Weitz, former head of the Jewish Agency settlement department, writing in *Davar* shortly after the Six-Day War (September 29, 1967), recalls his diary entry of 1940: "Between ourselves, it

must be clear that there is no room in this country for both peoples.
. . . The only solution is Eretz Israel, at least the Western Israel,
without Arabs, and there is no other way but to transfer the Arabs
from here to the neighboring countries—to transfer them all—not
one village, not one tribe should be left." And so on. Proceeding
with such examples, one could construct a rather grim picture of Israeli intentions.

Such a picture would no doubt be distorted. I would recommend
similar skepticism with regard to the widely current descriptions of
Arab society and intentions. Although it is natural to think the
worst of one's opponents, it is not necessarily correct. It is commonly argued that prudence requires that one assume the worst
case, but this too is extremely dubious. What this postulate overlooks is the dynamics of conflict. There are, no doubt, situations in
which a conciliatory and sympathetic approach may intensify the
aggressiveness of one's opponent. But I think that the opposite is
also and perhaps more frequently true.

One should not underestimate the potential dangers that Israel
faces in the long term. But at present, it is in a very strong position; with respect to the Palestinian Arabs, it is in a position of
overwhelming military dominance. In part, the tragedy of the
Palestinians is that they face hostility on all fronts—from the
great powers, from the Arab states, and from Israel, which,
though small, is an advanced, fundamentally Western society,
with a high technological level and, in Middle Eastern terms,
tremendous military power. Recall the terrific beating that Egypt
was taking prior to the cease-fire of 1970—the cities along the
Suez Canal almost totally destroyed by bombardment, perhaps
500 men killed per week along the canal in the two months preceding the cease-fire. In contrast, the Israeli government reports
181 Israeli soldiers killed on all fronts (most on the Suez Canal
front) during the year 1970 (Reuters, *New York Times*, January 4,
1971). The comparison gives some indication of the relative military strength at the moment.

Military writers in the Israeli press regularly emphasize the
great Israeli military advantage. For example, Reserve General

Mattityahu Peled (generally described as a dove) writes in *Maariv* (January 29, 1971) that in the event of a breakdown of the cease-fire, Israel should cross the canal, destroy the Egyptian armies between the canal and the Nile, and drive the Russian fleet from Port Said and Alexandria. "There is no doubt," he writes, that Israeli forces "will succeed from a military point of view" in these actions. (The United States, of course, would have to intervene to prevent an all-out Russian response with strategic weapons.) In *Ha'aretz* (February 4, 1971), B. Amidror explains (under the heading "the Egyptians do not understand that they have ceased to be an independent and serious military power") that strategic bombing can destroy the Aswan Dam, causing catastrophic flooding in the settled areas of Egypt. Quite generally, Israeli experts appear to be very confident of their substantial and growing military advantage over the Arab states. (The guerrillas they describe as at worst a nuisance, from a military standpoint.) As the Israelis see it, the "economic balance" too is developing in their favor, just as the "strategic balance" is. In *Israelis Reply* (March 1970), a bulletin published by Israeli students of Middle East affairs, it is reported that the Israeli GNP will reach that of Egypt in 1971 (Israeli GNP per capita is more than ten times as great) and will rapidly pull ahead, if current tendencies continue.

The situation might alter, but at present Israel appears to be in a strong position. It is difficult to see how its position would be weakened or threatened if it were to recognize, unequivocally, the national rights of the Palestinians; or to permit free political action in the occupied territories—which would entail permitting political, though not military, support for Palestinian guerrilla organizations; or to pursue plans such as those apparently suggested by Dayan and in some form reiterated by Sadat regarding the Suez Canal; or to make explicit commitments concerning withdrawal from the occupied territories, which might be demilitarized in some fashion. Though there are no "riskless policies"—including present policies—it might be argued that such moves would be realistic, from the point of view of perceived security interests, as well as just.

One might imagine a resolution of the fundamental issue—the conflict between Israeli Jews and Palestinian Arabs—that would accord, more or less, with the principle I cited earlier; perhaps a federation of predominantly Jewish and predominantly Arab areas, each preserving national institutions and retaining a high degree of self-government, but moving step-by-step toward closer integration, with parity between the two national communities, if conditions and the growth of mutual trust permit. However, I will not go on to speculate about such possibilities, because they seem to me remote. A rather different outcome seems to be taking shape, for the near future at least, based on a number of important factors.

The first is the Israeli military and technological predominance, already noted, which appears to be considerable and growing. To cite some additional facts, the Israeli aeronautical industry has been growing at greater than 30 percent a year since 1967, and projections are the same for 1971. The general manager of the aeronautical industry expects the industry to do quite well in international sales. Production includes aircraft as well as Gabriel rockets and other electronic systems (*Davar*, December 28, 1970; TADMIT Newsletter, January 1, 1971). CIA chief Richard Helms is reported to have informed Congress that Israel has achieved the capacity to manufacture and deliver nuclear weapons (*New York Times*, July 18, 1970). According to the same report, Israel has received two-stage solid-fuel missiles from France that are capable of carrying nuclear warheads and are presumed to be intended for this purpose; and Israel is reported to be manufacturing solid propellants and engines for such missiles and perhaps mobile erector platforms for them along with test facilities. The French MD-660 missiles are reported to be guided missiles with a range of 280 miles (cf. John Cooley, *Christian Science Monitor*, October 24, 1970). Recall that Golda Meir recently warned that the Russians were providing the Egyptians with Frog missiles— unguided missiles, with a range of thirty miles, according to press reports (ibid.).

In a careful analysis of the aerial power balance in *New Middle East*, May 1970, Neville Brown writes:

The conclusion that emerges indisputably is that Israel retains a marked superiority in every class of combat aircraft and airborne weapon system. What is equally certain is that sociological and organizational factors serve to reinforce it. My own view is, however, that too much has been made of differences in "fighting spirit"; already there have been enough instances of Arab pilots joining battle against manifestly hopeless odds. But what is desperately lacking on the Arab side is the combination of administrative and technical professionalism needed to guarantee, for example, high serviceability and sortie rates.

According to Robert D. Beasley (*New Middle East*, August 1970), the Israelis claim that the Gabriel missile—designed and produced entirely by the Israel aircraft industry—is "possibly the best sea-to-sea missile in the world." One would imagine that it can also be adapted to use as a ground-to-ground missile. Although it is alleged that Egypt has a local superiority in artillery and, of course, troop level at the Suez Canal, Israeli military experts, as noted earlier, seem to feel that this is more than compensated by other factors (unless there is direct Russian intervention, in which case an entirely new situation arises, with a potential escalation to global nuclear war).

If these reports are correct, the Israeli military advantage in offensive weaponry is even greater than previously supposed. Recall that the Israeli Phantom jets are unmatched by any other aircraft in the Middle East (outside of Iran) in their combination of range, speed, and bomb-carrying capacity, according to the information that has so far been made public. Israel is becoming a relatively advanced industrial society. It has, for the moment, a high growth rate and enormous per capita aid from abroad. One can expect that in the near future it will retain and probably increase its advantage relative to the other forces in the region.

A second important factor is that the Palestinian guerrilla movements appear to have been severely weakened, if not virtually destroyed. A report in the London *Times* (January 30, 1971), commenting on the most recent events in Jordan, states that "the guerillas are now officially out of business," having been forced to hand in their arms. The Jordanian prime minister, Wasfi at-Tal, states over BBC that guerrillas would no longer be allowed to operate from Jordanian territory. The journal of the Fatah central committee has suspended publication as of January 27, 1971. The commander of the Palestine Liberation Army stated in an interview in Beirut that "the PLO is about to be destroyed. Its offices, establishments, and apparatus have been all but paralyzed, and its existence has been rendered only symbolic" (*Christian Science Monitor*, January 28, 1971).

A third factor is that the Soviet Union appears to have rather limited ambitions in the Middle East, so far as can now be determined. Evidently, it wants the Suez Canal opened, and it will no doubt attempt to maintain its dominant position in Egypt, but there is no indication that it is intending to initiate or support further military action in the Middle East. Apparently, the Soviet Union has been urging for over two years that the canal be opened (*Christian Science Monitor*, October 21, 1970). Opening of the canal would not only reduce the probability of large-scale military aggression but would also presumably stop any "war of attrition" across the canal. A Russian peace plan announced a few months ago suggests "*de jure* ending of the state of war and the establishment of the state of peace" after the first stage of withdrawal of Israeli troops, and stationing of UN forces on both sides of the frontier, along with Big Four or Security Council guarantees (*New York Times*, October 16, 1970). At no time has the Soviet Union supported the political demands of the guerrillas or given any concrete indication of a desire for further military conflict in the region.

Furthermore, although the United States appears to have little interest in the opening of the canal, it too has no wish for a war in the Middle East. The oil is flowing fairly well—even from Algeria, which will be supplying natural gas to the United States, it appears. Problems over oil persist, but they also involve conflicts between the West and such states as Iran, which have been pretty firmly within the Western orbit.

An additional factor of importance is that Israel is gradually carrying out some settlement in the occupied areas. Again, the details are unclear, but I think a pattern is emerging. Here are a few recent examples. I mentioned the settlement plans near Hebron. According to *Davar* (December 24, 1970), Welfare Minister Michael Chazani told Hebron settlers that they will be citizens of Israel. He was presented with a list of industrial projects that private entrepreneurs want to establish in Hebron (TADMIT Newsletter, January 1, 1971).

On January 5, 1971, the *New York Times* published a Reuters dispatch reporting the first Israeli civilian agricultural settlement in the Sinai desert, between Rafah and El Arish, noting that there are already several paramilitary villages in the Sinai.

Peter Grose reports (*New York Times*, January 12, 1971) that the Israeli government seems to be moving to make the Jerusalem area predominantly Jewish, so that—critics claim—"any return of conquered territory around Jerusalem . . . would be a practical and a human impossibility." He reports that in northern Jerusalem a new Jewish town of 40,000–50,000 residents is being proposed and cites reports that large Israeli housing projects are under way throughout the area.

John Cooley, in the *Christian Science Monitor*, December 24, 1970, reports that some 4,000 acres of Arab land were expropriated in 1970 within the new and greatly expanded city limits of Jerusalem. Israel plans to double the Jewish population of 200,000 within five years. A new housing project in the Ramat Eshkol area, on 150 acres of seized Arab land, is to include 2,500 housing units, 150 to be allotted to Arabs, according to the Israeli housing minister.

In the Golan Heights area, little of the former Arab population remains, apart from the Druze. There have been reports of new Israeli settlements in the area. I have seen no published confirmation.[2]

What these and other reports suggest is a pattern of slow settlement in the occupied areas that will continue, if the status quo persists. Israel may well try to preserve the status quo and the cease-fire, which are to its short-term advantage. It may accept some token withdrawals and perhaps permit some form of home rule in the West Bank, but it is difficult to foresee any other developments, in the near future at least.

This could be a reasonably stable situation for the near future. How attractive it is depends on one's point of view. It is hardly in doubt that the Arab population will remain second-class citizens in a Jewish state, or in protectorates on its borders, perhaps in parts of the West Bank. This second-class status need not be a matter of law; it may be enforced by administrative decree and local practice. As in the case of American ethnic minorities, it is often not easy to spell out or identify the precise mechanisms by which discriminatory arrangements are preserved. It is frequently claimed—I am in no position to verify or refute these claims—that Jewish urban areas are kept largely free of Arab settlement by the application of laws that require permits for transferring one's residence.

The pattern of land expropriation and resettlement has undoubtedly led to substantial Jewish settlement in formerly Arab areas as the Jewish population has rapidly increased. Lower levels of the military administration over the Arab population were dismantled in 1966 (the military governors retain their authority), but again, it is an open question what that has meant in practice. There are reports that the civilian police administration in effect took over the tasks formerly carried out by the military and that practices were not modified in any significant fashion. I have been able to find very little specific information on this subject. There appear to be only dim prospects for first-class citizenship for the Arab population of Israel. I very much hope that my skepticism about this matter will be proven wrong.

If Israeli control, direct or indirect, extends over 1 million Palestinian Arabs, as appears not unlikely at the moment, then obviously the seeds exist for future troubles, quite apart from the partially un-predictable flux of international politics or the changes that might occur in the surrounding Arab states. What is now happening in Gaza might be a forewarning. The details are still unclear, but it appears that there is a good deal of violence, much of it among Arabs, and harsh repression by the Israeli Border Police. Perhaps Israel will succeed—as it would of course prefer—to institute a liberal occupation policy and create tolerable material conditions for its Arab population. Conceivably, there will be substantial withdrawal and some degree of autonomy for the presently occupied areas, with the establishment of a Palestinian state of some sort. Personally, as I mentioned earlier, I believe that a more desirable outcome might be imagined, but, increasingly, I doubt that it can be achieved.

II

The tendencies noted in the preceding remarks have become more pronounced in the sixteen months that have passed since they were formulated. The Palestinian movements have been crushed. Israeli economic and technological superiority is increasingly evident, as is the Israeli preponderance in offensive military capability.[3]

Steps toward integration of the "administered areas" with Israel are proceeding. At one level, the integration is economic, as Israel increasingly comes to rely on Arab workers in construction and other branches of manual labor. At another level, settlement in these areas is creating the facts of the future. A likely future will see some form of Israeli control over the presently occupied areas, with a scattering of Jewish paramilitary and civilian settlement in the West Bank; a greatly expanded Jerusalem and probably some new Jewish towns; denser settlement in the Gaza strip; only Jewish and Druze settlement in the Golan Heights, now virtually free of other Arabs; and permanent occupation of Sharm al-Sheikh and the communications links to it and very probably much or all of the Sinai peninsula. Very likely, some degree of home rule will be permitted in the West Bank, and perhaps Egypt will be offered the right to carry out civilian administration in parts of the Sinai peninsula, as long as Israeli military control is maintained. These appear to be quite plausible prospects for the foreseeable future.

If Israel succeeds in integrating the "Oriental" Jews successfully into the society now dominated by European (and American) settlers and their descendants, there will be three classes of individuals within the areas that remain under de facto Israeli control: Jews, Israeli Arabs, and other Arabs. The Israeli Arabs will be second-class citizens in a Jewish state. The remainder of the Arab population will be effectively deprived of political rights beyond the local level. It is possible that with relative peace and continued economic growth, the treatment of the second- and third-class strata of the society will be fairly decent and that their level of consumption may increase. However, as observers who are by no means unsympathetic to Israel have pointed out: "There is little doubt that this Palestinian minority will become, in the long run, a reservoir of over one million human time-bombs, already ticking away, already becoming a living promise of tears, blood and explosions"; "the Israelis, too, will discover that men who have been deprived of honour and dignity cannot be trusted for ever not to attempt to regain them."[4]

Responding to the Hussein plan for a Jordanian federation on March 15, 1972, Premier Golda Meir stated that

Israel will continue to pursue her enlightened policy in Judea and Samaria and will maintain the policy of open bridges. She will continue to look after the provision of services to the inhabitants of Judea and Samaria, and will respect every peaceful and law-abiding citizen.

The Israeli Parliament added: "The Knesset has determined that the historic right of the Jewish people to the Land of Israel [understood as including the West Bank] is beyond challenge" (cf. New Middle East, May 1972). This declaration is the first official statement to that effect. Strictly speaking, it does not imply that the occupied territories are to be permanently retained; some who speak of the "historic rights of the Jewish people" nevertheless add that these "rights," from two millennia ago, should not be enforced. Taken in context, however, the declaration strongly suggests the intention to stand by these "historic rights." And it has been so understood by knowledgeable and sympathetic correspondents. Walter Schwarz writes:

> In reality, the Israeli statements mean exactly what they say. The Israelis have raised their sights. It is no new phenomenon. Zionism began without insisting on a state at all. At every stage, Arab intransigence has created new situations, invited new claims, and opened up new horizons. All the while, genuine fears for security have been insidiously mixed up with dreams of a bigger country, embracing more, if not all, of the historical borders of ancient Israel.[5]

It is difficult to see in Hussein's proposal, whatever its defects may be, a further sign of "Arab intransigence" which "invites new claims." It would, I think, be more reasonable to interpret the Israeli response as an indication of the intention, perhaps not yet fully conscious or explicit, to maintain Israeli control over "Judea and Samaria." There is no doubt that this response constituted a hardening of the Israeli position with regard to the West Bank. Minister Israel Galili, Premier Meir's political adviser who directs policy on settlement in the administered areas, stated on television that the River Jordan should become Israel's "agreed border—a frontier, not just a security border." The Allon Plan, hitherto the minimal Israeli position, employed the term "security border" in referring to the Jordan River, suggesting the possibility of semi-independence for the West Bank. Mrs. Meir added: "We do not agree that between Israel and Jordan there should be a Palestinian state." Such a state "could have only one simple purpose and that is to be a state which will press against Israel to 'liberate' the Palestinian homeland for the Palestinian people—that is, to throw the Israelis into the sea."

Given the actual balance of forces, the comment can only be reasonably interpreted as signifying a refusal to contemplate any form of independence for a "Palestinian entity." She went on to say that Israel would "certainly not encourage any organization or any voice which will say the West Bank is a separate Palestinian state, because our policy is against it."[6] The phrase "not encourage" is something of a euphemism. With some justice, the liberal Israeli commentator Amnon Rubinstein sees in the Israeli government declaration the "increasing influence of the Herut movement [the 'nationalist, anti-Arab, and extremist religious' right wing of Israeli politics] over the Labor Party."[7] This is an important matter, to which I will briefly return.

Whatever the conscious intentions of the Knesset may have been in announcing the historic rights of the Jewish people to the full Land of Israel, some form of indefinite Israeli occupation is implicit in the dynamics of the post-1967 situation. A headline in the journal *Maariv* stated that "'General Time' is working for the benefit of Israel in Judea and Samaria" (December 31, 1970). The article quotes Sheikh Muhammad Ali al-Jaabari who points out that "as the months pass, Israeli rule will be consolidated in these territories." In a speech that aroused some controversy, Defense Minister Dayan, by no means an extremist within the framework of Israeli political life, suggested that Israel should regard itself as the "permanent government" (*memshelet keva*) in the occupied territories. A criticism from the right in the journal of the National Religious Party questioned the public statement of such views, suggesting rather that "whatever has to be done can be implemented without an explicit statement which could be viewed by the world as a proposal for official annexation."[8]

Left-liberal Israeli commentators have pointed out that the consequences of maintaining the present borders are "becoming either a binational state or another Rhodesia."[9] Rejecting these prospects, many have called for withdrawal from the occupied territories and a clear policy of support for UN Resolution 242. One may sympathize with them and respect their motives, but in fact, their program is unrealistic. Unless great power pressure is employed—an unlikely as well as ugly prospect—the argument against withdrawal will always be persuasive within Israel. The Arabs, it will be urged, cannot be trusted; security can only be guaranteed through force; we can rely only on ourselves; genocide awaits if we relax our guard. Stability will always seem preferable to the risks of tentative accommodation and compromise. No military force in the region can compel withdrawal or raise the costs of occupation to a significant level, and the great powers have no interest in imposing an alternative solution by force. "General Time" will take care of the longer run.

Under these circumstances, integration of the occupied territories will appear to many to be the humane course, as suggested by Mrs. Meir's remarks, quoted above. After all, the Arabs must exist within some organized structure, and their standard of living may well rise under Israeli administration. Dissidents will be expelled or silenced. Collaborators will be found for local administration. Settlement will proceed in accordance with the long-standing policy of "dunam after dunam," a policy that had progressive content under the British occupation in opposition to the reactionary forces of political Zionism, and that is now second nature to the leaders of Israeli society whose point of view was formed in that period. As General Dayan explained:

> We must devise a pattern of living and of situations which can be tolerated by the Arabs. By this I do not mean arrangements which are to their liking, but those they can live with, if they so wish.[10]

If they do not so wish, they can emigrate, with official blessings. Israel has the capability to develop a program of this sort, and there is every reason to expect that it will continue to receive public support.

Public opinion polls reinforce this natural expectation. The Jerusalem *Post* reported on January 8, 1970, that 41.5 percent of the population believe Israel should integrate the occupied territories into Israel and 86.4 percent favor widespread settlement throughout the areas,[11] surely the prelude to further integration, in the real world. A year ago, the Israpol public opinion survey reported the following response to the question, "What territories should Israel be ready to relinquish in exchange for a peace settlement with the Arab countries?": Sinai—48 percent; Judea and Samaria—21 percent; the Gaza strip—17 percent; Sharm al-Sheikh—3 percent; the Golan Heights—2 percent; Jerusalem—0.6 percent; no territory whatsoever—30 percent.[12] A more recent poll indicates that 31 percent of the population want to retain the whole of Sinai, 56 percent the whole West Bank, 73 percent Gaza, 91 percent Sharm al-Sheikh, and 92 percent the Golan Heights.[13] Surely it is reasonable to expect that these attitudes will harden, if explicit decisions have to be made.

At the time of the Six-Day War in June 1967, I personally believed that the threat of genocide was real and reacted with virtually uncritical support for Israel at what appeared to be a desperate moment. In retrospect, it seems that this assessment of the facts was dubious at best. Some Israeli military experts take a very different view. Reserve General Mattityahu Peled, a member of the Israeli general staff during the Six-Day War, wrote recently that Israel has, in his view, been in no real military danger from Arab attack since 1948 and that there was no threat of destruction in 1967; rather, Israeli forces greatly outnumbered the Egyptians in the Sinai, not to speak of the technological balance.[14] By now it is clear that the potential dangers to Israel, in the short run at least, are not military. They are real, but they lie elsewhere.

One continuing danger, recently emphasized by the brutal massacre at the Lod airport, is that of terror, a weapon of the weak and the desperate which may continue to plague Israeli life. But there are other dangers, more subtle, but no less real, and disturbing to liberal Israelis. Professor Yehoshua Arieli, at the convention of the Movement for Peace and Security in February 1972, warned that current trends would lead to increased dependence on the United States, the consolidation of a "vested interest" of war profiteers, reliance on Arabs for unskilled manual labor, the deterioration of the democratic structure of the country: "If the status quo continues, the internal situation is likely to veer sharply toward nonhomogeneity, nonidentification with the goals of the Jewish State [meaning internal democracy, social justice, and the fundamental values of independent Jewish labor], a lower intellectual level, internal disunity, and fragmentation."[15]

Events in the Gaza region, mentioned briefly at the end of section I, illustrate a continuing danger, not military, but moral. To update these remarks, in recent months it has been reported that families of wanted terrorists from the Gaza strip have been held for a year at a desert camp and permitted to return home only when the hunted man is killed or captured.[16] In the Gaza area, thousands of acres have been fenced off by the Israeli army and thousands of Bedouins evacuated, their wells blocked to prevent return, and some homes and cultivated areas destroyed. The intention appears to be to "dissect the strip," to establish Israeli settlements, urban and rural, paramilitary and civilian, and a new Israeli port town. According to an estimate in the journal of the Labor Party, about one-third of the Gaza strip is to become "state land" (*Davar*, March 20, 1972). The expulsion of the Bedouins was revealed by members of neighboring Mapam Kibbutzim in violation of military censorship, setting off public protests by Israeli peace groups.[17]

Protests may continue, but new facts are being created, in accord with the declaration of Minister Galili in 1969: "It can be said with absolute certainty that the Gaza strip will not be separated from the State of Israel again."[18] Peter Grose reports (see note 17) that the Gaza strip "is gradually being assimilated into Israel" with "a pattern of carrot-and-stick tactics by the occupation administration"; economic integration with Israel is well advanced, and controversial preparations are under way for new Jewish settlements on land occupied in the 1967 Arab–Israel war." There is an "apparent program not officially announced—to settle Jews in the rich farmlands of Gaza" and to resettle 3,000 Gaza residents yearly elsewhere in the region, he reports, quoting also a statement by Galili (March 27, 1972) that "Gaza will not again be separated from Israel."

Quite apart from the injustice of such deplorable policies as the use of families as hostages and population expulsion, the impact on Israeli society will surely be significant. In the first place, there will be protest and resistance. There are, for the first time, a number of resisters in Israeli prisons, refusing to serve in occupied areas. In the natural cycle, resistance will lead to repression. As an example, a sixteen-year-old boy, Eytan Grossfeld, has been confined for two months of psychiatric observation for participation in Black Panther demonstrations (*Ha'aretz*, January 30, 1972). It is not impossible that dissident groups within the Oriental Jewish community, such as the Black Panthers, will find some common ground with Arabs in Israel and the occupied territories, in which case Israel will have many more than "one million time bombs" to concern it. This is particularly likely if the state, devoting substantial resources to military purposes, finds itself unable to deal with pressing internal social needs. But far more serious than resistance in its implications for Israeli society would be acceptance of the Gaza pattern as the norm, as an unpleasant necessity. This would surely have a corrosive effect on Israel democracy and social life.

Israel will have to come to terms somehow with the fact that it is a Jewish state governing a society that is in part non-Jewish. This fact, rarely faced in a serious way, has always been the Achilles' heel of political Zionism. If a state is Jewish in certain respects, then in these respects it is not democratic. That much is obvious. If the respects are marginal and merely symbolic—the color of the flag, the timing of state holidays, and the like—the departure from democratic principle is not serious. If the respects are significant, the problem is correspondingly severe. The problems of achieving democratic goals in a multinational or multiethnic society are not trivial ones. It is pointless to pretend that they do not exist.

It has frequently been suggested that the Jewish state is to be Jewish only in the sense that France is French or England is English. This is patently impossible, however. An immigrant who receives French citizenship is French. If there is some form of institutional discrimination against him, if he is not "truly French" in the eyes of the law or administrative practice, this will be regarded as a departure from the democratic ideal. A citizen of the Jewish state, however, does not become Jewish. This is a matter of principle, not a departure from some ideal norm toward which the society strives. Since it is a matter of principle within a Jewish state, there will be no remedy through slow progress.

The respects in which Israel is a Jewish state are not trivial or merely symbolic, and there is no indication that this situation will change. A non-Jewish citizen suffers various forms of discrimination. He is not permitted to lease or work on state lands or lands owned "in the name of the Jewish people." He is not able to reside in all-Jewish cities, such as Karmiel, built on lands confiscated from Israeli Arabs. To mention a recent case, a Druze, formerly an officer with twenty years' service in the Israeli Border Police, was denied the right even to open a business near Karmiel by decision of the Israel Land Authority (*Yediot Ahronot*, February 8, 1971).

According to a publication of the Israeli League for Civil and Human Rights (August 1971), there are tens of thousands of stateless Israeli Arabs, unable to satisfy the requirements of the Israeli Nationality Law; and the number is increasing, since statelessness is inherited. Arabs born to parents without citizenship, who may not even be aware of this fact until they apply for passports or other documents, do not acquire Israeli citizenship by virtue of the fact that they are born in Israel, in villages where their families may have lived for generations. Arabs do not receive benefits from laws that remunerate families of members of the Israeli armed forces, i.e., virtually all Jewish families and, apart from the Druze, no others. In myriad ways, Arabs will not enjoy the full rights of citizenship. It is for such reasons as these that left-wing elements in the Zionist movement were always wary about the idea of a Jewish state, which did not, in fact, become official Zionist policy until 1942, at the time of the destruction of European Jewry by Nazi terror.

The problem is not a small one, no matter what the size of the Arab population in Israel, but it takes on major dimensions when this population is very large, as it will be if the tendencies noted earlier persist. The High Court of Israel has recently ruled that "there is no Israeli nation apart from the Jewish people, and the Jewish people consists not only of the people residing in Israel but also of the Jews in the Diaspora." The Court so ruled in rejecting the contention of Professor George Tamarin that Israel is separate from the Jewish people, and thus denied his appeal to change the designation "Jew" in his identity card to "Israeli."[19] The ruling no doubt expresses the implicit content of political Zionism. It also reveals that the legal structure of the state, as well as its customary social practices, will be inherently discriminatory. Liberal Americans oppose laws that discriminate against blacks, and would be appalled if New York City should adopt an urban development program to preserve the "white character" of the city. It is unclear why they should react differently when Minister Shimon Peres outlines a plan for development in Jerusalem that is to perpetuate its "Jewish character"[20] or when non-Jews are excluded from the extensive state or national lands, or even from the grant of citizenship.

The fact is that Israel is already a binational state, at least in the sense that it is a state that contains two identifiable national groups, Israeli Jews and Palestinian Arabs. Even this is misleading, in that some may choose to identify themselves differently (like Professor Tamarin), and Arabs may understand their associations in very different terms. While all of this may have seemed a secondary issue before 1967, after the Six-Day War it became a major problem. If the analysis of current trends outlined above is accurate, it is a problem that will become increasingly serious. The operative question, in my opinion, is how Israel will deal with the fact of binationalism.

One approach is to try to change the fact by Israeli withdrawal from the administered territories. As I have mentioned, left-liberal forces in Israel have urged such a policy. I think that they are justified, and should be encouraged in this effort. Though it would not, in my personal opinion, be the optimal solution, it might still be a tolerable one, and for Israelis who actually take part in the internal debate, it is a proper position to uphold. Nevertheless, it seems to me futile, for reasons already mentioned. If I may interpolate a personal note, shortly after the Six-Day War I became convinced, for the reasons cited, that the fact of binationalism was unalterable in the short run at least, that Israeli withdrawal from the occupied territories was a highly unlikely prospect. I have expressed this view since in personal communication with Israeli friends (very few of whom agree), and in public lectures and articles. It now seems to me increasingly apparent that this assessment was correct and that the expectation of Israeli withdrawal and establishment of an independent Palestinian entity of some sort is illusory. If so, the first approach to the fact of binationalism is not a feasible one.

A second approach is the South African or Rhodesian model, not necessarily with the brutality or viciousness of the white racists of Africa, but with a similar institutional structure. Surely this is an intolerable outcome, though it is far from obvious that it is not a likely outcome. General Dayan, in a recent television interview, stated:

> First we must be in a position to control the entire West Bank absolutely from a military point of view, should the need arise. . . . Second, the West Bank is not a "bank" but Judea and Samaria, which must be open to Jewish settlement. Any agreement must be such that allows Jewish settlement everywhere. Third, what is needed is an entirely different, much closer tie between Israel and the West Bank, if the West Bank areas do not remain in our possession. I say "if" for I do not think it likely that we'll have to part with them.

Commenting, Israeli journalist Victor Cygielman observes that under this plan, the West Bank would be "a sort of Israeli protectorate, a reservoir of cheap labor for the Israeli economy, and a market for Israeli industrial goods."[21] While Dayan added that "all citizens of Israel, including Arabs, must be equal citizens," this remains, in fact, a virtual impossibility in a Jewish state. Dayan, in the past, has been realistic in his commentary, and there is no reason not to take his remarks quite seriously.

A third approach would be "population exchange," which means, in effect, expulsion of much of the Arab population. As noted in section I, this has been seriously suggested. In the article cited above in *Davar*, Yosef Weitz wrote that the "demographic problem" is the most serious problem faced by the state, since the "territorial victory" in the Six-Day War did not lead to the flight of most of the Arab population. He recalls that many years earlier he had concluded that it would be necessary to transfer all Arabs from the area west of the Jordan ("at least"). Rethinking the matter after the Six-Day War, he observes that a substantial Arab population "is likely to destroy the foundations of our state," a judgment which may well be accurate. Weitz does not go on to consider the implications of his analysis, under the condition of permanent Israeli occupation of the West Bank. It is difficult for me to believe that Israeli public opinion would accept what appears to be the natural conclusion, that the Arab population must, under these conditions, be removed.

A fourth possible approach is the American "melting pot" model. But this is inconsistent with Zionist ideology, and will almost surely not be acceptable within Israel. Mayor Teddy Kollek of Jerusalem has stated that "we have no intention of creating a melting pot for Arabs and Jews along American lines." But he adds, quite properly, that "if, in a few years, the educational and social gaps between Jews and Arabs in Jerusalem do not disappear some day . . . there will be an explosion."[22] He then goes on to explain that "this year we are building 6,000 dwellings for Jews" and "only 100 housing units for Arabs"—although he would prefer to see 300. He does not go on to comment that the disparity revealed is not a mistake or an oversight, but is rather inherent in the concept of a Jewish state with non-Jewish residents. Furthermore, even in the unlikely event that social, educational, and economic gaps disappear, the "gaps" in political rights are in principle insurmountable, given the legal doctrine that "there is no Israeli nation apart from the Jewish people," which includes the Jews of Israel and the Diaspora.

A fifth approach is the federal model, for example, along Yugoslav lines, with federated republics, each dominated by one national group, and efforts, one would hope, to achieve social, economic, and political parity. With all of its problems, this approach has possibilities. The inevitable discrimination in a multinational society in which one group dominates might be relieved through the federal structure. One might imagine that a regionally based federation might gradually evolve toward closer linkages, if forms of association along other than national lines prove to be meaningful and firm. A federal approach would imply that in the short run, at least, Palestinian Arabs who wish to return to their former homes within the Jewish-dominated region would have to abandon their hopes; and, correspondingly, that Jews who wish to settle in the Arab-dominated region would be unable to do so. Personally, I feel that among those policies that are at all realistic, given present circumstances, some kind of federal solution is the most desirable.

Other possibilities may be envisioned: for example, parallel national institutions throughout the whole territory with a free option for each individual; and also the option of dissociation from national institutions with retention of full rights of citizenship for those who prefer. I will not sketch out details, though it might be a useful exercise, because it is, for the present, purely an academic exercise. Before such questions can even be faced, it is necessary to come to terms first with certain overriding realities: Israel is a binational society; the concept of a "democratic Jewish state" with non-Jews as citizens (or residents in "administered areas") is inherently flawed.

There is, to be sure, still another approach to these problems: to bury one's head in the sand and pretend that they do not exist. Unfortunately, this approach is characteristic of many Americans who regard themselves as supporters of Israel. Whether or not they are supporting Israel in a meaningful way by adopting this attitude is another question. One of the few articles that even attempts to deal with these problems, by political scientist Michael Walzer,[23] can serve as an illustration. Walzer blandly asserts that "if one could draw the line between an Arab and a Jewish entity, few people would object to making it a dotted line and compromising in small or even insignificant ways the absolute independence of the two political systems" in a federal arrangement.

It is, however, quite untrue that "few people would object." As noted earlier, many Israelis object to abandonment of Israeli control over any significant part of the occupied territories, and the Israeli political leadership explicitly rules out any notion of a Palestinian state. To my knowledge, support for compromising Israeli independence is virtually nonexistent in Israel. Of course, it is true that "few people would object" to a dotted line on the Jordan and the Nile (or perhaps even through the mid-Sinai) with no compromise of absolute political independence, but that would leave the essential problem of a Jewish state with a million Arabs unresolved. As to this problem, Walzer has nothing to say, except that the problems can be "smoothed by helping people to leave who have to leave." He considers it sufficient to deride those who "disdain Jewish aspirations to statehood or suggest that Jews (especially) should seek nobler ends" and asserts that "to respond to such people . . . no elaborate argument is necessary."

In Walzer's view, "a democratic secular state called Israel . . . already exists in substance (despite the power of Orthodox Jews)," and he criticizes contemporary advocates of binationalism, who "deny the existence of a *nation* of Jews capable, as Greeks, Poles, and Germans are capable, of rescuing and rehabilitating their fellow nationals." Again, the fallacious argument that Israel will be Jewish only in the sense that France is French. Since he makes no explicit references, it is unclear whose views he has in mind in these comments. But it is evident that he is simply missing the point. Even if the power of Orthodox Jews were to diminish to zero, the real problems of a Jewish state with a non-Jewish minority would not disappear, and it would not in any meaningful sense be a democratic secular state, for obvious reasons already noted.

These problems are serious enough to require an "elaborate argument." They have nothing to do with "disdaining Jewish aspirations" or suggesting that Jews "seek nobler ends," and they are raised precisely by people who recognize the validity of Jewish national goals and associations. Vague and misleading references, in the currently fashionable mode, to "upper-class radicals who are impatient with working-class materialism" also contribute nothing to solving the real problems which Walzer merely evades.

It is, I think, important that some Israelis are seriously facing the facts. After participating in a protest, which he helped to organize, against the expulsions in the Gaza region, Amos Kenan wrote that if, as maximalist groups argue, "one who believes that he has no right to Gaza must also doubt his right to Tel Aviv," then he, Amos Kenan, will "begin to doubt if indeed I have a right to Tel Aviv—at least to Tel Aviv as it now is: a Jewish city, in a Jewish state with a million Arabs deprived of rights" (*Ha'aretz*, April 18, 1972). "Today," he writes, "we are not living in a Jewish state, but in a binational state." The old Israel came to an end in June 1967, and "a colonialist Israel," which he finds "ugly," was born at that time. The "dynamics of Israel 1972 has already left behind it the protestors of the past," those who called for withdrawal. Presently, the state of Israel rules over a million non-Jews who lack the rights of equal citizens and who now "furnish Israel with cheap labor, without which its high standard of living cannot be preserved." These are the bitter comments of a person who has struggled courageously to prevent the permanent occupation that is now taking shape with its inevitable consequences for a "democratic Jewish state."

I noted earlier Amnon Rubinstein's observations on the increasing influence of Herut on the Labor Party. He adds that Menachem Begin is correct in claiming that the government declaration on the "historic right" of the Jewish people to the Land of Israel is an expression of the traditional point of view of the Herut movement and its Revisionist predecessors:

> In fact we observe here a strange process, in which the influence of Herut is growing without any relation to an increase in its electoral strength. This increase strengthens the significance of the Herut movement and the point of view that prevails in it.

The process that Rubinstein describes has historical roots. The Revisionists were forced out of the Zionist movement because of their advocacy of a Jewish state, but their position was officially adopted, years later, in the wake of the Holocaust. In both cases, one can point to external factors that led to the growing influence of right-wing nationalist views, though I believe that the present example is far less justifiable than the decision of the 1940s, understandable at the time, to adopt the program of a Jewish state.

Throughout the history of Zionism, there has been a certain tension between radically opposed conceptions, one socialist and "universalist," the other nationalist and exclusive. On the one hand, the Jewish settlement (Yishuv) in Palestine, later Israel, developed the most advanced democratic socialist institutions that exist anywhere, institutions that might be described—without exaggeration, in my opinion—as a model in microcosm for decent human survival. These represent the positive side of a revolutionary development that combined socialism and nationalism.

At the same time, the Zionist movement incorporated expressions of the value of national identification and racial purity that I, at least, find quite objectionable. To cite one case, Joachim Prinz wrote in 1934[24] that the "German revolution" signifies the end of the liberal era and the decline of parliamentary democracy: "The development from the *unity of man* of the Enlightenment to the *unity of nation* of the present contains within itself the principle of the development from the concept of mankind to the concept of the nation," a development that he appears to regard favorably and which, he states, places the "Jewish question" in a new light. In place of assimilation, natural in the era of liberalism, he proposes the principle of "recognition of the Jewish nation and the Jewish race." "A state which is built upon the principle of the purity of nation and race can have esteem and respect for the Jews only when they identify themselves in the same manner." Jews must therefore identify themselves as people "of one nation and one race."

Putting aside the fact that an emphasis on Jewish nationhood and racial purity would hardly have been likely to awaken respect among the Nazi gangsters, there are unpleasant overtones in these remarks. The Zionist opposition to assimilationist tendencies was, in my opinion, justifiable, but not if it leads to an emphasis on the profound significance of purity of nation and race. Even if it were accurate to claim that the enlightenment view of human unity is disintegrating, I cannot accept the view that this process of disintegration is to be regarded with favor (nor is the "enlightenment view" incompatible with forms of social organization that permit those who wish to retain ties of national identification). Embodied in the political institutions of a Jewish state, concepts of purity of nation and race can prove quite ugly. The legal debate in Israel over "who is a Jew" is an example, in my opinion.[25]

The point is that the tension among competing elements in the Zionist tradition remains unresolved, and has become a matter of fundamental importance under the conditions that now exist in Israel. The problems, of course, can only be faced and dealt with by those who are on the scene. Sympathetic outsiders might be able to be helpful, if it becomes possible to create an intellectual and emotional climate in which rational discourse on the topic is possible.

In the United States, at least, this has hardly been the case. Since the Six-Day War, critics of one or another aspect of Israeli policy have been subjected to ridiculous accusations and childish distortion. They have been portrayed as supporters of terrorism or even genocide, or as opponents of democracy. They are asked why they do not denounce Iraqi and Syrian oppression and atrocities, surely quite real, and are told that only those who prove their good faith by "support of Israel" are permitted to criticize the policies of the state. A generation ago, left-wing critics of the Soviet Union were told that only true supporters of the "revolution" had the right to criticize the Soviet regime and society, and they were asked, "What about the lynchings in the South?" With such defenders as these, Israel hardly needs enemies.

Examples are many. It is, for example, common to identify bi-nationalism with the PLO position in support of a "democratic secular state."[26] This is a gross error. The PLO (Fatah in particular) has always opposed binationalism in quite explicit terms. This kind of confusion contributes to the unfortunate tendency to identify any critical discussion of current Israeli policy, and any speculation about alternative political arrangements in the Middle East, as "support for terrorism." In chapter 5, I will return to many other examples. In many cases, problems of Israel and the Middle East are incidental to domestic political issues and are cynically exploited as a device for undermining the peace movement and the New Left.

The problems of the Middle East are serious enough in themselves. It is quite improper to infuse them into internal American political debate. There is extensive and quite natural sympathy for Israel within the United States. We can all agree, I presume, that it is no service to Israel or to the search for a just peace when this sympathy is exploited for personal political vendettas.

Surely it is obvious that a critical analysis of Israeli institutions and practices does not in itself imply antagonism to the people of Israel, denial of the national rights of the Jews in Israel, or lack of concern for their just aspirations and needs. The demand for equal rights for Palestinians does not imply a demand for Arab dominance in the former Palestine, or a denial of Jewish national rights. The same is true of critical analysis that questions the existence of the state institutions in their present form.

If one were to propose that the time is ripe for consideration of a South Asian federation, say, linking India, Pakistan, Bangladesh, and Kashmir, it would be appropriate to object on various grounds, but senseless to assert that the person raising this suggestion is "advocating the destruction of India," something which no person of goodwill can tolerate. If someone were to insist that discussion of the problems of South Asia must proceed on the assumption that "the survival of democratic India is an urgent moral-political necessity,"[27] and that anyone who suggests alternative social and political arrangements has therefore removed himself from the domain of moral-political discourse, he would not be demonstrating his sympathy and concern for democracy or for the people of India and their just aspirations, but merely revealing a degree of dogmatism that is of little service to these people.

In every part of the world, there are certainly possibilities other than the system of nation-states; they have their merits and defects, which should be rationally discussed. The problems are particularly acute in multinational societies that are dominated by one national group, with the inevitable violation of democratic principle and practice that results. Neither abuse nor evasion of serious issues makes any contribution to the amelioration of problems that are stubborn and simply will not fade away.

The Fourth Round

When Syrian and Egyptian armies invaded Israeli-occupied territories on October 6, 1973, the reaction in Israel and the West was one of amazement and disbelief. The visible military preparations had been discounted, as were the extensive maneuvers, including amphibious operations, a few months earlier. The prevailing assumption was that it would be suicidal for the Arab states to provoke the Israeli juggernaut—"lunacy," as Golda Meir put it. "Action against Israel is clearly out of the question," the well-informed correspondent of the *Guardian* wrote shortly before the war broke out,[1] expressing a virtually unanimous view. General "Arik" Sharon, commander of the Southern Front and now a leading figure in the right-wing coalition Likud, informed an Israeli political meeting last July that Israel is more powerful than any European NATO force and is capable of conquering the area from Khartoum to Baghdad to Algeria within a week, if necessary.[2] When Israeli Chief of Staff David Elazar announced in his first press conference that the tide had already turned and that Israeli forces would soon "break the bones" of their enemies, few doubted the accuracy of his prediction.

Events proved otherwise. Israel reconquered the Golan Heights and moved deeper into Syria, but the Syrian army was not destroyed and conducted vigorous counterattacks until the cease-fire. Correspondents in Syria detected no sense of urgency and wrote of "astoundingly high" morale and "relatively few" casualties, more civilian casualties than military in one Damascus clinic.[3] In Egypt, reports indicate that "the demoralization, not to say decomposition, of Egyptian society which the endless no-war no-peace situation had produced has been replaced by a true cohesion," so that now "Sadat can ask of his people sacrifices which were inconceivable before the war broke out."[4] Earlier this year, David Hirst comments, a war budget had to be withdrawn under popular pressure. No longer. The Suez battle remained a stand-off until the last days before the cease-fire, when Israeli armor succeeded in breaking through the Egyptian lines and crossing the Suez Canal. It was only after the cease-fire that Israeli troops surrounded the Egyptian III Corps, threatening a military catastrophe that led Sadat to call on the great powers to enforce the cease-fire, provoking a carefully stage-managed superpower confrontation.

Israel plainly was unable to "trample Arab faces in the mud," as its Arabic-language broadcasts promised.[5] Still less did it prove that it could conquer most of the Middle East and North Africa within a week. Rather, as one Israeli officer stated, "we have learned that given Soviet supplies to the Arabs, we cannot fight a two-front war simultaneously against the Egyptians and the Syrians"—"a very sad lesson," he added.[6] Without a massive U.S. military supply effort continuing without let-up after the cease-fire,[7] Israel might have been compelled to abandon parts of the occupied territories, and Israeli urban centers might have been exposed to bombardment—as Damascus and other Arab cities were—by the still intact Arab air forces. The U.S. government was sufficiently concerned to dispatch combat marines aboard two helicopter carriers to the Sixth Fleet. Merely a "normal replacement," Defense Secretary Schlesinger explained as he attempted to convince the public that the worldwide alert of conventional and nuclear forces was justified by the ambiguous indications that the Russians were preparing to dispatch airborne troops.[8] To be sure, the severity of the confrontation was not great, since the world understood that it was largely contrived for domestic political purposes in the United

States and that the local issue was enforcement of the cease-fire before the destruction of the trapped Egyptian forces. But American concern over the fortunes of the Israeli military was real enough.

Sadat's "Operation Spark" seems to have been a successful gamble. New forces were set in motion in the Arab world, and the United States may be impelled to reassess its policy of de facto support for permanent Israeli occupation of the territories gained in 1967. Earlier efforts by Egypt and other Arab states to achieve this end had failed, but it may be a result of the October fighting. Certainly, the basic assumptions of U.S. policy have been shaken, if not undermined. The oil producers and the great powers were compelled to involve themselves directly in the conflict. A potentially serious rift was exposed between the United States and its NATO allies. By disrupting regional stability and posing a threat to the fundamental interests of the superpowers, Egypt and Syria may have set the stage for an imposed settlement much along the lines of their earlier demands.

Israeli policy since 1967, and American support for it, have been based on the premise that Israel is a military superpower by the standards of the region and that its technological predominance will only increase. Though Sharon's bravado was excessive, his basic point was a commonplace. The Syrian minister of information observed that "America has based its Middle East policy on the assumption of overwhelming Israeli military superiority," and the leading paper of Kuwait warned that, in the light of Arab military successes, "America should realize that Israel is no longer a suitable protector" for its interests. In emphasizing that "Israel (and the United States) will never seriously consider concessions unless the Arabs show Israel is incapable of keeping the lid on the Middle East,"[9] Arab commentators were offering their own version of principles expressed as well by Israeli spokesmen. Thus General Yitzhak Rabin assured his countrymen that "Americans have given us weapons . . . so that we should use them effectively when necessary," adding that the

West is coming to understand that "if some medieval-type rulers really mean to endanger the oil needs of hundreds of millions of people in the civilized world, then the West is permitted to take tough steps to prevent this."[10] The implications of these— possibly prophetic—remarks seem obvious.

Confident in its power, Israel pursued the policy of gradual in- corporation of the occupied territories already described.[11] With the August 1973 electoral program (the "Galili Protocols"), the dominant Labor Party took a position that implied virtual an- nexation of the occupied territories. It thus outflanked the right- ist opposition from the right, as the liberal Israeli commentator Amnon Rubinstein noted, by adopting in effect Dayan's princi- ple that Jews and Arabs can live together only under Israeli mil- itary occupation. According to Rubinstein, Dayan's statement to this effect had been received "with deafening applause" at the graduating ceremony of Tel Aviv University.[12] It is hardly likely that such programs can have been adopted without U.S. govern- ment backing.

Until October, American policy seemed a qualified success. The major military powers in the region, Israel and Iran, were firmly in the American camp, as were Jordan and Saudi Ara- bia. In important respects, the policy of reliance on Israel as a threat to radical nationalism represented a point of conver- gence of the interests of these powers, as was clear when the Palestinians were crushed in September 1970. Furthermore, Egypt had expelled Russian advisers and was appealing for American support. Even during the war, final negotiations continued with the Bechtel Corporation and Kidder Peabody Investment bankers over an oil pipeline that is to be the biggest Egyptian undertaking since the Aswan Dam.[13] In Egypt, the leftist opposition had been eliminated. Syria had closed down the Palestinian radio station. A de facto settle- ment favorable to American interests seemed to be taking shape, a settlement which also coincided with domestic polit- ical needs of the Nixon administration.

It is important to bear in mind, however, that the United States has other policy options, which it will not hesitate to pursue if its basic interests are endangered. It might attempt to organize reactionary Arab regimes explicitly in an alliance that might well incorporate an Israel compelled to abandon its 1967 territorial gains. These were the implications of the Rogers Plan, discarded in favor of tacit support for permanent Israeli occupation. The latter policy is no law of nature, however, and the famous Jewish vote and Zionist lobby will be no serious barrier to reversing it if circumstances so require, just as they did not prevent Eisenhower from forcing Israeli withdrawal from the Sinai in 1956 or the Democratic administrations from giving twice as much aid to Egypt as did the Soviet Union during the Five-Year Plan of 1960–1965.[14]

The policy of supporting Israeli occupation carried serious risks, despite its appearance of success. It was unacceptable to Syria and Egypt, and there was always a danger—now quite real—that the Saudi Arabian regime might be compelled by nationalist pressures to withdraw its tacit acquiescence and to modify its close association with the United States. The U.S. government is not prepared to see the world's largest petroleum reserve slip from the control of American oil companies. Sadat's military success called forth gestures of support from Saudi Arabia and the Gulf oil producers. They have already cut back production and restricted export to the United States. Taking their pronouncements at face value, Aramco profits would be seriously reduced and the East Coast of the United States faced with a severe oil shortage. The matter would be still more serious if the oil producers were to expand state control or shift allegiance to Japanese or Western European state and corporate power. There is little indication of any such moves, and if they were to take place on any significant scale, this would signal a major conflict within the capitalist world, with unpredictable consequences.

There is little doubt that the regimes of the major oil-producing states would prefer to remain in the American orbit (as, it appears, would Sadat). If the United States comes to the conclusion that the major premise of its policy is now "inoperative," it can move toward an alternative policy option, and, with Russian support, impose a settlement along the lines of UN Resolution 242 of November 1967. There is every reason to expect Russian cooperation. The major goal of the Soviet Union remains an international arrangement (détente), under which it is free to control its imperial domains and suppress internal dissidence while benefitting from badly needed trade and investment and adapting itself, in general, to the requirements of American global policy. If the United States moves in this direction, Israel will have no choice but to submit, abandoning the policy of creeping annexation.

To establish the validity of the premise that was the foundation of its policy and American support for it, Israel had to win a quick and decisive victory. This it failed to do. The United States might therefore conclude that "Israel is no longer a suitable protector." One can imagine an imposed solution with a return of civil control to Egypt and perhaps Syria in occupied territories and a superpower guarantee of demilitarization, and perhaps a federation of parts of the West Bank (a "Palestinian entity") with Jordan, along the lines of Hussein's proposals.[15] For the Palestinians, the most tragic victims of the endless conflict, such a solution offers little. But it has long been clear that the rights and interests of the Palestinians are the concern of none of the contestants, apart from some inconsequential rhetoric. Every organized force in the region and the great powers as well will be more than pleased if the Palestinian plea for justice is stilled.

Such an outcome, essentially of the Latin American variety, seems not too unlikely. The basic logic of the approach would be support for reaction throughout the Arab world and continued suppression of the Palestinians and other disruptive forces. What would be the effect within Israel of such a shift in American policy? Loss of the post-1967 élan would be the most likely immediate effect. Just before the Six-Day War, the outlook within Israel was not overly optimistic. There was substantial emigration and an economic recession, largely overcome since by the expansion of war-related industry and the availability of a cheap Arab labor force. Arrangements of this sort might persist even after an imposed "Rogers Plan," and it is possible that with a shift to the right in Israeli politics, which should be welcome to the Nixon administration, Israel could be incorporated into an American-dominated alliance in the region as part of a general "peace settlement."

It remains true that Israel is the most advanced technological society and the major military force in the region. Within Israel, in the short run, the hawks will appear to have won a major political victory. But it is hard to believe that it will last. Implicit in the Israeli policy of gaining security through strength is the expectation of repeated military confrontations, in each of which Israel is likely to prevail. Plainly, in the long run, the policy is suicidal, since Israel can lose only once; and the need to rely on a single superpower and to accept increasing international isolation is no less risky from the standpoint of security. Recent events simply show that "the long run" may not be so long as anticipated. The war was very costly and much more of a close call than anyone expected. The isolation of Israel and the United States was remarkable. Even Ethiopia broke diplomatic relations with Israel. Turkey is reported to have permitted Russian overflights; Greece and Spain refused to permit the use of bases for resupply; and other NATO powers were so uncooperative as to call forth a rebuke from the U.S. government. The handwriting seems to be on the wall, and only the hopelessly irrational will ignore it.

There are, in fact, some indications that Israel has begun to lose its advantage in technical rationality—a very serious matter. General Sharon's comments, cited above, are only one of many indications that have been noted with dismay by sympathetic observers.[16] I believe that the growing irrationality and arrogance within some circles in Israel may be traced to the problem of living with the eternal contradiction of a "democratic Jewish state" with non-Jewish inhabitants, and since 1967, with a subject population in territories that were being gradually assimilated. Under such circumstances, it is natural that a doctrine of historic national mission will arise, accompanied by some form of colonialist ideology and the belief that the natives are better off under external control, incapable of acting in any effective way on their own. The recent war may well provide a shock to any such system of belief, just as it seems to have already had the complementary effect of reviving Arab confidence.

The war leaves the three societies that were directly engaged battered and wounded. Even more than before, they are subject to the will of external powers and dominated by reactionary forces within. It is likely that, in the short run at least, articulate groups will be still more firmly committed to the belief that only through military strength can their minimal demands be met. The domestic consequences of this commitment are plain. Unless other tendencies develop or the superpowers impose a solution by force, the stage will be set for another more brutal episode with still more awesome weapons and still greater destruction. Even now, the contending states may well be better armed than before the outbreak of the conflict. Western analysts seem to agree that Israel has the capability to produce nuclear weapons; the head of the French Institute of National Defense Studies asserts that it "certainly" possesses nuclear weapons.[17] Israel has long-range missiles that can carry nuclear warheads, and Sadat has claimed that Egypt possesses missiles of comparable range and probably similar character. In a moment of desperation, such weapons may well be used.

Quite apart from these dangers, the constellation of forces and the prevailing tendencies offer grim prospects for the people of the former Palestine. Yet their interests are perhaps not irreconcilable, and there is, perhaps, a slender hope that they may come to realize that the pursuit of their common interests, possibly in conflict with other regional or global powers, offers the best long-term hope for survival, as well as for a settlement that will satisfy the just demands of both peoples. This can only mean a program of socialist binationalism, which might take various forms. Realists on both sides will dismiss such possibilities, insisting that nations must organize themselves in a system of competing states for the purposes of mutual destruction and oppression. People who are willing to face reality may not be so sure.

The Peace Movement
and the Middle East

In November 1969, *Liberation* published a symposium on the
Middle East. The editors' introduction had this to say:

> The peace movement and the American left have generally
> adopted a stance of pained indifference to the conflict in the
> Middle East. The apparent hopelessness of finding a just resolu-
> tion is almost overwhelming. Moreover, many of us, without nec-
> essarily supporting the Arab or Palestinian position, have recoiled
> from the pro-Israeli chauvinism of the American Jewish commu-
> nity. The strenuous efforts by Zionist fund-raisers to picture Israel
> as a "free-world bastion" exploits and reinforces cold war idiocies.
> The celebration of the "fighting Jew" further alienates those of us
> who are not thrilled by Prussian efficiency.

A few months later, I was asked to discuss the topic "Israel
and the New Left" at a Zionist conference.[1] I gave a fairly extensive review of "New Left" literature expressing a wide range
of attitudes and concluded that there is no identifiable "New
Left doctrine" on the Middle East. "Rather, there is confusion,
unhappiness, some—though limited—debate, and a great deal
of sympathy, often at a rather intuitive and barely articulated
level, for socialist elements within the Jewish and Arab national movements, combined with a general fear that national
movements can do enormous harm if they subordinate the
struggle for social reconstruction to purely national aims." I
cited the remarks just quoted from *Liberation* as accurate, to my

knowledge, in expressing attitudes widely held in the peace movement and the left, and also in pointing out that such anti-Israel feeling as exists "is in part in reaction to the behavior of the American Jewish community . . . which has always been predominantly on the right, in the spectrum of world Zionism."

In the same symposium, other commentators drew a very different picture of New Left doctrine on Israel. Irving Howe wrote that "Jewish boys and girls, children of the generation that saw Auschwitz, hate democratic Israel and celebrate as revolutionary the Egyptian dictatorship." Taken in their context, these remarks imply that such is "the ideology of the New Left." He gave no examples of any celebration of the Egyptian dictatorship. In fact, he did not refer at all to the scanty New Left literature on the subject he was discussing. Nathan Glazer went still further: "It is clear," he asserted, "that the New Left has an overwhelming and unbendable tendency to support the Arabs and to oppose Israel." Glazer presented no evidence whatsoever to support this categorical judgment and was unperturbed when presented with substantial evidence showing that it was false.[2]

Still more interesting was the contribution of Seymour Martin Lipset. He contributed to the symposium a slightly revised version of an article that had appeared in *Encounter* (December 1969), the contents of which I have discussed elsewhere.[3] The revisions give a particularly clear insight into just what Lipset is up to in this study of left-wing anti-Semitism. In the original, Lipset identified I. F. Stone and me as "older left-wing critics of Israel [who] cannot be accused of ignorance concerning the Israeli socialist movement or its radical institutions." Stone and I, according to Lipset, have

> a commitment which currently involves defining the Al Fatah terrorists as "left-wing guerrillas" and Israel as "a collaborator with imperialism," if not worse. One doubts whether even the most so-

phisticated presentation of Israel's case could ever regain their support.

Note the quotation marks around the phrases "left-wing guerrillas" and "a collaborator with imperialism," the implication being, presumably, that these phrases were taken from our writings. Lipset also stated that

> Chomsky, in fact, was a long-time member of Hashomer Hatzair, the left-wing Zionist youth movement, which prided itself on its Marxism-Leninism and its loyalty to communist ideals.

All of this is complete fabrication. The alleged quotations do not exist. I had discussed Fatah, not identifying it as a left-wing movement, which would be nonsensical, but pointing out that it contains left-wing elements, as of course, it does. I had quoted Chaliand's observation that Fatah appears to be analogous to the early Kuomintang and that it might be supplanted by more revolutionary groups, as in China, if it fails (cf. chapter 1, note 26.) Neither Stone nor I have ever written anything expressing the commitment Lipset attributes to us (without reference), though it is easy enough to find explicit refutations of these views.

As for my longtime membership in an organization priding itself on its Marxism–Leninism, I was never a member of Hashomer Hatzair, precisely because I was opposed to its various Stalinist and Trotskyist tendencies. But, as Lipset knows, a little red-baiting is always helpful in a pinch.

In a letter published in *Encounter*, I pointed out these errors, and Lipset duly revised his article—in a revealing way. In the revision published in the symposium, Lipset withdrew without comment his inventions with regard to my personal background. He then reformulated the commitment that Stone and I allegedly share as follows:

> [They] are today committed supporters of the international revolutionary left. And that left currently defines the Al Fatah

terrorists as "left-wing guerrillas," and Israel as "a collaborator
with imperialism," if not worse. One doubts whether even the
most sophisticated presentation of Israel's case could ever regain their support.

It is conceivable that the false statements that appeared in the
original article were the result of carelessness. The revisions introduced in response to my letter cannot be explained in this
way. Knowing that he cannot support his allegations, Lipset attempted to insinuate what he knew very well to be false. Thus, if
Stone and I are committed supporters of the international revolutionary left, which defines al-Fatah as "left-wing guerrillas" and
Israel as "a collaborator with imperialism," if not worse, then it
will be concluded by Lipset's readers that Stone and I accept
these positions of the movement to which he claims we are committed. Naturally, Lipset makes no attempt to document his false
allegations.

It would be interesting to learn just what Lipset takes "the international revolutionary left" to be, or to learn how Stone and I
have demonstrated our committed support for this international
movement and its doctrines. But perhaps it is pointless to pursue
these fantasies any further.

Irving Howe took up the cudgels again a few months later.[4]
"Anyone who keeps an eye on our intellectual life," he wrote,
"must know that the turn against Israel reflects a complex of
values and moods verging on the pathology of authoritarianism." Specifically, the "turn in sentiment [against Israel] among
portions of our 'left' academics" results from two factors: anti-
Semitism and "the growing distaste, the downright contempt, a
portion of the New Left intellectuals shows towards the very
idea of democracy." Those who "yearn for a charismatic-au-
thoritarian Maximum Leader . . . will despise Israel not because
of her flaws but because of her virtues," that is, because Israel
offers "as good a model as we have for the democratic socialist
hope of combining radical social change with political freedom." Again, no facts, no argument. If everyone "must know"

these truths, then presumably it is unnecessary to establish them. Rather, in an attempt at parody, Howe explains how Israel might regain "the favor of the campus Guevarists, Trotskyists, Maoists, and Panthers who lead the assault against her." The method would be to institute a fascist dictatorship in a bloody revolution. Then, Howe writes, we would observe the following response:

> Everywhere the New Left rejoices. Brigades of youth from Scarsdale, Evanston, and Palo Alto race to Israel to help with "the planting." The *New York Review* plans a special issue. And Jean-Paul Sartre and Mme. de Beauvoir take the next plane to Israel, prepared to write a thousand pages in four weeks on *The Achievements of the Israeli Revolution* (while getting the street names of Tel Aviv wrong).

These are the kinds of slanders that one does not even bother to refute. I am quite certain that Howe knows that his insinuations are outrageously false. But he also understands very well a convention of American political discourse. When the target is activist elements of the peace movement or the left, slander and abuse are permissible, argument and evidence are superfluous. In this particular diatribe, Israel and the Middle East are really quite irrelevant, as are the facts. Howe is simply exploiting the natural and overwhelming sympathy for Israel in the United States to attack his political enemies. How convenient to have these enemies committed to the destruction of Israel and bloody, fascist revolutions, irrespective of the facts.

Howe returns to this theme in a recent lament that "intellectual prominences are silent" while Israel faces destruction.[5] "Some leaders of the Vietnam opposition, with trained capacities for public speech, have not said a word in behalf of Israel," while others denounce Israel. One might ask why, in an article that is ostensibly about Israel and its problems, there should be so much ado about "young professors and academics . . . whose minds are filled with the notions of Fanon, Guevara, and Mao" and who are

"contemptuous of Israel" precisely because it is a democracy advancing toward socialism. Such people, if they exist, are politically irrelevant in the United States, as Howe very well knows—
just as Lipset knows what merit there is in his claim that "the most
important political event affecting Israel in Western politics in recent years has been the rise of the New Left."[6] In both cases, Israel and the Middle East are incidental to private political feuds.

It is difficult to imagine any other reason why Howe, with the
familiar sneer, should bring up fund-raising parties for the Black
Panthers—how much more civilized was his response when Fred
Hampton and Mark Clark were assassinated by the Chicago police. And it may explain why he deplores the "self-denying tradition" among "prosperous or suburban Jews" and "some Jewish
New Left students soliciting help for Al-Fatah." Wealth . . . sub-
urbs . . . New Left. Is the reader perhaps intended to conjure up
the image of the suburban New Left, always one of Howe's fa-
vorites? Recall his earlier parody on the New Left "from Scars-
dale, Evanston, and Palo Alto" rejoicing over a fascist revolution
in Israel, while the democratic socialists soberly continue their
work in Harlem, Gary, and Watts.

Howe writes that "to be deeply involved with the fate of Israel is no longer very chic," especially "at Elaine's in Upper
Manhattan," though "Israel may be strong in the lower-middle-
class neighborhoods of Brooklyn and Queens." It would be interesting to see the data on which this sociological observation
is based. It would be interesting to test this claim against the
experience of fund-raisers for Israel. I suspect that, as a statement of fact, it is about on a par with Howe's insinuation that
New Leftists regard Saudi Arabia (no less) as a progressive
Third World regime and that they oppose Israel precisely because of its democratic and socialist structures. The rhetoric is
useful for Howe's domestic political purposes; facts can be
cheerfully ignored.

The same motivation can perhaps explain why Lipset and
Glazer are unperturbed when their assertions and judgments are
demonstrated to be false. These judgments express a deeper

truth: they provide an ideological weapon that is useful for cur-rent political battles. So much the worse for the facts.

All of this is at about the same level of intellectual integrity as Joseph Alsop's allegation that people who attack "America's will and America's power" (I am cited as the prime, though ex-treme, example) are virtually inviting the Russians to destroy Israel. To enliven the story, Alsop even invented a meeting in which an unofficial emissary of the Israeli government at-tempted to explain to me the relation between "the defense of the United States" and "the defense of Israel." (I dismissed this out of hand as part of the Alsopian fable.) Alsop then turns to that other notorious anti-Semite, I. F. Stone, who, he claims, "hurled the first stone at Israel from the New Left,[7] in a slimy article on the Six-Day War that was closely comparable to his book on the Korean war." The reference is to an article of Stone's in the New York Review (August 3, 1967), in which Stone, speaking from the point of view of someone "closely bound emotionally with the birth of Israel," describes the con-flict as a "tragedy," "a struggle of right against right"; expresses his faith in Israeli "zeal and intelligence" while giving no word of support to the Palestinian Arab movements; argues that "Jewry can no more turn its back on Israel than Israel on Jewry"; and urges that Israel should find "acceptance as a Jew-ish state in a renascent Arab civilization." Not even Alsop's imagination can construct a comparison between this article and Stone's book on the Korean War. The point, of course, is not to present a rational argument, but rather to plant a useful association: "slimy" attack on Israel, skepticism about the Ko-rean War, assault on America's will and power. With a skillful exploitation of the general sympathy for Israel and a few well-chosen innuendos and misrepresentations, Alsop can finally end by warning Senator Jacob Javits to stop "whacking away at our own national defense."[8]

These examples illustrate a phenomenon of some generality. Left-liberal criticism of Israeli government policy since 1967 has evoked hysterical accusations and outright lies. Anyone

associated with the peace movement or the American left who
has opposed expansionist or exclusivist tendencies within Israel has been reviled, without documentary evidence, as a supporter of terrorism and reactionary Arab states, an opponent of
democracy, an anti-Semite, or if Jewish, a traitor afflicted with
self-hatred. In some instances, the explanation is transparent.
Thus Joseph Alsop will apparently grasp at any straw to try to
undermine opposition to the policies of militarism and intervention that he supports. Similarly, one need not search very
far to explain the denunciation of Daniel Berrigan by John
Roche, "intellectual in residence" at the White House in the
latter part of the Johnson administration and one of the last
defenders of the American war in Vietnam. As such, Roche
has little affection for "that gentle Christian, Daniel Berrigan,
S.J.," who, Roche alleges, "delivered himself of some of the
most venomous remarks on Israel that I have seen outside of
the Arab and anti-Semitic press." Particularly disturbing is the
"premise" that Roche alleges is "fundamental," namely, "the
premise that the Israelis have been sitting around, like Spar-
tans, for the last 25 years conspiring to enslave the 70-odd million Arab neighbors." Roche does not reveal where Berrigan
expressed this fundamental premise, but "as one Irishman to
another," he informs Berrigan that his views on the Middle
East "may be politely defined as ten pounds of dung in a five-
pound sack." To refute Berrigan's alleged errors, Roche treats
us to such historical insights as the observation that the Jews
in the Arab states "had lived in virtual slavery for a millen-
nium or more." Plainly, Berrigan has much to learn from this
eminent political scientist.[9]

It is also not very difficult to explain why Abba Eban should
present the following analysis of Israel's problems with the New
Left:

Let there be no mistake: The New Left is the author and the
progenitor of the new anti-Semitism. One of the chief tasks of
any dialogue with the Gentile world is to prove that the dis-

tinction between anti-Semitism and anti-Zionism is not a distinction at all. Anti-Zionism is merely the new anti-Semitism
. . . I do not believe that any argument, however sophisticated,
can probably change the convictions of Noam Chomsky or of
I. F. Stone, whose basic complex is one of guilt about Jewish
survival.[10]

Naturally, Abba Eban will seek to identify anti-Zionism and
anti-Semitism. Then any criticism of the policies of the state he
represents can be dismissed at one. Resort to this device is common enough. Lipset claims that, at a private meeting he attended, Martin Luther King admonished black students that
criticism of Zionism is simply anti-Semitism; this he found "an
experience which was at once fascinating and moving." Howe
attributes Israel's dangerous international isolation to "skillful
manipulation of oil" and that "sour apothegm: *In the warmest of
hearts there's a cold spot for the Jews.*" If this is all there is to it, it
is unnecessary to consider the impact of Israel's policies of annexation, as many Israeli commentators do.[11] As for Eban's
comments on the infamous duo Stone–Chomsky, I doubt that he
knows anything at all of our expressed views; the rhetoric suggests that he is simply paraphrasing Lipset, and it is possible that
he regards Lipset as a responsible scholar. But whatever the
facts, his analysis is again convenient. If criticism of Israeli policy by Jews is simply a neurotic complex, then it too can be dismissed with amateur psychoanalysis of the Lipset variety, and all
criticism is neutralized: Non-Jews are anti-Semites; Jews are
guilt-ridden neurotics.

Eban's remarks are of interest only because he is regarded as an
Israeli dove. Perhaps it is true that Eban represents a less militant
and more conciliatory position within the Israeli government,
but it must be understood that he is the kind of "dove" who argues, before the Knesset, that:

To raise the question of a Palestinian identity different from
the people living in Jordan would be a distortion of history and

the facts. . . . Most of the Palestinians are Jordanian citizens, and most of the Jordanians are Palestinians. Moreover, the dissociation of the concepts of "Palestinians" and "Jordanians" is meaningless. . . .

The views of Eban, the dove, are indistinguishable in this respect from those of Golda Meir, who is quite sure that "there is no Palestinian people wandering in the world without knowing where to go."[12] The Labor Party insists that there is no Palestinian people and no issue of Palestinian national rights (cf. introduction, pp. 19–20), and it is natural therefore that Eban should try to dismiss any concern for this mythical entity.

Abuse directed against the peace movement and the left with regard to Middle East problems can easily be explained when it originates from spokesmen for the Israeli government or for American militarism. It is more interesting when the source is left-liberal American opinion, as in several of the examples I have discussed. Had there been any effort to support the remarkable allegations I have cited or any concern over the obvious falsehood of many of the charges, we would be within the domain of rational discourse over factual issues and complex problems that can be variously interpreted and understood. But this is not the case. Therefore, it is appropriate to seek some explanation.

I have already suggested a plausible one. The problems of Israel and the Middle East are incidental; the overwhelming sympathy for Israel since 1967 is simply being exploited by certain embattled liberals and "democratic socialists" in an effort to regain a position of credibility that was seriously threatened in the late 1960s by the mass popular opposition to the Vietnam war and to American militarism. This development was deeply troubling to many left-liberals, who were unwilling to associate themselves with this movement, and who lost their position as the critics of American society from the left. Their own ambiguous attitudes toward the American war in Vietnam[13] became a serious embarrassment by the late 1960s. Particularly disturbing were the developments that placed the movement against the war in opposition to state power, often in direct resistance. To deal seriously with the issues was not easy. It was much more convenient to denounce one's enemies as totalitarians, radical-chic suburbanites, anti-Semites, or backers of Arab genocide.

Furthermore, with the right in disarray over Watergate,[14] there are new opportunities for those segments of the liberal intelligentsia that naturally gravitate toward state power. I will not discuss here whether this is a good or bad thing, or what the impact on state policy is likely to be.[15] It is sufficient to remark that the prospects for a political success are quite real.

A few ingredients are missing, however. If Camelot is to be rebuilt, it will be necessary to achieve a new élan, a sense of moral purpose and legitimacy. To this end, a few adjustments in the historical record will be helpful. The war in Vietnam was a ghastly failure, and too many people think of it as the liberals' war. Thus, it will be necessary to create a new past in which everyone really abhorred and opposed the war, from the start. The Berrigan brothers, latecomers to the general cause, opposed the war in one way; and the Bundy brothers—who were not simply bent on martyrdom and self-glorification—opposed the war in their more serious and effective way. So did McNamara, the Americans for Democratic Action, and democratic socialists pondering the question whether the "value of peace" outweighs our commitment to democracy. The Jason scientists struggled against the war under their slogan "Gravel Mines for Peace." Government consultants ruminating on "forced-draft urbanization" opposed the war, along with crusading editors and liberal historians who prayed that Joseph Alsop would be right, but feared that he would not. Everyone opposed the war, although the serious efforts to bring it to an end were often impeded by the tantrums of that part of the "peace movement" that was actually visible, and confusion was sown in the minds of the guilt-ridden upper middle class by moralists who do not understand the awesome dilemmas faced by responsible leaders.

Since the intelligentsia are the custodians of history, we can anticipate that the 1960s will be reconstructed to meet the need.[16]

It is in this context, I believe, that one can understand much of the vilification of the New Left under the guise of discussion of the Middle East. In the late 1960s, I. F. Stone was a proper target for slanderous attacks; his criticism of the Vietnam war was beyond the limits of responsible opinion.[17] And in 1973, who could be a more appropriate target than Daniel Berrigan, the very symbol of resistance to the state?

As I write, there is much furor over an address that Daniel Berrigan delivered before an Arab-American audience on "sane conduct" in the Middle East, on October 19, 1973, in the last days of the fourth Arab–Israeli war.[18] It is instructive to investigate with some care the responses to Berrigan's address.

Berrigan announced himself to be no expert. He predicted that "the present course . . . leads to the same dead end for both sides" and that the local antagonists are in danger of becoming clients of the superpowers, thus losing the independence for which they have fought. He condemned both sides in harsh terms. He refused to "take sides" and urged nonviolence. He paid "tribute to the great majority of the Jewish community" in the United States who did not let "their acute and legitimate concern for Israel" become "a weapon against Vietnamese survival," thus rejecting the bait that Nixon had offered them. He stated terms that he found "reasonable" for a cease-fire: "a declaration of de facto respect [by the Arab states] for the existence of Israel, a de facto state . . . a return to the boundary lines which existed before the 1967 war, and some justice for the Palestinian people." He expressed his personal dismay that Jews, who had taught him a "vision . . . of human conduct in a human community," should resort to "the violence and repression of the great (and little) powers, a common method, a common dead end."

Predictably, these remarks provoked a storm of protest. I have yet to read protest against Berrigan's unmitigated condemnation of the Arab states for "their capacity for deception, which is remarkable even for our world . . . their contempt for their own poor . . . their willingness to oil the war machinery of the superpowers . . . their cupidity masked only by their monumental indifference to the facts of their world." Hardly a balanced analysis. The recent history of Kuwait, Syria, and Egypt, for example, is not simply a record of "contempt for their own poor." But Berrigan's rhetorical excesses in this regard passed unnoticed.[19] That is not surprising. Such characterizations are common enough in American political discourse, [20] so much so that James Wechsler could write in the *New York Post* that "in its totality, the lecture had the quality of a simplistic Arab propaganda tract delivered before a fan club."

But Berrigan's remarks about Israel evoked the usual response. He has been denounced as an anti-Semite, a Father Coughlin, a totalitarian, and so on through the familiar litany. Still, the predictability of the response does not in itself justify dismissing it as simply another outbreak of the deplorable fanaticism of the past few years. Perhaps, for once, the criticism is well taken and the charges accurate. I will not attempt to review the full range of responses to Berrigan. Rather, I will consider in some detail two of the more serious examples, which are, I think, typical and instructive both for the insight they provide into the critical reaction to involvement of the "peace movement" with Middle East problems, and for the illustrations they provide of some of the misconceptions that underlie much of the current discussion of the Arab–Israeli conflict.

One of the first and most widely quoted responses to Berrigan was by Rabbi Arthur Hertzberg, president of the American Jewish Congress. [21] Hertzberg describes himself as an early and vigorous opponent of the Vietnam war; thus he is no Alsop or Roche. He also describes himself as "slightly notorious also for being a 'dove' on the Israel–Arab conflict." Hertzberg sees Berrigan's remarks as "old-fashioned theological anti-Semitism," a severe charge that deserves a careful analysis. Consider now Hertzberg's reasoning.

Hertzberg attributes to Berrigan the claim "that the Arabs were right and the Jews were wrong" and urges that he "not malign Israel with unique venom." But he nowhere mentions Berrigan's condemnation of the Arab states, already cited, or his condemnation of the Arab resistance for its "rhetorical violence and blind terrorism." Nowhere does Berrigan suggest that the Arabs were right and the Jews wrong. Rather, he consistently adheres to his refusal to "take sides." We can therefore dismiss this charge as simply another fabrication.

According to Hertzberg, Berrigan's recognition of the injustices to the Arab refugees leads him to "assert . . . that an end be made of the state of Israel." Discussing Berrigan's "horror stories," Hertzberg alleges that concern over the refugees has led some (by implication, Berrigan) to argue that "only Israel must be refused the right to exist at all," though "moral hysterics" over other refugee displacements have long since ceased. Again, fabrication. Berrigan nowhere suggests that an end be made of the State of Israel. Rather, he insists that the Arab states at once declare "de facto respect for the existence of Israel, a de facto state."

Hertzberg does not tell us, incidentally, whether the concern of the Zionist movement over the displacement of Jewish refugees two thousand years ago was also an example of "moral hysterics."

Hertzberg then accuses Berrigan of misrepresenting the relation between the American Jewish community and its leaders:

> Berrigan asserts that the great majority of the American Jewish community "refused the bait offered by Nixon and peddled by their own leaders"—that is, they resisted Zionism. This distinction of his has absolutely nothing to do with the truth.

What has absolutely nothing to do with the truth is Hertzberg's rendition of Berrigan's statements. Berrigan nowhere suggests that American Jews resisted Zionism. On the contrary, immediately after paying tribute to the Jewish community in the remarks Hertzberg cites, Berrigan went on as follows (emphasis mine):

> Their *acute and legitimate concern* for Israel never became a weapon against Vietnamese survival. They refused that immoral choice offered them by a leader who would make a price of the safety of one people, the extinction of another.

Thus Hertzberg attributes to Berrigan the exact opposite of what he clearly stated in remarks that Hertzberg partially quotes.

To Berrigan's statement that Israel is deficient in "the Jewish passion for the poor and forgotten," Hertzberg offers the following rebuttal:

> What does he think that Israel's hospitality since 1948 to hundreds of thousands of refugees from the Arab lands has represented? For that matter, why are Israel and the world Jewish community fighting so hard with Soviet Russia about the right of emigration?

Surely this is too much. Israel's acceptance (indeed, encouragement) of Jewish immigration is hardly evidence for "the Jewish passion for the poor and forgotten." Rather it was an effort, justified or not, to establish a Jewish majority in a Jewish state. Before the establishment of Israel, the Zionist movement gave no encouragement to resettlement of Jewish refugees outside of Palestine. That is an understatement. "For Zionists a national homeland in Palestine was so clearly the answer that to divert money and energy to resettlement elsewhere was akin to heresy. . . . The bitter truth seems to be that in order for mass rescue [of European Jews] to have succeeded, the effort in Palestine would not only have had to be supplemented by other resettlement ventures but also by mass infiltration into established states,"[22] and to this project the Zionist movement was always opposed. The same is true today. The world Jewish community is fighting hard to compel Russia to

permit Jews to emigrate and is expending considerable resources to bring Russian Jews to Israel and settle them there.
Millions of dollars of U.S. government aid have been specifically allocated by Congress to this purpose. I imagine that
there might be some Russian Jews interested in coming to the
United States, and "passion for the poor and forgotten" would
certainly motivate some concerted efforts on their behalf. I am
aware of none.

I suspect that a Palestinian Arab who had been evicted from
his home might find Hertzberg's rebuttal a bit cynical on this
score.

On the matter of the flight of refugees, Hertzberg has the following to say:

> As a matter of fact, the Arab refugee problem began in the war of
> 1948 in large part because the Arabs . . . chose to leave as part of
> a tactical maneuver.

The evidence for this claim, at present, is slight indeed. Earlier
claims were thoroughly demolished by Erskine Childers, who
also exposed numerous propaganda fabrications in the process.[23]
No doubt the case is not settled, but Hertzberg's "matter of fact"
might better be labeled "a highly dubious claim" or "a probable
fabrication."

Hertzberg objects to Berrigan's unremitting denunciation of
Israeli society and his failure to find any good in it—in particu-
lar, his assertion that Israel has failed "to create new forms of po-
litical and social life for her own citizens." In this case,
Hertzberg's criticism is justified. He is quite right to refer to the
Kibbutz as an outstanding example of new forms of political and
social life, as is commonly done in literature of the New Left.[24]
Berrigan does not give a balanced appraisal of Israeli society, any
more than he gave a balanced account of the policies of the
Arab states.

But when Hertzberg gets down to specifics, his criticism again
falls wide of the mark. He objects to Berrigan's discussion of "the

price in Israeli coinage" for the policies of the past years: the "creation of an elite of millionaires, generals and entrepreneurs," with the price "being paid by Israel's Oriental Jews, the poor, the excluded, prisoners." These observations, however, are not only reasonably accurate, but also commonplace.[25]

The remainder of Hertzberg's accusations are too vague for comment. On the whole, his response is careless and inaccurate and supports none of his conclusions. Rather, it falls squarely within the tendencies described earlier. Since there is no reason to suspect that Hertzberg is motivated by domestic political concerns, one can only conclude that he, like Eban, simply hopes to stifle discussion.

The conclusion is strengthened by a look at Hertzberg's ideas on an appropriate policy for Israel. Berrigan advocates a peace treaty with recognition of Israel within its 1967 borders; it seems that he supports something like the Rogers Plan. Hertzberg's position is quite different. Speaking in Israel at a meeting of Jewish organizations, Hertzberg warned that Nixon and Kissinger "now need an impressive diplomatic victory" because of Watergate and are therefore putting pressure on Israel:

> We—and now I refer to Israel and American Jewry—are unable to accept this pace and this arrangement under pressure and ultimatum. Kissinger proposes as a first step Israeli withdrawal to the Mitla and Giddi passes, and the Arabs want this to take place tomorrow. From a historical and psychological point of view—not to speak of other considerations—the matter cannot be handled in this way. A government that agrees to this would be overturned and assassinated at once. Jews in the Diaspora who agree to this will be called traitors. And from the psychological point of view, this is correct.[26]

Interesting views for a "slightly notorious dove," assuming that he was not badly misquoted. In rather similar language, the right-wing Likud opposed the January 18 Egyptian–Israeli agreement that called for Israeli withdrawal to the Mitla and

Giddi passes. Comparing Hertzberg's position with Berrigan's, we see that there is indeed a difference worth discussing. Hertzberg would have done a service had he made this clear. But this would presuppose a willingness to have these crucial issues aired, and I suggest that to prevent this is precisely the purpose of personal attacks and distortions of the kind I have been discussing.

I have suggested that much of the commentary on Israel and the New Left is motivated by domestic American concerns and by a desire to forestall debate that might reach serious issues. Hertzberg's attack on Berrigan as an old-fashioned theological anti-Semite falls into the second category. Irving Howe's comments, discussed earlier, fall within the first. It is therefore interesting to consider his response to the Berrigan address.[27]

Howe denounces Berrigan as "arrogant," elitist," with "little taste for mere 'formal' liberty," moved only by "his own persuasion of righteousness." Berrigan's address is, furthermore, "an extreme instance"—of what, Howe does not make clear. A charitable interpretation of Howe's critique would make Berrigan an extreme instance of erosion of support for Israel. But since the preceding paragraph refers to unnamed New Leftists "whose minds are filled with the notions of Fanon, Guevara, and Mao" and who therefore are "contemptuous of Israel" precisely because of its "advanced social legislation, progress towards socialism, the kibbutz experiments, ebullient democracy," perhaps Howe is trying to tell us that Berrigan, with his distaste for mere "formal" liberty, is an extreme instance of this type. Whatever Howe may have in mind exactly, these are plainly serious accusations, not to be made lightly. Let us consider then the evidence that Howe adduces to support these charges.

Howe's argument rests on two observations. First, "it does not stir the heart" of Father Berrigan "that, in a moment when the whole country feels itself in the utmost peril, the Israelis set an example of democratic openness and debate, running an election with God alone knows how many parties (including two Communist parties, one of which has long been pro-Arab)." Second, while Berrigan preaches resistance against the state, "to get himself arrested, to maneuver himself into the condition of 'resistance' [in Israel], he would have to do something really extreme, like providing military help to Egypt or Syria."

Howe's second observation is false outright; his first suffers from important omissions. But even if correct, Howe's two observations would not substantiate his charges. They would simply show that Berrigan ignored positive features of Israeli society, which is true, just as he ignored positive developments in the Arab states. When Howe denounces Egypt as a "rigid dictatorship," overlooking entirely all constructive programs undertaken by Nasser, are we to conclude austerely that Howe has little taste for mere human needs (subsistence, education, welfare)? Adopting his style of argument, that is exactly what we would conclude. What is more serious, the deficiencies in Howe's two observations, as we shall see directly, are traceable to a single cause: he has little concern for the condition of Arabs in the Jewsh state. Are we to conclude, then, reasoning in Howe's style, that Howe is simply a racist? That would hardly be just, though to ignore substantive evils while engaging in fulsome praise of a regime is a serious fault—far worse than overlooking much that is praiseworthy while condemning substantive evils.

Now a look at Howe's premises. Take first the matter of resistance. Uri Davis spent five months in prison, not for providing military help to Egypt or Syria, but for entering a "military zone" without a permit. The "military zone" consisted of land expropriated from Arabs on the pretext of "security" and then converted into an all-Jewish settlement area from which Arabs are officially excluded. Even a Druze veteran of the Israeli Border Patrol, in a recent scandal, was denied the right to open a business there.[28] It would take a vivid imagination to interpret Davis's act of resistance as a case of providing military help to Egypt or Syria or the like.

Davis was apparently the first Jew to be arrested under the Emergency Regulations of 1945, previously applied only to Arabs (since 1948). These regulations were described in 1946 by Y. S. Shapira, later to be attorney general of Israel and minister of justice, as "unparalleled in any civilized country; there were no such laws even in Nazi Germany." They are still in effect, although the first Knesset, in 1951, declared them "incompatible with the principles of a democratic state."[29]

Davis is not the only example of a resister who managed to get himself arrested without approaching the extremes that Howe suggests are necessary in Israel. Since 1967, a number of people have been imprisoned as resisters for their refusal to serve in the armed forces in the occupied territories. Are they guilty, by Howe's standards, of giving military help to Egypt or Syria or the like? Or consider the case of Rami Livneh, sentenced in 1973 to ten years in prison for failing to report to the authorities a meeting with a Palestinian alleged by the prosecution to be a "foreign agent." No proof was offered that Livneh had given military aid to Egypt, Syria, the Palestinians, or anyone else. The court stated in its decision that "replacement of the present structure of the state by an Arab–Jewish regime (as was the central purpose of the organization [to which the defendants belonged]) constitutes an attack on the sovereignty of Israel." Since Israel was established as a Jewish state, the court held, advocacy of a Jewish–Arab state is equivalent to advocacy of overthrow of the state.[30]

Howe regards Berrigan's remarks on resistance in Israel as so ridiculous that he asks, "Does he know what he has in mind?" I suspect that Berrigan knows all too well some things that Howe has yet to learn, not only about Israel but about state power and propaganda in general. We have already noted Howe's scorn for Sartre and de Beauvoir for their alleged superficiality and factual inaccuracy. They would have little difficulty in returning the compliment, with ample evidence.

Consider next Howe's comment on elections. True, Israel is a Western democracy, with relatively high standards of freedom and justice—for its Jewish citizens. Arabs may take part in political life, but under certain understood conditions. On

one occasion, an Arab nationalist group (the al-Ard group) attempted to form an Arab political party (all-Jewish parties,
e.g., the governing Labor Party, have been the rule). This attempt was blocked by the district governor on grounds that it
had the object of "prejudicing the existence and security of the
State of Israel." Upholding the ban, the High Court held that
"it has never happened in history that in countries where there
is a sound democratic regime, monopolistic fascist movements
have been allowed to operate against the state, using the rights
of freedom of speech, freedom of the press and freedom of association, in order to organise destructive activities under
cover of these freedoms."[31] Since the Court invoked the analogy of Weimar—a slight exaggeration, perhaps—it might be
useful to recall the record of the judiciary under the Weimar
Republic:

> It is impossible to escape the conclusion that political justice is
> the blackest page in the life of the German Republic. The judi-
> cial weapon was used by the reaction with steadily increasing in-
> tensity.[32]

In Israel, Arab–Jewish communist parties are permitted to function, but not Arab parties that might prove effective in rallying
popular support for Arab rights.

Howe assures us that one of the communist parties (Rakah) is
"pro-Arab," a testimonial to Israeli democracy. It is always useful in such cases to listen to those who are suffering from discriminatory practices. The well-informed Israeli Arab lawyer
Sabri Jiryis, who was himself restricted to Haifa for over a year
under the Emergency Regulations, though charges were never
brought against him, and who now lives in Beirut, describes
Rakah as "the Communist sector of the Israeli establishment."
Nevertheless, "most of the Arab members of the party's leadership, including the members of its Political Bureau, its newspaper editors and correspondents, and its village branch secretaries
and youth leaders, are subject to various restrictions" under the

Emergency Regulations. But "these restrictions have never once been imposed on Jewish members of the Party." From these and many similar examples, Jiryis concludes, judiciously and I think plausibly, that in the area of democratic freedoms

> . . . the authorities do not practise discrimination against individuals or groups on the basis of purely national or communal considerations. It is when ethnic differences are combined with opposition to their basic political and social concepts that they allow themselves to be influenced by racial differences.[33]

In short, by no means South Africa, but not quite an "ebullient democracy" either.

This is within Israel proper. In the occupied territories, no serious form of political organization has been tolerated. Dissidents are quickly taken care of. To cite only the most recent case, on December 10, 1973, Israeli troops expelled eight prominent Palestinians, marching them blindfolded into Jordan. This provoked a protest at a junior college (Bir Zeit) in the occupied West Bank. Israeli troops closed the college, giving the students and staff six hours to leave.[34] The incident was described as follows in the Israeli press:

> The last straw was a demonstration, which took place in the institution, last week, protesting the deportation of 8 Arab notables to Jordan. Once more the teachers and students were warned that they are exploiting freedom of speech in Israel too far, and when they did not comply with the warnings, it was decided to silence them and close other channels of activity by less delicate means.[35]

If Howe would attend to the issues instead of simply berating his enemies, he would perceive at once that his unqualified praise for Israeli democracy could not possibly be accurate. Israel is a Jewish state with non-Jewish citizens. By law and administrative practice it must be—and is—a state based on discrimination and exclusivism.[36] It will not do simply to assert that "there is no perfection in this world, and the case for Israelis rests on no claim that they are perfect," while describing this "ebullient democracy" progressing toward socialism[37] as being "about as good a model as we have for the democratic socialist hope of combining radical social change with political freedom." Howe must be aware that there are Arabs, as well as those who might not choose to identify themselves as Jews, in the Jewish state. But nowhere does he face the problem of their status.

One might argue that the essentially flawed democracy of a Jewish state (equivalently, an Arab state) is the least unjust solution available, given the objective realities. That is a rational position, one that can be respected and discussed. But Howe attempts no such argument. His method, with regard to this issue at least, is to try to bury difficult and uncomfortable facts in a heap of invective.

I do not mean to suggest that New Left positions on the Middle East, or criticisms of Israel expressed by people associated with the peace movement, are beyond criticism—far from it. In fact, I find myself in strong disagreement with much of the peace movement and the left over these issues (see chapter 2). Reasonable criticism can only be welcomed. But the examples I have discussed here and in the references cited do not fall within this category. I think that they are to be explained by a combination of the two factors mentioned: fear of critical analysis, and the desire to exorcise the heresies of the 1960s so that "respectable" left-liberalism can regain its position of moral authority.

The authors of the denunciations I have discussed describe themselves as supporters of Israel against those who seek its destruction. I happen to think that many of them bear a measure of responsibility for the October 1973 tragedy and for further conflicts that are likely, if the policies they advocate are pursued (see introduction, pp. 12–13, 22, 24). I do not therefore castigate them as "supporters of Arab genocide," though their stand may well contribute to the ultimate destruction of Israel. But I do reject their claim that they "support Israel" against its enemies.

Contrary to their belief, this self-characterization requires an argument, not merely declamation, no less than their accusations against their political enemies.

In fact, a rational person will be wary about such phrases as "support for Israel." Are Sakharov and Solzhenitsyn enemies of the Soviet people when they denounce atrocities committed by the Russian state? Or Daniel Berrigan, when he supports Russian dissidents, who, no doubt, are quite isolated from the mainstream of Russian opinion? Was A. J. Muste supporting or attacking the United States when he called for American withdrawal from Vietnam, virtually alone, at a time when democratic socialist *Dissent* was explaining that American withdrawal "would mean something quite as inhumane" as the policy of "hopeless attrition of the Vietnamese people"?[38] Were American resisters and deserters enemies of the United States, or were they defending the interests of the American people and their professed ideals? The semantic trap is obvious. Apologists for state power are always quick to identify opposition and resistance to state policy as an attack on the society and its people. In the case at hand, support for policies of the Israeli state may or may not be "support for Israel" in any reasonable sense of this notion, and criticism of these policies must also be analyzed on its merits.

The matter is not academic. Quite apart from questions of right and justice, it is far from obvious that Israeli policy since 1967 has been motivated by considerations of security, though these are, of course, invoked in Israel as elsewhere for the purposes of the state. It is not very surprising that Moshe Dayan should bitterly attack the professorial doves who have been pointing out, with some accuracy, just where his policies of annexation are leading. For Dayan, the role of the professors is to "contribute to faith and strengthening," not to "humiliation and depression," as they have been doing by discussing the likely consequences of his policies. "Were they a lion cub?" Dayan asks rhetorically, "or a worm of Jacob?"—adding, "I don't mean just the worm of Jacob Talmon."[39]

I have given my own views on the matter of security, and referred to those of some Israeli doves, including those denounced by Dayan (cf. introduction, pp. 23–24). These views are surely debatable and are perhaps incorrect, but it is striking to see how the relevant questions are ignored in some of the eloquent pleas that we raise our voices in support of Israel. Irving Howe is again a case in point. He asks a question that "haunts us: why is it that some people—Jews, liberals, intellectuals, persons conspicuous for developed political and moral sensibilities—refrain from expressing such anxieties" over the fate of Israel? The silence of opponents of the Vietnam war is particularly troubling to him, almost as troubling as the antagonism to Israel on the part of the two people he specifically names: Daniel Berrigan and me.

When Berrigan speaks of the Israelis as "a people in danger," of the "acute and legitimate concern for Israel" on the part of American Jews, of the "dead end" to which Israeli policy is leading, of the possiblities for a peaceful solution involving recognition of Israel by the Arab states, could it be that he is, in fact, expressing anxieties over the fate of Israel? Howe makes the familiar point that "the Israelis need only suffer one serious defeat in order to face extinction." I have been writing the same thing for years and arguing that the policies of the Israeli state are leading in that very direction. Could it be that, in so doing, I am expressing the anxieties that Howe feels? Such questions are apparently incomprehensible to him. One finds absolutely no awareness in his writings of the problems of security and the many discussions of them. He simply takes it for granted that his views, whatever they may be, constitute "support for Israel." Anything else must be a form of radical chic, "romantic authoritarian delusion," or the "radiant sincerity" of ideologists blind to fact. Argument and evidence are, as always, quite beside the point.

I wrote, "his views, whatever they may be." The reason is that it is not easy to determine what these views are. An examination of Howe's treatment of the issue—or better, nontreatment—gives

some insight into the attitudes toward Israel of substantial segments of the left-liberal intelligentsia. We know what Howe rejects. Judging by his comments on Berrigan, we may conclude
that he rejects Berrigan's suggestion that Israel be recognized by
the Arab states within its 1967 boundaries. Howe writes that he
sympathizes with the proposal that Israel should give up "most of
the occupied territories, provided that secure borders followed,"
but it must have "the kinds of borders that would allow the Israelis to establish their own guarantee" of security. Just what borders would suffice for this purpose? Evidently, the borders of September 1973 did not. With these borders, Israel suffered serious
losses and came perilously close to disaster. Still wider borders,
perhaps? But Howe supports withdrawal from most of the occupied territories. It is impossible to make sense out of such incon-
sistencies.

Howe adds that unless Israelis are in a position to guarantee
their own security, "they will be left in a state of economic decline and political debacle, and gravely wounded in national
morale," facing destruction. Perhaps he means to suggest that
with a settlement of the sort that Berrigan advocates or the very
similar principles of the Rogers Plan, the situation in Israel will
revert to something like 1966, a period of serious economic and
psychological crisis, with emigration exceeding immigration—
the "most serious crisis" in Israel's history, when its "entire social,
economic and ideological structure was at risk."[40] But if this is
the reason for opposing withdrawal, then let us say so directly
and not invoke the problem of security.

Howe's few remarks explaining why he objects to compelling
Israeli withdrawal from the occupied territories are remarkably
like those heard from extremist right-wing and chauvinist elements within Israel. Eliezer Livneh, an Israeli writer who is one
of the spokesmen for the expansionist Greater Israel Movement,
explains his opposition to UN Resolution 242 "or any other formulation of the Kissinger plan" on the following grounds. The
result will be, he says,

a militaristic Israeli society, a state in siege. It will not have sufficient manpower and resources to absorb immigrants. The realization of Zionism will be strangled at the height of its impetus.
The breaking up of Israel and the heavy curbs on her development will erode the impulses for immigration. Just as victory in
the Six Day War and the restoration of large areas of the homeland gave tremendous impetus to the desire for immigration from
the Soviet Union, so the retreat from the liberated areas will
bring about a Zionist depression. And is it not possible that the
reverse movement, that of emigration from Israel, will be renewed, if the Zionist lever, which gives purpose and sense to Israeli society, is broken?[41]

Left-liberal commentators in Israel and conservative doves have
taken pains to refute Livneh's argument, which is virtually the
same as Howe's. Howe's remarks on security and morale also recall to mind those of General Ezer Weizmann, air force commander in 1967 and a leading right-wing political figure. Speaking of the 1967 war, Weizmann stated that he would

accept the claim that there was no threat of destruction against
the existence of the State of Israel. This does not mean, however, that one could have refrained from attacking the Egyptians, the Jordanians and the Syrians. Had we not done that,
the State of Israel would have ceased to exist *according to the
scale, spirit and quality she now embodies*. . . . We entered the Six-
Day War in order to secure a position in which we can manage
our lives here according to our wishes without external pressures. . . .[42]

In fact, it is obvious that neither Israel nor any other small
country can guarantee its own security. Talk of "guaranteeing
one's own security" is either a sign of serious confusion or a euphemism.[43] Security is not strictly a military concept. Its foundations are political. It rests on international opinion, regional
settlement, and, ultimately, on the interests of the superpowers, much as we may deplore the fact. Howe derides the "U.S.

'guarantee' of [Israel's] future survival," and with some justice, though again he seriously misunderstands the basic problem. It is foolish indeed to place one's fate in the hands of a great power—as Israel has done, and will continue to do if it follows Howe's prescription. The escape from this predicament lies not in a mythical capability to guarantee one's own security, but in local and regional accommodation. But this path leads to consideration of social and political policy that Howe, like so many "supporters of Israel," always ignores. With his insistence that Israel be in a position to establish its own guarantee of security, Howe lends his support, not to Israel, but to the most dangerous and ultimately self-destructive tendencies in its recent policy: the displacement of politics by reliance on power. Howe says that he sympathizes with Israeli doves, but it is precisely this tendency in Israeli policy that they have most insistently condemned. They have insisted, and rightly so, that the policy of annexation favored by General Weizmann does not "secure a position in which we can manage our lives here according to our wishes without external pressures." This policy does not guarantee security, but only further conflict. It leads precisely to "political debacle," as Israel becomes isolated internationally and thus compelled to rely on a "U.S. 'guarantee' of future survival." It does not preserve "national morale," at least in any sense congenial to those who value Israeli democracy, which cannot survive the annexation of territories inhabited by Arabs—the famous "demographic problem" that I have discussed before. (See the introduction, p. 19, and chapter 3, pp. 93–94, 101ff.)

Whatever Howe may have in mind exactly, his remarks on security and its basis, while vague and confused, nevertheless tend in the direction of extremist right-wing elements in Israel. As in the case of Rabbi Hertzberg, once again we have an American dove who sounds, by Israeli standards, strangely like a hawk. Again we see an illustration of the association of American Zionism to right-wing and chauvinist tendencies within Israel—and formerly, world Zionism (cf. chapter 1, p. 42, and this chapter, p. 139).

Howe urges that we "keep our voices in readiness" and continue with "the work of politics, pressure, persuasion." We are to persuade those in power that . . . That what? That Israel not be destroyed? But on this issue I am aware of no disagreement in the United States, except for the most marginal and inconsequential groups. There are real disagreements over security and how it is to be achieved. But on these matters, Howe is silent.

There are also real disagreements over the question of what would constitute a just and proper solution to the multitude of problems that arise in the Arab–Jewish conflict. But like many others who ask us to raise our voices in support of Israel, Howe has no more to say about these questions than about the problem of security. There are a number of possibilities that might be considered, each with several variants (see chapter 3, section II): (1) an Arab state with those Jews who are permitted to remain granted second-class citizenship as a tolerated minority (Qaddafi); (2) a Jewish state with Arabs as second-class citizens, after population transfer (right-wing Zionism); (3) a Jewish and a Palestinian state, side by side in cis-Jordan, perhaps part of a broader federation (some Zionist doves); (4) a democratic secular state (PLO); (5) an Arab–Jewish binational state (the Zionist left until 1947; Ihud; Ben-Gurion and other Zionist leaders in the early 1930s); (6) a Jewish state in most of cis-Jordan with Arabs as second-class citizens, with some areas returned to Jordanian administration and a division of Sinai with Egypt (doves of the Eban variety, if we consider the actual meaning of their proposals). Evidently, Howe rejects (1), (2), and (4). Alternative (3) seems ruled out by his vague remarks about the need for Israel to guarantee its own security. He makes it clear, with the obligatory insults and with arguments that deserve no comment, that he regards socialist binationalism of the sort I have discussed as an absurdity. Thus, (5) is ruled out. We are left, by elimination, with (6): that is, Israel is to remain a Jewish state in most of *cis*-Jordan, hence necessarily a discriminatory state with a substantial class of second-class Arab citizens—given current demographic trends, a very substantial class, and perhaps even a majority before too long (or does Howe support the population-transfer concept of his fellow "democratic socialist" Michael Walzer[44] and the outright Jewish Qaddafis?).

But can this be? After all, Howe insists, "I have never been a Zionist; I have always felt contempt for nationalist and chauvinist sentiments." Furthermore, as a democratic socialist Howe is surely committed to the universality of such values as democracy and equal rights. The circle seems complete. An explanation would be helpful, but instead we are treated only to denunciation and abuse and to the plea that we speak out for Israel.

Like many other left-liberal American Zionists whose writings I have discussed, Howe always skirts the crucial questions: What is the relation between "security" and annexation of the occupied territories? How can a Jewish state with non-Jewish citizens be a "democratic state," let alone a socialist society? How are American liberals or socialists to respond to the blatantly discriminatory legal and administrative structures that are the foundation of the state of Israel? These are nontrivial questions. The ostrich approach is decidedly unhelpful.

Given that Howe has "always felt contempt for nationalist or chauvinist sentiments," we search with interest for his expression of concern for the Palestinians, let us say, those who have been expelled from their lands to make room for all-Jewish settlement. We find these ringing declarations of principle: "I think Golda Meir inadequate on the Palestinian question. . . . I believe that some of the Arab claims, especially in regard to the Palestinian problem, have an element of validity." That is all. It is good to learn that Golda Meir's position—that the Palestinians do not exist—is "inadequate."[45] It would be still more interesting to learn how the "element of validity" in Palestinian claims is to be dealt with.

For example, is there an "element of validity" in the claims of the villagers of Aqraba on the West Bank, whose fields were defoliated in 1972 and then turned over to a nearby Jewish settlement? Or the villagers of Kaffr Kassem, whose claims we discover in the following news item (emphases in the original):

> Kaffr Kassem, east of Petah Tiqva, was the place where a trigger-happy army killed some women and peasants that had returned from the fields, where they had neither been told that the *Sinai war* (1956) had broken out, nor that a curfew had been imposed on their village. This week, the mayor of the small Arab town came to the Knesset to protest against the *confiscation of most of the land* cultivated by his village. The New Force Party has taken up the problem.[46]

According to the Palestinian historian and geographer Aref el-Aref of Ramallah, 475 Arab villages existed before 1948 within the 1967 borders of Israel. Today, 90 remain. In many cases, there is no record of what has happened, and even the sites are now unknown.[47] Is there, perhaps, some "element of validity" lurking in the background here? Of these matters too, we hear nothing.

Israeli leftists and civil libertarians are deeply concerned over these issues. There have been protests and demonstrations in particular instances, though the impact on state policy has been negligible. The protestors do not thereby become "enemies of Israel," whatever Moshe Dayan may think. Or Glazer, Lipset, Howe, et al.

Unfortunately, much of the discussion of the Middle East conflict in the United States not only overlooks such critical issues as those I have mentioned here and in the preceding essays, but also seriously misrepresents others. This is true even on the part of commentators from whom one has come to expect a much higher degree of accuracy and clarity. Thus Hans Morgenthau writes:

> Four times the Arabs tried to eliminate Israel by war. . . . it is an undisputed historic fact that none of the violent encounters in

the Middle East between the Arabs and the Jews—from the 20s to the Six Day War—had anything to do with the boundaries of the Jewish State. They concerned first the presence of Jewish settlers in Palestine, and then the existence of a Jewish state in the midst of the Arab world.[48]

Surely one cannot characterize the 1956 Israeli–British–French aggression against Egypt in these terms. Earlier terrorist incidents also relate directly, in some cases at least, to the boundaries of the Jewish state (cf. introduction, note 20). As for the 1967 war, the situation was far more complex. Israeli Chief of Staff Rabin observed that "there is a difference between concentrating forces in order to get into a war and making a move that, while it might end up in war, is not aimed at war but at something else. . . . [Nasser] preferred the danger of war to backing down."[49] I have already cited Rabin's analysis of the 1973 war (cf. introduction, note 48). The interaction over the years has been far more complex than Morgenthau's remarks indicate. If there is to be useful analysis and discussion of the complex and painful problems of the conflict between Jews and Arabs, it must proceed on firmer grounds than these.

In past years, many people in the peace movement felt that problems of the Middle East should, to preserve the unity of popular opposition to the war in Vietnam, be given a wide berth. I am sure that this is one reason for the "stance of pained indifference" noted by the editors of Liberation (cf. above, p. 123). Furthermore, it was always obvious that opponents of the movement against the war, including some who were unhappy about the course the war had taken, would eagerly seize upon any departure from Zionist orthodoxy (with its predominant right-wing character in the United States) as a means to undermine the mass popular opposition that developed. Perhaps it was justifiable to keep away from the problem on these grounds, but it is no longer.

I think that Israel has suffered, and will continue to suffer, from efforts in the United States to stifle discussion, slander critics, and exploit Israel's problems cynically for domestic political purposes, as it suffers from the general tendency in the United States to support the more chauvinistic and militaristic elements in Israeli society. We should, at the very least, be able to duplicate here the range of discussion and debate that exists in Israel itself. We should, in fact, be able to do better, a step removed from the immediate conflict. In Israel, the "peace list" (Reshimat Shalom) was known as "the Professors' Party." In the United States, the American Professors for Peace in the Middle East (APPME) publishes statements that, to me at least, suggest the rhetoric of the Greater Israel movement, and often appears to be serving virtually as an organ of Israel state propaganda.[50] The contrast is striking and reflects a most regrettable situation.

The United States, with its vast military and economic aid[51] to several countries in the region and with the massive investments of American corporations in petroleum and increasingly other projects, is deeply involved in affairs of the Middle East. The structure of international capitalism and relations with the state socialist system depend crucially on how the problems of this region evolve. In no other region of the world are the problems so likely to lead to devastating regional conflict and possible global war. Furthermore, for Israeli Jews and Palestinian Arabs, problems of justice and even national survival are posed in stark and threatening terms. I have suggested that these problems have only been aggravated by the irrationality and intolerance that has dominated discussion in the United States. It will be most unfortunate if this state of affairs persists.

II

The Intifada, Israel, and the United States at the Turn of the Millennium

The "Peace Process" in U.S. Global Strategy

My primary concern here is the "peace process," its content and its prospects. To summarize in advance, the Madrid–Oslo process should be understood, in my opinion, as an impressive vindication of the rule of force in international affairs, at both the policy and the doctrinal level. The basis for this judgment, which bears directly on the prospects, should become clear, I think, when we attend to the actual terms of the agreements, and even more so, the general framework within which the process took shape. Needless to say, the influence of the United States has been overwhelming in this region for many years; not surprisingly, the Madrid–Oslo process is an expression of that fact. I will begin with a few remarks about U.S. global strategy, then narrow the focus to the Middle East, and finally to the peace process itself, its origins and substantive content.[1]

I will keep to the period since World War II, when the United States became the dominant world power. It had been by far the largest economy in the world long before, but its global reach did not extend much beyond the Caribbean–Central America region and the Pacific (Hawaii, the Philippines).

Oil policy was an exception. In the late 1920s, the United States demanded and received a share in the control of Middle East oil, dividing these resources with Britain and France. Even earlier, the United States had moved to bar Britain, its major rival, from Venezuela, virtually taking over this richly endowed country, which was the world's leading oil exporter from the

1930s until 1970, and which in the mid-1990s has again become the main source of U.S. oil imports, rivaling Saudi Arabia.[2] The United States itself was by far the main oil producer when Britain was expelled from Venezuela by the Woodrow Wilson administration and remained so for almost half a century, but planning in this crucial domain has often been long-range.[3]

The basic principle of oil policy, enunciated by the Wilson administration and then more forcefully during World War II, was that the United States must maintain its "absolute position" in the Western Hemisphere, "coupled with insistence upon the Open Door principle of equal opportunity for United States companies in new areas."[4] In brief, what we have, we keep, closing the door to others; what we do not yet have must be open to free competition. This is, incidentally, the way "free trade" and the "open door" commonly function in practice.

During World War II, Washington was able to displace Britain and France from the Western Hemisphere, establishing a regional system under its control, in violation of the rules of world order it sought to impose elsewhere. The United States was at last able to achieve an early foreign policy goal: excluding imperial rivals from the hemisphere under the Monroe Doctrine. The operative meaning of the doctrine was spelled out in internal deliberations of the Wilson administration. Secretary of State Lansing observed privately that "[i]n its advocacy of the Monroe Doctrine the United States considers its own interests. The integrity of other American nations is an incident, not an end. While this may seem based on selfishness alone, the author of the Doctrine had no higher or more generous motive in its declaration." President Wilson found the argument "unanswerable," though he felt it would be "impolitic" to state it openly, particularly at this peak moment of American "idealism" in international affairs. With the doctrine finally imposed, Latin America was to assume its "role in the new world order": "to sell its raw materials" and "to absorb surplus U.S. capital."[5]

The model is an important one to bear in mind when considering the Middle East, as recognized by Washington's British rivals/allies, who understood its significance well enough. As World War II ended, Lord Killearn wrote, "I often wished that in years gone by we had followed America's wise example and established a sort of Monroe doctrine in this area," making it clear to the locals that we have the "powder in the gun" and will "discharge it" if need be. A few months earlier, as Washington was again making clear to the British its intention to take over Saudi Arabia, the British minister protested that "this is not Panama or San Salvador," so he erroneously thought, though (having little choice) "the British did acquiesce in American treatment of Saudi Arabia almost as if it were a Latin-American country," William Roger Louis observes.[6]

After World War II, Washington sought to extend a version of the Monroe Doctrine to the Middle East oil-producing regions, in uneasy alliance with Britain. In accord with the Wilsonian interpretation, within the reach of the Monroe Doctrine and its extensions, the United States reserves the right to act as it chooses, without interference by the United Nations, the International Court of Justice, the Organization of American States (OAS), or anyone else. That position was reaffirmed in February 1997 when the United States rejected World Trade Organization (WTO) jurisdiction over its sanctions against Cuba in response to a complaint brought to the WTO by the European Union. The Clinton administration "argued that Europe is challenging 'three decades of American Cuba policy that goes back to the Kennedy administration,' and is aimed entirely at forcing a change of government in Havana," the New York Times reported.[7] The legitimacy of the goal is beyond controversy. Washington had taken the same stand in dismissing the order of the World Court to terminate its "unlawful use of force" (that is, international terrorism) against Nicaragua and to pay substantial reparations.[8] On the same grounds, the United States has repeatedly barred UN resolutions calling on all states to observe international law, supported only by Israel (occasionally also Micronesia, Albania, or some other marginal actor), a regular pattern on a wide range of issues concerning world order and human rights. Israel's reliability is one sign of its dependence on the United States, which has no counterpart in world affairs.

Under Clinton, Washington has extended these aspects of the Monroe Doctrine to the Middle East as well. Secretary of State Madeleine Albright, then UN ambassador, informed the Security Council that in this region too the United States will act "multilaterally when we can and unilaterally as we must," because "[w]e recognize this area as vital to U.S. national interests" and therefore recognize no limits or constraints, surely not international law or the United Nations.[9]

These are the prerogatives of overwhelming power. The peace process finds its place within this context.

Let us return to World War II, which left the United States in a position of global dominance with no historical parallel, possessing half the world's wealth and enjoying great advantages in every domain. Not surprisingly, "[f]ollowing World War II the United States assumed, out of self-interest, responsibility for the welfare of the world capitalist system," in the apt words of diplomatic historian Gerald Haines, also senior historian of the Central Intelligence Agency (CIA). As an executive of the Standard Oil Company of New Jersey phrased the matter in 1946, the United States "must set the pace and assume the responsibility of the majority stockholder in this corporation known as the world."[10]

The first postwar task was domestic. Articulating a broad consensus, the business press pointed out that advanced industry "cannot live without one kind or another of governmental support."[11] It was quickly realized that the Pentagon system would be the best device to socialize cost and risk while privatizing power and profit, in part because it is easy to disguise "subsidy" as "security," as the Truman administration observed. That has been the basis for most dynamic sectors of the economy ever since and helps explain why the Pentagon budget remains at Cold War levels, currently increasing on the insistence of congressional "conservatives," while social spending is cut.

The second postwar task was to reconstruct the industrial economies, restoring the traditional order (including Nazi and fascist collaborators) while dispersing the antifascist resistance and its popular base. That should be chapter 1 of a serious postwar history, beginning with Italy in 1943.[12]

In the case of Italy, as of course Greece and Turkey, Middle East oil was an important concern. "U.S. strategic interests" require control over "the line of communications to the Near East outlets of the Saudi-Arabian oil fields" through the Mediterranean, a 1945 interagency review observed, adding that these interests would be threatened if Italy were to fall into "the hands of any great power" (meaning, other than the United States).[13] Washington took the matter quite seriously. The first memorandum of the newly formed National Security Council (NSC) secretly called for military support for underground operations in Italy, along with national mobilization in the United States, "in the event the Communists obtain domination of the Italian government by legal means" in the 1948 elections. The influential planner George Kennan wanted to go further, outlawing the Communist Party, which was expected to win a fair election, even though he thought this would probably lead to civil war, U.S. military intervention, and "a military division of Italy."[14] Italy remained a prime target of CIA subversion at least until the 1970s, when the available internal record runs dry.

The commitment to subvert Italian democracy, a large factor in the enormous rise in corruption and crime, was not limited to government initiatives. The U.S. oil companies Exxon and Mobil, as well as Britain's BP and Shell, provided substantial funding to political parties, recognizing that their "best interests" would be served by "extending financial support to the major non-Communist Italian parties," as a Mobil executive put it. Foreign contributions to U.S. political parties are illegal and, when revealed, are considered a major scandal that undermines the democratic process. U.S. intervention in the electoral process abroad, which is massive in scale, is routinely praised as a generous contribution to democracy enhancement. The criteria are the same as those that define terrorism as "the plague of the modern age" when it is directed against the United States or its clients but as noble support for freedom fighters, or perhaps inadvertent errors or silly shenanigans that got out of hand, when agent and victim are reversed.[15]

Greece was officially regarded as part of the Middle East, not Europe, until the overthrow of the U.S.-backed fascist dictatorship in the 1970s. It was part of the peripheral region required to ensure control over Middle East oil, which the State Department described as "a stupendous source of strategic power, and one of the greatest material prizes in world history," "probably the richest economic prize in the world in the field of foreign investment"—the most "strategically important area in the world" in Eisenhower's view, describing the Arabian peninsula. As Gendzier comments, "by 1947, the importance of the eastern Mediterranean and the Middle East to U.S. policy was beyond argument. Economic and strategic interests dominated calculations of U.S. policy, whether in Turkey, Iran, Saudi Arabia, Palestine, or Lebanon," while "to the consternation of British allies," the economic programs of the (highly selective) Open Door policy "locked the eastern Mediterranean and Middle East into U.S. foreign economic policy, if only because the region was both an indispensable source and a passageway" for oil. Concerns reached far beyond, not only to southern Europe but also to India, where "domination . . . by the USSR would be certain to cost us the entire Middle East," Eisenhower warned in 1954, referring primarily to trade and diplomatic relations, not conquest, of course.[16]

The third postwar task was to restore the former colonial world to its traditional service role. Each region was assigned its "function" for the "welfare of the world capitalist system." High-level planning documents identify the major threat as "economic nationalism" ("radical nationalism," "ultranationalism"), which "embraces policies designed to bring about a broader distribution of wealth and to raise the standard of living of the masses," on the principle that "the first beneficiaries of the development of a country's resources should be the people of that country." These dangerous tendencies must be terminated: the prime beneficiaries are to be U.S. investors and their counterparts elsewhere, who must be assured a favorable climate for business operations and free access to the human and material resources of the service areas. In the Middle East, that translates to the concern that the people of the region might seek to be the beneficiaries of its enormous riches, which are to flow to the United States and its allies. The principles are spelled out frankly and explicitly in internal documents, which often have a vulgar Marxist tone, as is common in the business press as well.

The particular quotes just given,[17] which are typical, happen to concern Latin America, where there was not a remote hint of Soviet involvement at the time, just as there was virtually none in the Middle East. In later years, policies often became entangled in the Cold War conflict, but the basic thrust was essentially the same and persists into the post–Cold War era with some tactical revisions, facts that are again important for understanding the peace process.

How little things would change was revealed when the Berlin Wall fell in November 1989, ending any possible Cold War issue. The United States immediately invaded Panama, killing hundreds or perhaps thousands of civilians; installing a puppet regime of bankers, businessmen, and narcotraffickers; vetoing two Security Council resolutions condemning the aggression; and ignoring the condemnation of the OAS and the Group of Eight Latin American democracies, which had suspended Panama and now expelled it as a state under military occupation. Also ignored were continuing protests within Panama, including the client government's own human rights commission, which years later continued to denounce the "state of occupation by a foreign army," condemning its human rights abuses.[18]

At the same post–Cold War UN session, Washington also vetoed a Security Council resolution condemning Israeli abuses in the occupied territories and (joined only by Israel) voted against two General Assembly resolutions calling on all states to observe international law, one condemning U.S. military aid to the terrorist forces attacking Nicaragua,[19] the other its illegal embargo against Nicaragua. The United States and Israel were joined by Dominica in voting against a resolution opposing acquisition of territory by force (151–3). The resolution once again called for a diplomatic settlement of the Arab–Israeli conflict with recognized borders and security guarantees, incorporating the wording of UN Resolution 242, and the principle of self-determination for both Israel and the Palestinians, the latter unacceptable to the two rejectionist states. I will return to the background of their unwavering rejectionism, now given formal status in the peace process.

The Cold War was definitely over, but the U.S.–Israeli stand on international law, force versus diplomacy, human rights, and the United Nations remained unchanged.[20] Contempt for international law is so extreme that in the debate over the Panama invasion, the U.S. ambassador informed the Security Council that the UN Charter permits the United States to use force "to defend our interests," eliciting no public comment.[21]

The invasion of Panama was a mere footnote to history, apart from two innovations. First, it was not in "self-defense against the Russians," no longer available as a threat; rather, the motive was to capture the criminal Noriega—indeed a criminal, whose major crimes had been committed while he was on the CIA payroll, but who became an authentic criminal when he began to act too independently and was not cooperating properly with the U.S. war against Nicaragua. Second, as pointed out by former Undersecretary of State Elliot Abrams, with the Soviet deterrent gone, the United States was now able to "use force" more readily to attain its ends, opportunities that had been discussed earlier by U.S. policy analysts and that were causing no slight alarm in the Third World.[22]

The immediate reaction to the final end of the Cold War is instructive. Policies continued much as before but with new pretexts and fewer constraints, effects soon to be seen in the Middle East as well.

There were other continuities. President George Bush took the occasion of the Panama invasion to announce still more assistance to his friend and ally Saddam Hussein. Shortly afterward, the White House submitted to Congress its annual budgetary request for the Pentagon. It was virtually unchanged, apart from justifications. In the "new era," the statement explained, "the more likely demands for the use of our military forces may not involve the Soviet Union and may be in the Third World"—just as before, though now without invoking a Soviet threat. Furthermore, it will remain necessary to strengthen "the defense industrial base" (meaning most of high-tech industry) and to create incentives "to invest in new facilities and equipment as well as in research and development," maintaining the public subsidy, no longer because of the Soviet threat but, rather, to counter "the growing technological sophistication" of the Third World—which the United States was seeking to enhance through sales of sophisticated armaments, with increasing fervor after the Gulf War, which was used frankly as a sales promotion device. Military intervention forces must also be maintained, still primarily targeting the Middle East, because of "the free world's reliance on energy supplies from this pivotal region," where the "threats to our interests" that have required direct military engagement "could not be laid at the Kremlin's door," contrary to earlier doctrine, which was no longer functional. "In the future, we expect that non-Soviet threats to these interests will command even greater attention."[23]

In reality, the "threats to our interests" had always been indigenous nationalism, a fact recognized internally, and sometimes even publicly.

The threats to our interests could also not be laid at Iraq's door. At the time (March 1990), Saddam Hussein was a favored friend and trading partner and remained so until August, when he committed the first crime that mattered: disobeying orders. He then lost the status of "moderate," which had been unaffected by such acts as gassing Kurds and torturing dissidents, a replay of the story of Noriega and many others.

In any event, with the fall of the Berlin Wall, it was at least conceded that the core "threat to our interests" has been independent nationalism, often with Cold War entanglements. One useful effect of the end of the Cold War is that the clouds have lifted somewhat and reality is coming into clearer view.[24]

Let us look more closely at how the Middle East fits into the general picture. The crucial issue has remained "history's greatest material prize." A high priority has been to assure that control over the world's cheapest and most abundant energy reserves is in U.S. hands. Immediately after World War II, France was unceremoniously expelled from the Middle East on the interesting legal argument that it was an enemy country, having been occupied by Germany. Britain was permitted a subsidiary role. As one elder statesman of the Kennedy administration put it, Britain may "act as our lieutenant (the fashionable word is partner)."[25] Britain has preferred to hear the fashionable word, though its diplomats understood as the war ended that Britain would be no more than a "junior partner in an orbit of power predominantly under American aegis." The United States was already exercising "power politics naked and unashamed," going well beyond the traditional "spheres of influence" approach, Foreign Secretary Ernest Bevin complained in internal discussion.[26] Foreign Office records reveal few illusions about "the economic imperialism of American business interests, which is quite active under the cloak of a benevolent and avuncular internationalism" and is "attempting to elbow us out." Americans believe "that the United States stands for something in the world," the minister of state at the British Foreign Office commented to his cabinet colleagues: "something of which the world has need, something which the world is going to like, something, in the final analysis, which the world is going to take, whether it likes it or not." Not an inaccurate perception, though not approved for public consumption.[27]

To organize and control the Middle East region, Washington took over the basic structure of the system that Britain had designed. Local management was assigned to an "Arab facade," with "absorption" of the colonies "veiled by constitutional fictions as a protectorate, a sphere of influence, a buffer State, and so on," a device more cost-effective than direct rule (Lord Curzon and the Eastern Committee, 1917–18). The facade should receive only "the outward semblance of sovereignty," the high commissioner for Palestine and Transjordan explained, describing the steps to evade UN demands for decolonization in 1946. But we must never run the risk of "losing control," John Foster Dulles warned as the United States took over the British system.[28]

The conception is conventional. Similar ideas have guided U.S. policy in the Western Hemisphere, the USSR in Eastern Europe, South Africa in the Bantustan era, and the United States and Israel in today's peace process, among many cases. Even outright colonies like India under the Raj were ruled in much the same way, by a local facade.

The facade must be dependable, therefore weak. In the Middle East, family dictatorships are preferred. They are tolerated, even honored, no matter how brutal their behavior, as long as they direct the flow of profits to the United States, its British lieutenant, their energy companies, and other approved projects. If they perform that function, they are amply rewarded by the U.S. taxpayer, who knows nothing about it. To illustrate, "the amount of U.S. dollars flowing from the American Treasury to Arab oil producers dwarfed the amount of U.S. foreign aid to Israel from 1950 until 1973," Yale University economic historian Diane Kunz observes, though the funds, based on tax manipulation, could be interpreted as a gift from the taxpayer to oil companies. In comparison, even before 1967, Israel received the highest per capita U.S. aid of any country, a substantial part of the unprecedented capital transfer to Israel from abroad that constituted almost all of its investment, Harvard Middle East specialist Nadav Safran alleges. Kunz estimates "American private transfers to Israel" (much of it tax deductible, hence U.S. government aid) represented 35 percent of Israel's annual budget in the 1950s. Later the amounts were far greater.[29]

After 1973, the temporary rise in oil prices required measures to recycle petrodollars to the U.S. Treasury through arms sales, construction projects, and other devices, one reason why the United States did not particularly oppose the price increase. Another was the extraordinary profits of U.S. oil companies as the price of oil rose (along with other commodity prices, including major U.S. exports). These factors provided the United States with a positive trade balance with Middle East OPEC (Organization of Petroleum Exporting Countries) members in 1974–1975, also yielding huge profits for U.S. corporations and a flow of billions of Saudi dollars to U.S. Treasury securities.[30]

But since the facade must be weak and compliant, a problem arises: the danger of internal unrest by populations that fall prey to the idea that *they* should benefit from the region's resources. The facade must be protected from such "radical nationalism." That requires regional enforcers, local "cops on the beat," as they were called by the Nixon administration. These are preferably non-Arab: Iran (under the shah), Turkey, Israel, Pakistan. It is understood that police headquarters remain in Washington, though the lieutenant can share the responsibility. As British military historian John Keegan explained when Britain joined the United States in the Gulf War, the British have a "sturdy national character" and a proper tradition: they "are used to over 200 years of expeditionary forces going overseas, fighting the Africans, the Chinese, the Indians, the Arabs. It's just something the British take for granted," and the new task "rings very, very familiar imperial bells with the British," who have always understood the importance of "reserving the right to bomb niggers," as the eminent British statesman Lloyd George expressed the common theme.[31]

Rights are assigned by virtue of the role that actors play within the system. The United States has rights by definition; Britain too, as long as it "acts as our lieutenant" (not as it did in 1956, when it invaded Egypt without authorization and was quickly expelled; the regional gendarmes and the Arab facade have rights as long as they fulfill their functions. Those who contribute nothing to the system of power have no rights: Kurds, slum dwellers in Cairo, and others, among them Palestinians—who, in fact, have negative rights, because their dispossession and suffering arouse unrest. These simple realities explain a good deal about U.S. policies in the region, including the peace process.

Some useful instruction on these matters was provided by the influential neoconservative intellectual Irving Kristol. He pointed out that "insignificant nations, like insignificant people, can quickly experience delusions of significance," which must be driven from their primitive minds by force: "In truth, the days of 'gunboat diplomacy' are never over. . . . Gunboats are as necessary for international order as police cars are for domestic order."[32] Kristol's ire had been aroused by Middle East upstarts who had dared to raise the price of oil beyond what the master ordered. More sweeping proposals for dealing with this insubordination were offered at the same time by Walter Laqueur, another highly regarded public intellectual and scholar. He urged that Middle East oil "could be internationalized, not on behalf of a few oil companies, but for the benefit of the rest of mankind."[33] If the insignificant people do not perceive the justice and benevolence of this procedure, we can send the gunboats.

Laqueur did not draw the further conclusion that the industrial and agricultural resources of the West might also be internationalized, "not on behalf of a few corporations, but for the benefit of the rest of mankind," even though "by the end of 1973, U.S. wheat exports cost three times as much per ton as they had little more than a year before," to cite just one illustration of the sharp rise in commodity prices that preceded or accompanied the rise of oil prices.[34] Those who perceive an inconsistency need only be reminded of the crucial distinction between significant and insignificant people.

Palestinians are not only "insignificant people" but are much lower in the ranking, because they interfere with the plans of the world's most "significant people": privileged Americans and

Israeli Jews (as long as they keep their place). Worse yet, instead of sinking into the oblivion that becomes them, "Palestinian Arabs [are] people who breed and bleed and advertise their misery," Ruth Wisse explained in the prestigious neoconservative journal of the American Jewish Committee. That is "the obvious key to the success of the Arab strategy" of driving the Jews into the sea in a revival of the Nazi lebensraum concept, she continued. Then a professor at McGill University, she moved to Harvard to take a chair endowed by Martin Peretz, who advised Israel on the eve of its 1982 invasion of Lebanon that it should administer to the Palestine Liberation Organization (PLO) a "lasting military defeat" that "will clarify to the Palestinians in the West Bank that their struggle for an independent state has suffered a setback of many years." Then "the Palestinians will be turned into just another crushed nation, like the Kurds or the Afghans," and the Palestinian problem—which "is beginning to be boring"—will be resolved.[35]

One cannot fully understand the peace process without an appreciation of the cultural milieu from which it arises, illustrated not only by such thoughts of prominent Western intellectuals but also, and more significantly, by the fact that they pass without notice, apparently being considered quite natural, though changing a few names would elicit a rather different reaction.[36]

The general strategic conception explains the persistence of the huge military intervention apparatus aimed at the Middle East, with bases stretching from the Pacific through the Indian Ocean to the Azores. The unraveling of colonial relations has led to modifications in the system, but they are not very profound. A 1992 congressional study found that Washington had made, or was in the process of making, "access agreements" with about forty nations (Israel prominent among them) as a more cost-effective device than foreign bases. Middle East oil remains a prime concern. Visiting the Philippines to establish such arrangements after the closing of U.S. military bases, Admiral Charles Larson declared that "the Philippines may be used as a staging area for U.S. military operations should the U.S. initiate involvement in those areas" (Korea and the Mideast, where there are "brewing conflicts"). The Philippine defense minister expressed some concern that the Philippines might be "dragged into a war in the Mideast" as a result.[37]

Similarly the end of the Cold War has led mostly to tactical modifications. At a peak moment of Cold War tensions in 1980, Robert Komer, the architect of President Jimmy Carter's Rapid Deployment Force (later Central Command), aimed primarily at the Middle East, testified before Congress that its most likely use was not to resist a (highly implausible) Soviet attack but to deal with indigenous and regional unrest ("radical nationalism"). The same analysis had been stressed internally. At another critical moment, in 1958, Secretary of State John Foster Dulles informed the National Security Council that the United States faced three major foreign policy crises: Indonesia, North Africa, and the Middle East (all Islamic). He added that there was no Soviet role in any of these crises, and President Eisenhower took "vigorous exception" to the suggestion that others might be serving as Soviet proxies.

In Indonesia, the basic threat was democracy, as in Italy in 1948 and afterward: the fear that "Communists could not be beaten by ordinary democratic means in elections" and must be "eliminated." Such a program was undertaken successfully a few years later, with the slaughter of some half-million people, mostly landless peasants, eliciting unconstrained euphoria in the West—a revealing glimpse of Western civilization, best forgotten, as it has been. In North Africa the problem was the anticolonial struggle, which was interfering with U.S. intent that "North African states under France's benevolent tutelage develop into friendly partners which will be bulwarks of a strong France" (the same "function" that the former colonies were to fulfill for "the welfare of the world capitalist system" generally). In the Middle East as well the primary threat was "radical nationalism." As noted, the basic points are now publicly acknowledged.[38]

The system has worked well for half a century, a long period in human affairs. One index is the price of oil in the United States.

It has changed very little in fifty years, reaching its lowest level in real terms in 1995, though two qualifications are necessary. [39] First, the United States does not want the price to fall too low, because that would cut into profits of the energy corporations, mostly U.S.-based, and would undermine important markets for arms, construction, etc. Second, the actual price of oil is considerably higher than the official numbers indicate, because they fail to take into account many factors, among them the cost of the military forces deployed to keep the prices within an acceptable range. The direct costs amount to a 30 percent public subsidy to oil prices, according to one technical study by a Department of Energy consultant, who takes the results to show that "the current view that fossil fuels are inexpensive is a complete fiction."[40] Estimates of alleged efficiencies of trade and conclusions about economic health and growth are of limited validity if we ignore many such hidden costs.

Though the system has generally been a great success, providing important underpinnings for the "golden age" of state capitalism in the postwar period, problems have arisen. The first was a nationalist uprising in Iran, quickly suppressed with a U.S.-backed military coup that restored the shah. Full details of the operation will probably never be learned. The regular thirty-year archival declassification procedure (covering these events) was disrupted by Reaganite statist reactionaries, leading to the resignation of the State Department historians in protest. More recently it has been revealed that CIA records of the coup were "inadvertently" destroyed.[41]

A second problem arose when Britain, France, and Israel invaded Egypt in 1956. This was unacceptable to the United States, primarily because of timing, according to President Eisenhower, who quickly forced the three disobedient countries to withdraw.

There were also continuing problems with Syria and Egypt, which led to U.S. attempts to overthrow these regimes.[42] Secretary of State Dulles described Egyptian president Gamal Abdel Nasser as "an extremely dangerous fanatic." He was a "fanatic" because of his neutrality and independence and dangerous because the people of the region were "on Nasser's side," President Eisenhower recognized ruefully. Our "problem is that we have a campaign of hatred against us, not by the governments but by the people," he added. By January 1958, concerns were becoming quite serious. The National Security Council concluded that "in the eyes of the majority of Arabs the United States appears to be opposed to the realization of the goals of Arab nationalism. They believe that the United States is seeking to protect its interest in Near East oil by supporting the *status quo* and opposing political or economic progress." Washington's basic problem was that the perception was correct. As the NSC formulated the matter, "our economic and cultural interests in the area have led not unnaturally to close U.S. relations with elements in the Arab world whose primary interest lies in the maintenance of relations with the West and the *status quo* in their countries."[43] For reasons that are deeply rooted in policy formation and its institutional sources, the United States found itself on a collision course with independent nationalism in the Middle East, as elsewhere in the Third World.

These problems came to a head a few months later, in July 1958, when a military coup overthrew the British client regime in Iraq. Reactions in the United States and United Kingdom give a clear picture of interests and intentions and provide highly relevant background for what happened in 1990 when Iraq invaded Kuwait, with a significant impact on the peace process, to which I will return.

After the coup, the United States immediately landed Marines in Lebanon, with a presidential order to prepare for use of "*whatever* means might become necessary to prevent any unfriendly forces from moving into Kuwait" (Eisenhower's emphasis). Middle East scholar William Quandt, who also has a background in the national security apparatus, interprets this as a reference to use of nuclear weapons. British foreign secretary Selwyn Lloyd flew to Washington for consultations. These led to a recommendation that Britain grant nominal independence to Kuwait while maintaining its virtual colonial status. The only alternative considered was immediate British occupation of Kuwait, an option rejected because it might arouse further nationalist reactions in Kuwait and elsewhere. But Britain needed to be prepared "ruthlessly to intervene" if anything went wrong, "whoever it is has caused the trouble"—Kuwaiti nationalists, for example. Washington was to assume the same posture toward Saudi Arabia and the Persian Gulf principalities, agreeing that "at all costs these oilfields [in Kuwait, Saudi Arabia, Bahrain, and Qatar] must be kept in Western hands," Lloyd cabled to London.[44]

Kuwait was assigned to Britain. As senior partner, the United States took charge of most of the rest of the countries in the Middle East. Washington recognized that the British economy relied heavily on the wealth of the region and determined that the United States must be ready "to support, or if necessary assist, the British in using force to retain control of Kuwait and the Persian Gulf."[45] The major difference in 1990 was that power had shifted even more to U.S. hands.

The terminology should be noted: the United States and the United Kingdom were to *retain control* of the oil-producing regions, not to *defend* them. In public, there was a ritual appeal to the Soviet threat, but the internal record is again different. The perceived threat was the usual one throughout the service areas: radical nationalism.

In January 1958, the NSC had concluded that a "logical corollary" of opposition to growing Arab nationalism "would be to support Israel as the only strong pro-Western power left in the Middle East."[46] While this was an exaggeration, it was an affirmation of the general strategic analysis, which identified indigenous nationalism as the primary threat, as elsewhere in the Third World—with overwhelming clarity in Latin America and Southeast Asia.[47] The NSC analysis also affirmed the conclusions of the Joint Chiefs of Staff in 1948, when they were much impressed by Israel's military prowess and suggested that Israel might be a suitable base for U.S. power in the region, second only to Turkey.

Failure to look closely at the internal record, the timing of events, and the close similarity of policies throughout the world can easily lead to a misreading of their basic thrust, hence a dubious interpretation of current developments and prospects. One standard formulation is that "the Israel–Arab conflict was fueled by the Cold War, in which the United States regarded Israel as a reliable ally against the Soviet-backed regimes of some Arab states." I am quoting from an Israeli "post-Zionist" analysis, highly critical of standard interpretations, but in this case not critical enough. The statement is not literally false, but it is highly misleading.[48] Support for "local cops on the beat"—Israel, South Africa, and others—has regularly been seen as a "logical corollary" of opposition to indigenous nationalism in the service areas. The targets of subversion and attack often did turn to the USSR for support, sometimes for independent reasons as well, just as Islamic fundamentalist extremists in Afghanistan turned to the United States for support against Russian aggression. But the USSR did not attack Afghanistan in fear of U.S. support for Gulbuddin Hekmatyar. We should be careful not to confuse cause with consequences or to misconstrue the way the Cold War connections developed.

Much more accurate, in my opinion, is the interpretation of former chief of Israeli military intelligence Gen. Shlomo Gazit, who wrote after the collapse of the USSR that

> Israel's main task has not changed at all, and it remains of crucial importance. Its location at the center of the Arab Muslim Middle East predestines Israel to be a devoted guardian of stability in all the countries surrounding it. Its [role] is to protect the existing regimes: to prevent or halt the processes of radicalization and to block the expansion of fundamentalist religious zealotry.[49]

Religious zealotry is no problem as long as it is properly disciplined (as in Saudi Arabia, Afghanistan, or for that matter in the United States itself, which ranks high on the scale of "fundamentalist religious zealotry"), but it is an unacceptable form of "radical nationalism" if it escapes these bounds, whether or not it

turns elsewhere for support. In these terms, well supported by the
documentary and historical record, we can understand the highly
systematic character of policy and its essential continuity with
the USSR gone from the scene.

Returning to forty years ago, fear of the Nasserite disease did
not abate. By the early 1960s there was concern that it might infect even Saudi Arabia, the ultimate domino in the region.
Israel's military victory in 1967 put an end to these concerns,
earning the country the status of "strategic asset" that it has since
maintained and also arousing enthusiastic support for Israel
among American intellectuals, much impressed by the effective
use of force against people with "delusions of significance"—no
small issue in those years of Washington's difficulties in Vietnam.[50]

The aftermath is familiar. The "logical corollary" was translated into a major policy instrument. U.S. military and diplomatic support for Israel increased sharply again in 1970, when
Israeli muscle flexing deterred possible Syrian intervention in
Jordan in support of Palestinians under brutal assault there, a possibility that the United States regarded as a threat to the Arab facade. By the early 1970s, a de facto alliance was in place between
Israel and Iran, the two major local gendarmes within the newly
articulated Nixon Doctrine. The Senate's leading specialist on
the Middle East and oil politics, Henry Jackson, described these
partners as two "reliable friends of the United States," who,
jointly with Saudi Arabia, "have served to inhibit and contain
those irresponsible and radical elements in certain Arab States
. . . who, were they free to do so, would pose a grave threat indeed to our principal sources of petroleum in the Persian Gulf"—
sources that the United States then hardly used but that were
needed as a reserve and as a lever for world control, and for the
vast wealth they yield.[51] The formal conflict between Saudi Arabia and both Iran and Israel was only a technicality, as was the
theoretical opposition of the shah's regime to Israel's policies.

With the fall of the shah in 1979, Israel's importance as a regional gendarme increased. After the failure of President Carter's

emissary Gen. Robert Huyser to inspire a military coup in Iran, the United States, Israel, and Saudi Arabia tried to restore the tripartite alliance, with Saudi Arabia funding the sale of U.S. arms via Israel to elements of the Iranian military, who, it was hoped, would overthrow the regime. The goals and intended measures were described with brutal frankness at the time by Uri Lubrani (effectively, Israel's ambassador to Iran under the shah) and by Moshe Arens (then ambassador to the United States) and others.[52]

By that time, Israel's client relationship was firmed up on other grounds. Israel was performing important secondary services in Africa and Asia, but particularly in Latin America, where Washington was inhibited from providing direct support for the more brutal tyrants and killers by popular opposition and congressional human rights legislation that reflected the popular mood. Carter and, increasingly, by the 1980s, the Reaganites were able to turn to Israel to take over such tasks as part of an international terror network that also included Taiwan, Britain, Argentine neo-Nazis, and others, often with Saudi funding. Israeli cooperation in weapons development and testing under live battlefield conditions was also a matter of increasing interest in Washington, along with basing facilities for the U.S. fleet and for prepositioning of weapons, contingency planning, joint exercises, and the like, again within the general strategic conception, and independently of the Cold War. Thus policy persisted with no notable change. These matters are reported in Pentagon testimony to Congress and the writings of U.S.–Israeli strategic analysts. One interesting case is the analysis by Benjamin Netanyahu's close associate Dore Gold, spelling out Israel's role as an intervention force in "non-Soviet scenarios"— that is, against "radical nationalism"—thus "expand[ing] the range of American options."[53]

Let us turn to the diplomatic record, which is eminently understandable in the developing context just outlined.[54]

After the 1967 war, the great powers established UN Resolution 242 as the basic framework for a diplomatic settlement, calling for Israeli withdrawal from the conquered territories in return for a peace treaty between Israel and the Arab states. Though archival records are not yet fully available, enough has appeared—including a leaked State Department history—to establish that the United States understood UN 242 to require *full* Israeli withdrawal to the prewar borders, with at most minor and mutual adjustments, the position announced officially in the 1969 Rogers Plan.[55] Under Washington's interpretation, UN 242 called for full withdrawal in return for full peace. The Arab states refused full peace, and Israel refused full withdrawal, settling in 1968 on the Allon Plan, which has undergone various modifications over the years. The Oslo agreements laid the groundwork for implementation of a contemporary version, with slightly different variants as political power shifts between Labor and Likud coalitions.

Note that UN 242 is outright rejectionist, with no recognition of any Palestinian right of self-determination. That fact is of crucial importance for understanding the U.S.-run peace process.

The impasse over UN 242 was broken in February 1971, when Egyptian president Anwar Sadat accepted a proposal by UN mediator Gunnar Jarring, agreeing to full peace with Israel in return for Israeli withdrawal to the prewar Israel–Egypt border.[56] Again, the proposal was pure rejectionism, offering nothing to one of the two contestants for rights in the former Palestine; in fact it was limited to Israel–Egypt relations. Israel officially welcomed this as a genuine peace offer. In his memoirs, Yitzhak Rabin describes it as a "famous . . . milestone" on the path to peace.[57]

Israel's reaction is reported by Yossi Beilin in his detailed review of internal government rècords. At a high-level meeting a few days after Sadat's peace offer was received, no one advocated accepting it. Abba Eban proposed a conditional response, with "Israeli armed forces to withdraw from the cease-fire line with Egypt to secure, recognized, and agreed borders, which will be established in the peace agreement," not the borders assumed in UN 242 and the Jarring memorandum. Golda Meir's hawkish adviser Israel Galili objected even to this, suggesting instead outright rejection with the formula that "Israel will not withdraw to the pre–June 5, 1967, borders." Moshe Dayan and Yitzhak Rabin agreed and convinced the cabinet to accept Galili's proposal. Jordan had expressed its interest in a settlement through the 1967–1973 period in "direct secret meetings between the highest officials in Jordan and Israel" and in other ways, Beilin alleges, observing also that even Galili "did not deny the possibility for a peace settlement on the June 4, 1967, borders."[58]

Adopting Galili's formula, Israel rejected Sadat's peace offer, preferring expansion to peace. The reasoning was outlined publicly by Gen. (ret.) Haim Bar-Lev of the governing Labor Party:

> I think that we could obtain a peace settlement on the basis of the earlier [pre–June 1967] borders. If I were persuaded that this is the maximum that we might obtain, I would say: agreed. But I think that it is not the maximum. I think that if we continue to hold out, we will obtain more.

Ezer Weizmann added that if Israel were to accept UN 242 as interpreted by the United States and other great powers, it could not "exist according to the scale, spirit, and quality she now embodies."[59] Israeli commentator Amos Elon wrote ten years later that Sadat had caused "panic" among the Israeli political leadership when he announced his willingness "to enter into a peace agreement with Israel, and to respect its independence and sovereignty in 'secure and recognized borders.'"[60] As in other cases, the "panic" was overcome by holding fast. Sometimes resort to violence seemed a better means, as in Lebanon, when, to overcome the threat of PLO moderation, a "veritable catastrophe" for the Israeli government, Israel invaded in the hope of compelling "the stricken PLO" to "return to its earlier terrorism," thus "undercutting the danger" of negotiations, historian Yehoshua Porath pointed out shortly after the invasion, a judgment well supported on other grounds.[61]

In 1971, Israel chose the near certainty of military confrontation and terror, not the possibility of diplomatic settlement. One may debate the merits of the choice, but a choice it was. In Bar-Lev's terms the choice was justified: reliance on force rather than diplomacy did allow Israel to "obtain more" under the peace process.

Sadat's peace offer presented Washington with a dilemma. Egypt's position was in accord with the official U.S. stand; Israel's was not. An internal debate followed, with the State Department keeping to the earlier position and national security adviser Henry Kissinger advocating what he called "stalemate": no negotiations or diplomacy, just reliance on force. Kissinger gives reasons in his memoirs, but they are so outlandish that they can be dismissed (they are generally ignored in the professional literature).[62] Kissinger prevailed and soon took over the State Department, eliminating his rival, William Rogers, possibly his real motive in this affair. The United States accordingly changed its interpretation of UN 242 to permit only partial withdrawal, as the United States and Israel alone determine. Given U.S. power, that has been the operative meaning of UN 242 since 1971.

This was a major turning point in Middle East diplomacy and is of great significance today. Since that time, the United States has barred every diplomatic initiative based on UN 242 under its original meaning, in complete diplomatic isolation (along with Israel).

U.S.–Israeli isolation became even more extreme by the mid-1970s, as the international consensus shifted toward recognition of Palestinian rights. UN resolutions recognizing those rights were added to UN 242 in the diplomatic process—not given the name "peace process" because the world-dominant state opposed it. The issue reached the UN Security Council in January 1976, with a resolution incorporating the language of UN 242 but abandoning its rejectionism, now calling for a Palestinian state alongside Israel. The resolution was supported by virtually the entire world, including the major Arab states, the PLO, Europe, the nonaligned countries, and the Soviet Union, which was in the mainstream of international diplomacy throughout. According to Israeli UN ambassador Haim Herzog, later president, the PLO not only backed the plan but in fact "prepared it."[63]

Israel refused to attend the UN session. Instead, it bombed Lebanon once again, killing more than fifty villagers in what it called a "preventive" strike, presumably retaliation against UN diplomacy. By Western standards, such actions do not fall under "the plague of international terrorism."

The United States vetoed the resolution, as it did again in 1980. From the mid-1970s, the United States blocked all initiatives from the UN, Europe, the Arab states, the USSR, and the PLO, with increasing intensity from the early 1980s. Though the Security Council was eliminated by the U.S. veto, the General Assembly continued to pass such resolutions at its annual meetings, with overwhelming support, the United States and Israel opposed, as on many other issues. The last such vote was in December 1990 (144–2). The date is significant.

Virtually all of this is out of history, ignored or distorted even in scholarly work and flatly denied in journalism and intellectual discourse. Apparently the picture of the United States as the leader of the rejection front cannot be assimilated into the intellectual culture. Hence history has been rewritten, a rather impressive achievement, which I have reviewed elsewhere.[64] The facts have been available regularly in marginalized dissident literature, but rarely elsewhere.

More interesting is that the facts seem to have been erased from the memories of Israeli leaders who could not have failed to know them—for example, the generally realistic Moshe Dayan, who, in November 1976, said in a confidential interview that "there is a real hope that Egypt may want peace with us" someday, as perhaps may even other Arab states. Such reactions may be a symptom of the "panic" Elon described over the threat of a diplomatic settlement, which would undermine the "permanent rule" over the territories that Dayan had anticipated when serving as defense minister in the Labor government, prior to 1973.[65]

After the rejection of his 1971 peace offer, Sadat tried in many ways to gain Washington's attention. Among other initiatives, he expelled Soviet advisers, thereby "abandoning the Egyptian intention to destroy the Zionist reality," Dayan observed in the same interview.[66] Sadat also threatened war if the United States and Israel continued to reject a peaceful settlement. American diplomats in the Middle East, businessmen, and others urged Kissinger to take these threats seriously, but he dismissed them on prevailing assumptions about Israeli military dominance: for example, that Israel is a military power on a par with Britain and France and could immediately conquer the area from Khartoum to Baghdad to Algeria if necessary (Gen. Ariel Sharon) and would "trample Arab faces in the mud" if they forget that fact of life (Israeli radio), whereas "war is not the Arabs' game."[67]

The 1973 war dispelled these rather racist theses. Kissinger came to realize that Egypt could not simply be disregarded. The next best option was to remove it from the conflict, a policy that culminated in the Camp David agreements of 1978–1979, which left Israel free to integrate the occupied territories and attack Lebanon, as it proceeded to do with the Arab deterrent removed. These implications of Camp David were obvious at once and are now generally acknowledged, for example, by Israeli strategic analyst Avner Yaniv, who observes that the effect of the "Egyptian defection" was to "free" Israel "to sustain military operations against the PLO in Lebanon as well as settlement activity on the West Bank."[68] In reality, the military operations regularly targeted Lebanese civilians from the early 1970s, guided by the "rational prospect, ultimately fulfilled, that affected populations would exert pressure for the cessation of hostilities" and acceptance of Israeli arrangements for the region, Abba Eban observed. Eban's advocacy of international terrorism was in response to Prime Minister Menachem Begin's account of atrocities in Lebanon committed under the Labor government in the style "of regimes which neither Mr. Begin nor I would dare to mention by name," Eban observed, acknowledging the accuracy of the account.[69]

Sadat's 1977 initiatives were welcomed, turning him into a hero and a "man of peace" and very definitely entering history, though his proposals were far less acceptable to Israel than the suppressed and forgotten "famous milestone" of 1971, because he now called for Palestinian rights, in accord with the revised international consensus. The reason for the different reactions is simple: the 1973 war.

By the late 1980s, U.S.–Israeli extremism was running into difficulties. The intifada threatened Israel's control of the territories, and by late 1988, Washington was becoming an object of international ridicule for its increasingly desperate efforts not to hear the diplomatic initiatives from the PLO and others. By December, Secretary of State George Shultz gave up the game. Washington grudgingly "declared victory," announcing that the PLO had capitulated and uttered the "magic words"—namely, reiterating its unchanged position, which Washington could no longer ignore. The preferred version is the one that Shultz reports in his memoirs: before, Yasser Arafat had been saying in one place "'Unc, unc, unc,' and in another he was saying, 'cle, cle, cle,' but nowhere will he yet bring himself to say 'Uncle,'" in the style of abject surrender expected of "insignificant people."[70]

Washington announced further that as a reward for its sudden good behavior, the PLO would be permitted to have a "dialogue" with the United States, plainly as a delaying tactic. The protocols of the first meeting were leaked and published in Egypt and in Israel, where there was much jubilation over the fact that "the American representative adopted the Israeli positions." U.S. ambassador Robert Pelletreau stated two preconditions that the PLO must accept for the dialogue to proceed: it must abandon the idea of an international conference and call off the "riots" in the occupied territories (the intifada), "which we view as terrorist acts against Israel."[71] In short, the PLO must ensure a return to the pre-intifada status quo, so that Israel would be able to continue its expansion and repression in the territories with U.S. support.

The ban on an international conference followed from the unwillingness of the world to adopt U.S. rejectionism at that time. As Henry Kissinger had privately explained, his diplomatic efforts were designed "to ensure that the Europeans and Japanese did not get involved in the diplomacy concerning the Middle East" (also "to isolate the Palestinians" so that they would not be a factor in the outcome, and "to break up the Arab united front," thus allowing Israel "to deal separately with each of its neighbors").[72]

The background for Pelletreau's second precondition is made clear in another UN resolution barred by the United States: the 1987 General Assembly resolution condemning "terrorism wherever and by whomever committed." The offending clause is:

> [N]othing in the present resolution could in any way prejudice the right to self-determination, freedom and independence, as derived from the Charter of the United Nations, of peoples forcibly deprived of that right . . . , particularly peoples under colonial and racist regimes and foreign occupation or other forms of colonial domination, nor . . . the right of these peoples to struggle to this end and to seek and receive support [in accordance with the Charter and other principles of international law].

These rights are not accepted by the United States, Israel, or, at the time, their South African ally. The resolution passed 153–2, the United States and Israel opposed, Honduras alone abstaining. It was therefore effectively vetoed (also unreported and banned from history). For similar reasons, the United States rejected the declaration of the 1993 Vienna Conference on Human Rights that "any foreign occupation is a human rights violation," also unreported.[73]

On these assumptions, protests in the occupied territories are "terrorist acts against Israel."

A few weeks later, in February 1989, Yitzhak Rabin had a meeting with Peace Now leaders in which he expressed his satisfaction with the U.S.–PLO dialogue, which he described as "low-level discussions" that avoided any serious issue and granted Israel "at least a year" to resolve the problems by force. "The inhabitants of the territories are subject to harsh military and economic pressure," Rabin explained, and "in the end, they will be broken" and will accept Israel's terms.[74]

These terms were spelled out in the May 1989 plan of the Peres–Shamir coalition government, which stipulated that there can be no "additional Palestinian state" (Jordan already being a "Palestinian state") and that "there will be no change in the status of Judea, Samaria and Gaza other than in accordance with the basic guidelines of the [Israeli] Government." Furthermore, Israel would conduct no negotiations with the PLO, though it would permit "free elections," to be conducted under Israeli military rule with much of the Palestinian leadership expelled or in prison without charge.[75]

This proposal was praised for its "great promise and potential" by prominent American doves (Aaron David Miller of the State Department, Middle East commentator Helena Cobban), who mentioned only that Israel might allow "free elections." In December 1989, the State Department's James Baker plan officially endorsed the Peres–Shamir plan, offering Palestinians a dialogue on measures to implement it; no other issues were to be raised.

Again, the essential facts have yet to reach the American public, except at the margins.

There remained the problem of how to implement the extreme form of rejectionism advocated by the Labor–Likud coalition and the Bush administration, as by their predecessors. That problem was solved a few months later, in August 1990, when Saddam Hussein invaded Kuwait, having misunderstood the rules of world order, as dictators are prone to do in their isolation. Bush continued to send aid to Saddam until the day of the invasion, as did British prime minister Margaret Thatcher, and the State Department indicated to him that Washington would not object if he were to rectify a disputed border with Kuwait and shake his fist at other oil producers to induce them to raise prices. Saddam perhaps interpreted this as authorization to take over Kuwait. At that point, the principles enunciated in 1958 came into force.

The Bush administration feared that Saddam would immediately withdraw, leaving a puppet regime in place; that is, that he would duplicate what the United States had just done in Panama. No historical parallel is exact, of course. Civilian casualties in Panama were apparently higher than in Kuwait at that stage, and there were other differences. In internal discussion, chairman of the Joint Chiefs Colin Powell warned that in "the next few days Iraq will withdraw," putting "his puppet in," and "everyone in the Arab world will be happy."[76] Latin Americans, in contrast, were anything but happy about similar U.S. actions in Panama. But the major difference is that as the global superpower, the United States could veto Security Council resolutions and nullify other objections to its invasion of Panama and could mobilize rather unwilling international support to ensure that apparent Iraqi withdrawal initiatives would be dismissed and that the reaction would be "ruthless," as prescribed thirty-two years earlier. An instructive series of events followed; these are reviewed elsewhere.[77]

As bombs and missiles were falling on Baghdad and peasant recruits were hiding in the sands, George Bush announced the basic principle of the New World Order in four simple words: "What we say goes."[78] What "we say" was made crystal clear as the shooting stopped. Immediately, a rebellion in the Shi'ite regions of southern Iraq sought to overthrow Saddam, who launched a vicious counterattack. The United States stood by quietly, refusing even to allow rebelling Iraqi generals access to captured Iraqi military equipment to protect the population from Hussein's slaughter. The official reasoning was outlined by Thomas Friedman, chief diplomatic correspondent of the *New York Times*. "The best of all worlds" for Washington, he explained, would be "an iron-fisted Iraqi junta without Saddam Hussein," a return to the happy days when Hussein's "iron fist . . . held Iraq together, much to the satisfaction of the American allies Turkey and Saudi Arabia"—and, of course, their superpower patron.[79] But since no suitable clone could be found, it would be necessary to settle for second best: an iron-fisted junta run by the Beast of Baghdad himself. U.S.–UK policy was described by the chairman of the House of Commons Foreign Affairs Committee, David Howell, as saying to Hussein, "It is all right now, you are free to commit any atrocities you like."[80]

U.S. officials confirmed that the Bush administration would persist in its refusal to talk to Iraqi democrats or to raise questions about democracy in Kuwait. That would be inappropriate interference in the internal affairs of other countries, they explained. For Iraq, what mattered was "stability," and that meant support for Hussein as he crushed the southern rebellion under the eyes of Stormin' Norman Schwartzkopf and then turned to the north to crush the Kurdish uprising. In the latter case, an unanticipated popular reaction in the West forced Washington to put some limits on Hussein's atrocities, though he did receive vocal support from Turkey, brutally repressing its own Kurdish population, and from Israel, where military and political figures (including the retiring chief of staff and leading doves) warned that Kurdish autonomy might create a territorial link between Damascus and Tehran, so that the butcher should be allowed to carry out his necessary work. Turkish concerns received some mention in the United States, but not the Israeli reaction, which clashed too sharply with preferred imagery.[81]

The aftermath of the Gulf War offered both a need and an opportunity for the United States to implement its rejectionist program. The need arose from the ugly picture in the gulf region: the Beast of Baghdad back in charge, now with tacit rather than overt U.S. support as before; the uprisings violently crushed; the Arab facade safeguarded from democratic pressures; and reports beginning to come in from respected Western medical sources and human rights groups about thousands of Iraqi children dying from sanctions that were aimed at the civilian population, not Hussein. That was not a scene to be left in public memory, particularly after the jingoist frenzy and awe for the Grand Leader that had been whipped up by the doctrinal system. A triumph was badly needed.

The opportunity arose from the fact that the world now accepted the guiding principle of the New World Order: "What we say goes," at least in the Middle East. Europe backed away. Its only further role was to facilitate U.S. rejectionist programs, as Norway did in 1993. The Soviet Union was gone. The Third

World was in disarray, in part as a result of the economic catastrophe of the 1980s. The United States was at last free to implement the two basic principles it had upheld in isolation for twenty years: (1) no international conference; (2) no right of self-determination for the Palestinians.

That was the framework of the Madrid negotiations, which began in fall 1991 to great fanfare and applause. Negotiations dragged on while Israel continued its expansion into the territories with U.S. support, though Washington continued to prefer the style of Labor, which understands better than Likud how to present its actions so that they will be accepted rather than condemned. In other respects the differences are not great. The Clinton administration came as something of a surprise in its support for more extreme Israeli policies. There were also increasing challenges to Arafat within the Palestinian community, reported in Israel through the summer of 1993.

In September 1993, the Declaration of Principles was signed in Washington. It incorporated the basic principles of U.S.–Israeli rejectionism. First, the "permanent status" is to be based solely on UN Resolution 242, which offers nothing to the Palestinians, not on 242 *and other relevant UN resolutions* that the United States has barred since the mid-1970s because they recognize Palestinian rights. Second, UN 242 is to be understood in the terms unilaterally imposed by the United States since 1971 (meaning partial withdrawal) and incorporated in the Peres–Shamir–Baker plan of 1989. Presumably the United States and Israel will modify that plan at least rhetorically. It would make sense for them to use the term "state" to refer to whatever scattered cantons they decide to leave to local Palestinian administration, much as South Africa did when it established the "homelands" in the early 1960s—a program that merited the term "peace process" as much as the present one does but did not gain that status because it was not an expression of the rules of world order that are established by the powerful.

Whether the United States and Israel decide to call the cantons a "state" or something else—perhaps "fried chicken," as

David Bar-Illan elegantly suggested—the results are likely to re-
semble the Bantustan model.[82] No one familiar with the situation in the territories created by the Rabin–Peres–Netanyahu
governments and their predecessors (and successors) will fail to
recognize the picture given in a standard work of African history:

> South African retention of effective power through its officials in
> the Bantustans, its overwhelming economic influence and secu-
> rity arrangements gave to this initiative [of elections] elements of
> a farce. However, unlikely candidates as were the Bantustans for
> any meaningful independent existence, their expanding bureau-
> cracies provided jobs for new strata of educated Africans tied to
> the system in a new way and a basis of accumulation for a small
> number of Africans with access to loans and political influence.
> Repression, too, could be indigenized through developing home-
> land policy and army personnel. On the fringe of the Bantustans,
> border industry growth centers were planned as a means of free-
> ing capital from some of the restraints that influx control imposed
> on industrial expansion elsewhere and to take advantage of vir-
> tually captive and particularly cheap labor. Within the home-
> lands economic development was more a matter of advertising
> brochures than actual practical activity although some officials in
> South Africa understood the needs from their own perspective for
> some kind of revitalization of the homelands to prevent their
> economies from collapsing even further.[83]

So far, Israeli officials have not recognized any need to keep the
economies of the cantons from collapsing even further, though
sooner or later they may see the merit in the demands of Israeli industrialists for a "transition from colonialism to neo-colonialism"
in the territories with the collaboration of "the representatives
of the Palestinian bourgeoisie," thus creating "a situation similar to
the relations between France and many of its former colonies in
Africa"—or the United States and Mexico, or Western investors
and the Third World that is being restored in Eastern Europe, or
international capital in southeast China, etc.[84]

As in the United States, the threat to transfer production
across the border can be used effectively to undermine unions,

lower wages, increase inequality, and diminish the threat of democracy. "If any union even thinks of striking, the manufacturers can close their factories and set up new ones in Gaza," Histadrut officers explained, a prospect that was particularly appealing to Yitzhak Rabin, who had "never concealed his animosity toward the Histadrut or his free-market leanings"—"free market" U.S.-style, with the economy based on massive state subsidy for wealth and privilege and spin-offs from military industry.[85] A model is suggested by events in Ofakim, where a factory was closed shortly after its owners received a substantial public subsidy and transferred across the border to enjoy much cheaper labor with few benefits, a good illustration of the promise of Peres's "new order" in the Middle East.

Israeli policies have continued to contribute to the further collapse of the Palestinian economy. The territories were not permitted to develop under Israeli rule and are now spinning rapidly downward, though Palestinians "tied to the system" and "with access to loans and political influence" can enrich themselves by stealing foreign aid with Israel's cooperation. Similarly, the United States winks at Israel's rampant corruption, for example, the diversion of billions of dollars of U.S. loan guarantees, theoretically for immigrants, to give "Israel's banking system (taken over by the government after the 1983 bank shares scandal) greater liquidity and willingess to extend credit to corporations, small businesses, and private individuals," enabling Israelis to "purchase automobiles, foreign travel, or speculate on the stock market" in an artificially rich country that now is competing with its sponsor for the lead in inequality in the industrial world. Widespread corruption in client states is considered no more of a problem than at home, as long as the "significant people" are receiving their due.[86]

The International Monetary Fund (IMF) reports that through 1996, and since the Oslo process began, unemployment nearly doubled in the territories and per capita income shrank 20 percent, while investment halved. The further devastation of the economy results in part from the closures, which were particularly harsh under Labor, and from Israel's policy of blocking Palestinian exports while maintaining a captive market for expensive Israeli imports, made even more costly as they pass through the monopolies established as payoffs by the Palestinian Authority. Meanwhile, the IMF reports, total Israeli exports grew by almost half, "nearly doubling in Asian markets opened up by the peace process, while foreign investment in Israel went up six-fold."[87] The UN agencies in the territories estimate the decline in per capita gross national product since Oslo I to be about 40 percent, accelerating "the retardation of development in the territories that began in 1967."[88] Other informed observers give still higher estimates of the decline.

In short, the peace process follows a rule of very great generality: it serves the interests of its architects quite nicely, while the interests of others are "an incident, not an end." As for the "insignificant people," the peace process has offered the United States and Israel new mechanisms to follow the advice of Moshe Dayan, one of the Labor leaders more sympathetic to the Palestinian plight, in the early days of the occupation: Israel should tell the Palestinian refugees in the territories that "we have no solution, you shall continue to live like dogs, and whoever wishes may leave, and we will see where this process leads." The suggestion is natural within the overriding conception articulated by Haim Herzog in 1972: "I do not deny the Palestinians a place or stand or opinion on every matter. . . . But certainly I am not prepared to consider them as partners in any respect in a land that has been consecrated in the hands of our nation for thousands of years. For the Jews of this land there cannot be any partner."[89]

Nothing fundamental has changed in the conception of the Labor doves and their U.S. sponsors, apart from new modalities.

At the peak period of Israeli rejectionism in mid-1988, Yitzhak Rabin called for a settlement leaving Israel in control of 40 percent of the West Bank and Gaza, an updated version of the Allon Plan. At Oslo II, he agreed to accept twice that much, though surely Israel will want to transfer more mostly useless land to local Palestinian administration while keeping control of the resources and valuable sectors, perhaps reaching Rabin's 1988 figure.

After Oslo II, Peres informed a gathering of ambassadors in Jerusalem that "this solution about which everyone is thinking and which is what you want will never happen." He continued to act resolutely to ensure that outcome with U.S. funding and support—for example, in February 1996, when his housing minister, Benjamin ("Fuad") Ben-Eliezer, announced the construction of 6,500 units for Jews only in the area of southeast Jerusalem that Israel calls Har Homa, with groundbreaking scheduled to begin in a year. Only a few days before Netanyahu was elected, dozens of Palestinians tried to block Peres's bulldozers paving the way to the planned settlement at Har Homa. Ben-Eliezer also announced other building plans that are more important, east of Jerusalem (Plan E-1). These developments will effectively split the West Bank into two cantons, with Ma'ale Adumim incorporated into "Greater Jerusalem," in accord with the plans announced and implemented by the Rabin–Peres administrations after the Oslo agreements and then pursued by their Likud successor. While attention was focused on the Har Homa (Jabal Abu Ghneim) constructions, falsely attributed to Likud initiatives, Defense Minister Yitzhak Mordechai announced that Labor's E-1 program would be implemented, with new housing construction and road building. Knesset member Michael Kleiner, the head of the expansionist Land of Israel Front (Hazit Eretz Yisrael), greeted the announcement with appreciation, observing that this plan, which "was the initiative of the former Housing Minister Benjamin Ben-Eliezer with the authorization of Yitzhak Rabin," is "the most important" of the front's demands, more so than Har Homa.

Ben-Eliezer also explained that "Fuad does everything quietly, with the complete protection of the Prime Minister," using such terms as "natural growth" instead of "new settlements" when he implements Labor's policies of expanding Greater Jerusalem to include Ma'ale Adumim, Givat Ze'ev, and Beitar as the "first circle" of settlements surrounding Jerusalem, to which another "chain of settlements" is to be added in a second circle. According to Labor dove Yossi Beilin, the Rabin government "increased settlements by 50 percent" in "Judea and Samaria" (the West Bank) after Oslo, but "we did it quietly and with wisdom," whereas you, Netanyahu, "proclaim your intentions every morning, frighten the Palestinians and transform the topic of Jerusalem as the unified capital of Israel—a matter which all Israelis agree upon—into a subject of world-wide debate."[90] The statement is only partially accurate, since the "quiet wisdom" extends well beyond Jerusalem.

The differences of style can presumably be traced to the constituencies of the two political groupings. Labor, the party of educated professionals and Westernized elites, is more attuned to Western norms and understands that the sponsors should be offered a way "not to see" what they are doing. Likud's brazen and crude methods of achieving basically the same results are an embarrassment to Western humanists and sometimes lead to conflict and annoyance.

The Labor/Likud program of establishing a Bantustan-style settlement cannot be accused of violating the peace process. Oslo I says nothing relevant, apart from the stipulations about the "permanent status" already mentioned, which establish the basic principles of the Peres–Shamir–Baker plan and long-term U.S.–Israeli rejectionism. Oslo II, in contrast, is quite explicit about many important topics. I have reviewed the details elsewhere and will not repeat them here.[91] In brief, Oslo II grants Israel permanent control over most of the crucial water resources and imposes purposefully humiliating conditions on Palestinians, even with regard to such matters as transit of Palestinian police on "Palestinian roads." These abominations are designed to make life for Palestinians as miserable as possible while Israelis and tourists speed to their destinations on the modern bypass highways that free them from the need to see the Arab inhabitants, who are to survive somehow, isolated from their families, workplaces, and institutions. With regard to land, the agreement allows Israel to do virtually whatever it likes. Oslo II even states that Palestinians "shall respect the legal rights of Israelis (including corporations owned by Israelis) related to lands located in areas under the territorial jurisdiction of the [Palestinian] Council"—that is, the whole of the

occupied territories—specifically, their rights related to government and absentee land, an indefinite category that expands at
Israel's whim, reaching perhaps 70 percent of the territories, according to the Israeli press.[92] Oslo II thus abrogates the stand of
the entire world, including technically the United States, that
legal rights cannot be attained by conquest, and rescinds even
the post-1971 U.S. interpretation of UN 242.

Palestinians and others are only deluding themselves and others when they say that Israel committed itself to "withdraw from
occupied Palestinian territories, including Jerusalem" in accord
with UN 242 or anything remotely like it; or that they agreed to
grant Palestinians "control over water, telecommunications and
transport, among other things"; or that George Bush's Madrid
initiative "involved the implementation of U.N. Security Council resolutions on Palestine" (Palestinian foreign minister Farouk
Kaddoumi). Or that "the terms of reference" for the peace
process are given by UN 242, the Oslo accords, and the Madrid
conference, "which enshrine the land-for-peace principle"
(Egyptian diplomat Abdalaleem El-Abayad).[93] Nothing of the
sort is true, as the documents make clear and the consistent practice even more so, unless we interpret such phrases as "land for
peace" with the cynicism that would have welcomed the South
African homelands policy.

Israeli doves may prefer what some observers have called a
state of "collective self-denial," avoiding the documents and the
historical context that gives them meaning, perhaps even "not
seeing" what is happening a few miles from where they live—
not a phenomenon unique to Israel, needless to say. The funders
and supporters elsewhere may also find the stance convenient.
But the realities remain.

The realities go beyond the occupied territories, including also
Israel within the Green Line, where South African analogies are
again unfortunately not inappropriate, if by no means exact. And
crucially, they extend to the Palestinian diaspora, particularly after President Bill Clinton broke with official U.S. policy since
1948 and (alone with Israel) rejected UN Resolution 194, which

spells out the concrete meaning of Article 13 of the UN Universal Declaration of Human Rights, adopted the preceding day. Since a negative U.S. vote is effectively a veto, the right of Palestinians to return or receive compensation is thereby formally abrogated. The endorsement was always hypocritical. There was no intention of implementing Resolution 194, even the right to compensation, which Israeli foreign minister Moshe Sharett estimated at $1 billion in 1950 (50 percent more than German reparations to Israel), amounting to $6 billion in current dollar value, even without interest.[94]

In 1948, Israeli government Arabists predicted that the refugees would either assimilate elsewhere or "would be crushed" and "die," while "most of them would turn into human dust and the waste of society, and join the most impoverished classes in the Arab countries."[95] If current plans succeed, these predictions may be fulfilled. Apart from privileged sectors that accommodate to the neocolonial settlement, those remaining in the territories can look forward to the bright future of Haitians toiling in U.S. assembly plants for a few cents an hour or the semislave laborers in China's foreign-controlled export industries. And Palestinians within Israel may expect to live as American Jews and blacks would if the United States were to become "the sovereign State of Christian Whites" throughout the world (to paraphrase Israeli law), not the state of its citizens.

Such consequences need not come to pass, but they might, and if they do, privileged sectors of American, Israeli, and Palestinian society will have a lot to answer for, in my opinion.

7

Prospects for Peace
in the Middle East

Before discussing the prospects for peace in the Middle East, let me make a few preliminary comments. The first is that peace is preferable to war. But it's not an absolute value, and so we always ask, "What kind of peace?" If Hitler had conquered the world, there would be peace but not the kind we would like to see.

My second comment is that there are many dimensions to the topic of the prospects for peace in the Middle East. There are several areas of ongoing serious violence—three in particular that I will say something about. One is Iraq, where the problem includes both sanctions and bombing. A second is Turkey and the Kurds, which is one of the most severe human rights atrocities of the 1990s, and a continuing problem. And the third is Israel and Palestine. There are many other issues, such as the question of the place of Iran within the region, that one can examine. Everywhere you look, virtually without exception, you see severe repression, human rights abuses, torture, and other horrors. So the question of peace in the Middle East has many dimensions.

My third and last comment is that the United States plays a significant and often decisive role in these cases. —Furthermore, however important a relative factor U.S. involvement might be, it should be central to our own concerns for perfectly obvious reasons—it is the one factor that we can directly influence. The others we may deplore, but we can't do much about them. That's a truism, or ought to be a truism, but it is important to emphasize it, because it is almost universally rejected. The prevailing doctrine is that we should focus on the crimes of others and lament them, and we should ignore or deny our own. Or more accurately, we should structure the way we view things so as to dismiss the possibility of looking into the mirror; we should shape discourse so the question of our own responsibilities can't even arise, or more accurately, can arise only in one connection, namely, the connection of how we should react to the crimes of others. So, for example, by now there's a huge literature, both popular and scholarly, about the so-called dilemmas of humanitarian intervention when others are guilty of crimes, as they often are. But you'll find scarcely a word on another question, a much more important topic—the dilemmas of withdrawal of participation in major atrocities. In fact, there are no dilemmas. That is a window that has to be kept tightly shuttered, or else some rather unpleasant visions will appear before us that we're not supposed to see.

Exactly how the evasion of the central themes is accomplished is an interesting and important topic about which there's a lot to say, but reluctantly I'm going to put it aside and keep to the special cases that concern us here. I should add that this shameful stance is by no means a novelty—in fact it is kind of a cultural universal. I think you would have to search very hard for a case in history, or elsewhere in the present, in which the same theme is not dominant. It's not an attractive feature of Homo sapiens, but a very real one.

Iraq

Let's begin with Iraq. The only serious question about the UN sanctions is whether they are simply terrible crimes or whether they are literally genocidal, as charged by those who have the most intimate acquaintance with the situation, in particular the coordinator of the UN humanitarian program in Iraq, Denis Halliday, a highly respected UN official who resigned under protest because he was being compelled to carry out what he called "genocide," as did his successor Hans von Sponeck.[1] It is agreed on all sides that the effect of the sanctions has been to strengthen Saddam Hussein and to devastate the population—and yet we must continue, even with that recognition.

There are justifications offered, and they merit careful attention. They tell us a good deal about ourselves, I think. The simplest line of argument to justify the sanctions was presented by Madeleine Albright when she was the U.S. ambassador to the UN. She was asked on national television by Leslie Stahl about how she felt about the fact that sanctions had killed half a million Iraqi children. She didn't deny the factual allegation. She agreed that it was, as she put it, "a very hard choice" but said, "we think the price is worth it."[2] That was the end of the discussion. That is the important fact, and it's very enlightening to see the reaction. The comment is hers; the reaction is ours. Looking at the reaction, we learn about ourselves.

A second justification that is given commonly is that Iraqi suffering is really Saddam Hussein's fault. The logic is intriguing. Let's suppose the claim is true: it is Saddam Hussein's fault. The conclusion that is drawn is that therefore we have to assist him in devastating the civilian population and strengthening his own rule. Notice that this conclusion follows logically if you say it is his fault but that we have to go on helping him.

The third argument that is given, which at least has the merit of truth, is that Saddam Hussein is a monster. In fact, if you listen to Tony Blair, Clinton, Albright, or almost anyone who comments on this, they repeatedly justify the sanctions by saying that this man is such a monster that we just can't let him survive. He has even committed the ultimate atrocity—namely, using weapons of mass destruction against his own people in his horrendous gassing of the Kurds. All of this is true, but there are three missing words. True, he committed the ultimate atrocity—using poison gas and chemical warfare against his own population—*with our support*. Our support in fact continued, as he remained a favored friend, trading partner, and ally—quite independently of these atrocities, which obviously didn't matter to us, as evidenced by our reaction. Our support continued and in fact increased. An interesting experiment that you might try is to see if you can find a place anywhere within mainstream discussion where the three missing words are added. I will leave it as an experiment for the reader. And it is an illuminating one. I can tell you the answer right away—you're not going to find it. And that tells us something about ourselves too, and also about the argument.

The same, incidentally, is true of his weapons of mass destruction. It is commonly claimed that we can't allow Hussein to survive because of the danger of the weapons of mass destruction that he might be developing. This is all correct, but it was also correct when we were providing him consciously with the means to develop those weapons of mass destruction, at a time when he was a far greater threat than he is today. So that raises some questions about that argument.

The fourth argument is that Saddam Hussein is a threat to the countries of the region. There is no doubt that he is a serious threat to anyone within his reach, exactly as he was when he was committing his worst crimes with U.S. support and participation. But the fact is that his reach now is far less than it was before, and the critical attitude of the countries in the region to the sanctions and bombing reveals rather clearly what they think of this argument.

That, as far as I know, exhausts the arguments we have been given. But those arguments entail that we must continue to torture the population and strengthen Saddam Hussein by imposing very harsh sanctions. All of that, as far as I can see, leaves an honest citizen with two tasks. One is to do something about it— remember that it is us, so we can. The second is intellectual—to try to understand what the actual motives are, since they can't possibly be the ones that are put forth.

I do not want to downplay the threat. There are very serious reasons to be concerned about the threat of Iraq and Saddam Hussein. There were even greater reasons during the period when we were helping build up the threat, but that doesn't change the fact that there are reasons today. More generally, there are reasons to be concerned about the threat of extreme violence and devastation in the region. And that is not just my opinion; it is underscored, for example, by Gen. Lee Butler, who was the head of the Strategic Command, the highest military agency that is concerned with nuclear strategy and the use of nuclear weapons, under Clinton. General Butler said, "It is dangerous in the extreme that in the cauldron of animosities that we call the Middle East, one nation [Israel] has armed itself, ostensibly, with stockpiles of nuclear weapons, perhaps numbering in the hundreds, and that inspires other nations to do so."[3]

Or it inspires them to develop other weapons of mass destruction as a deterrent, which has an obvious threat of a very ominous outcome. There is little doubt that General Butler is correct in that. Actually, the threat becomes even more ominous when we consider that the United States, the superpower patron of Israel, demands that other nations regard the United States as "irrational and vindictive" and ready to resort to extreme violence if provoked, including the first use of nuclear weapons against nonnuclear states. I am citing high-level planning documents of the Clinton administration, plans that were then implemented by presidential directives.[4] All this is on the public record, if anybody wants to learn something about ourselves and why much of the world is terrified of us.

In fact it is understood in the world that others are naturally impelled to seek weapons of mass destruction of their own as a deterrent. These are prospects that are recognized by U.S. intelligence and strategic analysts, who also recognize that the threat to human survival is enhanced by programs that are now under way. For example, almost every country in the world regards the U.S. National Missile Defense program as a first-strike weapon— quite realistically so. Potential adversaries will presumably respond by developing a deterrent of one sort or another. That is largely taken for granted by U.S. intelligence and strategic analysts and raises questions about why we insist on pursuing a policy that raises the threat of destroying ourselves as well as others. That is another question one might ask. The Middle East poses perhaps the primary danger in this regard—not the only one, but it certainly ranks high.

It is worth mentioning that in 1990 and 1991, on the eve of the Gulf War, these questions arose. They were raised by Iraq. Several days before the Gulf War began, Iraq offered once again (they had apparently made several such offers) to withdraw from Kuwait, but in the context of a settlement of regional strategic issues, including the banning of weapons of mass destruction. That position was recognized as "serious" and "negotiable" by State Department Middle East experts. Independently of this, that happened to be the position of about two-thirds of the American public according to the final polls that were taken a couple of days before the war.

We do not know whether these Iraqi proposals were indeed serious and negotiable, as State Department officials concluded. The reason we don't know is that they were rejected out of hand by the United States. They were suppressed to nearly 100 percent efficiency by the media. There were a few leaks here and there, but they were effectively removed from history. So we do not know. However, the issues remain very much alive, even though they have been removed from the agenda of policy and from public discussion.

Turkey and the Kurds

Let me turn to the second issue, Turkey and the Kurds. The Kurds have been miserably oppressed throughout the whole history of the modern Turkish state, but in 1984, the Turkish government launched a major war in the southeast against the Kurdish population.

If we look at U.S. military aid to Turkey—which is usually a pretty good index of policy—aid shot up significantly in 1984, at the time that the counterinsurgency war began. This increase had nothing to do with the Cold War, transparently. It was because of the counterinsurgency war. Turkey was of course a strategic ally, so it always had a fairly high level of military aid. The aid remained high, peaking through the 1990s as the atrocities increased. The peak year was 1997. In fact, in the single year 1997, U.S. military aid to Turkey was greater than in the entire period from 1950 to 1983, during which there were allegedly Cold War motivations. The end result was pretty awesome: tens of thousands of people killed, two to three million refugees, and massive ethnic cleansing, with some thirty-five hundred villages destroyed.

The United States was providing about 80 percent of Turkey's arms. Since you and I are not stopping it—and we are the only ones who can—the Clinton administration was free to send jet planes, tanks, napalm, and so on, which were used to carry out some of the worst atrocities of the 1990s. And these atrocities continue. Turkey regularly carries out operations both in southeastern Turkey and across the border in northern Iraq, where attacks are taking place in the so-called no-fly zones where the Kurds are being protected by the United States from the temporarily wrong oppressor.

The operations in northern Iraq are similar in character to Israel's operations in Lebanon during the twenty-two years when it occupied southern Lebanon in violation of the United Nations but with the authorization of the United States, so therefore legitimately. During that period Israel killed roughly on the order of forty-five thousand, judging by Lebanese sources. Nobody really knows because nobody counts victims of the United States and its friends.

How is all this dealt with in the United States? Very simply: with silence. You can check and see—I urge you to do so. Occasionally, the treatment of the Kurds is brought up by disagreeable people. And when it is brought up and can't be ignored, there is a consistent reaction: self-declared advocates of human rights deplore what they call "our failure to protect the Kurds." Actually we are failing to protect the Kurds roughly in the way that the Russians are "failing to protect the people of Chechnya."

Or it is claimed that the U.S. government is unaware of what is happening. So when Clinton was sending a huge flow of arms to Turkey (in this period, Turkey became the leading recipient of U.S. arms), he and his advisers did not realize that the arms were going to be used. It just never occurred to them that the weapons were really going to be used for the war that was then taking place. Those who bring the matter up and suggest otherwise are lacking in "nuance," sophisticated commentators observe.

Or sometimes it is argued that the United States is unable to find out what is going on. Actually, it is kind of a remote area. Who knows what's happening in southeastern Turkey? This is an area that happens to be littered with U.S. air bases, where the United States has nuclear-armed planes, and that is under extremely tight surveillance. But how could we know what is going on there? And of course nobody can read the human rights reports, which constantly describe in detail what is happening. But that is the reaction.

I mentioned that Turkey became the leading U.S. arms recipient in the world during this period. That is not quite accurate. The leading recipients, Israel and Egypt, are in a separate category. They are always the leading recipients. But aside from them, Turkey reached first place during the period of the counterinsurgency war. For a while Turkey was displaced by El Salvador, which was then in the process of slaughtering its own population and moved into the first place. But as they succeeded in that, Turkey took over and became first.

That continued until 1999. In 1999, Turkey was replaced by Colombia. Colombia has the worst human rights record in the hemisphere. And for the last ten years, when it has had the worst human rights record, it has received the bulk of the U.S. military aid and training. That's a correlation that works pretty closely, incidentally. Why did Colombia replace Turkey in 1999? Well, we are not supposed to notice that by 1999 Turkey had succeeded in repressing internal resistance and Colombia had not yet succeeded. Just by accident that happened to be the year in which the huge flow of arms to Colombia increased.

All of this is particularly remarkable because we have been inundated recently by a flood of self-adulation—unprecedented in history to my knowledge—about how we are so magnificent that for the first time in history, we are willing to pursue "principles and values" in defense of human rights. Especially in "crucial cases," to borrow President Clinton's words, we cannot tolerate violations of human rights so near the borders of NATO, and therefore we have to rise to new heights of magnificence to combat them. Again there are a couple of missing words. Apparently we cannot tolerate human rights violations near the borders of NATO countries, but we not only can tolerate them but in fact encourage and participate in them *within* NATO's borders. Try to find those missing words—you won't, and it will tell you something again.

Israel–Palestine

Let me turn to the third case—Israel–Palestine. Let's take a look at the current fighting, at what is called the al-Aqsa Intifada, and look closely at the U.S. reactions. This is the part that concerns me most and is the part that should concern us most.

The official U.S. position, which was reiterated in March 2001 by U.S. ambassador Martin Indyk is that "[w]e do not believe in rewarding violence."[5] That was a stern admonition to the Palestinians, and there are many others like it. It is easy to assess the validity of that claim. So let's assess it just in the obvious way.

The al-Aqsa Intifada, the violence that Indyk deplores, began on September 29, 2000, the day after Ariel Sharon went to the Haram al-Sharif, the Temple Mount, with about one thousand soldiers. That event passed more or less without incident, surprisingly. But the next day, which was Friday, there was a huge army presence as people left the mosque after prayers; there was some stone throwing and immediate shooting by the Israeli army and border patrol, which left half a dozen Palestinians killed and more than two hundred wounded.[6] On October 1, Israeli military helicopters, or, to be precise, U.S. military helicopters with Israeli pilots, sharply escalated the violence, killing two Palestinians in Gaza. On October 2, military helicopters killed ten people in Gaza and wounded thirty-five. On October 3, helicopters attacked apartment complexes and other civilian targets. And so it continued. By early November, the helicopters were being used for targeted political assassinations.

How did the United States react? In mid-September, before the fighting started, the United States sent a new shipment of advanced attack helicopters to Israel. Also in mid-September, the U.S. Marines carried out joint exercises with elite units of the Israeli army, the Israeli Defense Forces (IDF)—training exercises for the reconquest of the occupied territories. The role of the Marines was to provide new, advanced equipment that Israel didn't have and training in its use.

On October 3, the day that the press was reporting that military helicopters were attacking apartment complexes and killing dozens of people, the Israeli press announced, and then the international press repeated, that the United States and Israel had reached a deal—the biggest deal in a decade—for dispatch of U.S. military helicopters to Israel.[7] The next day leading military journals reported that this included new advanced attack helicopters and parts for the older helicopters, which would increase the capacity to attack civilian targets. Incidentally, the Israeli defense ministry announced that they cannot produce helicopters. They do not have the capacity, so they have to get them from the United States. On October 19, Amnesty International issued a report calling on the United States not to send military helicopters to Israel under these circumstances—one of a series of Amnesty International reports.[8] On February 19, 2001, the Pentagon announced that Israel and the United States had just made a half-billion-dollar deal for advanced Apache attack helicopters.[9] I've just sampled of course.

Let's look at how this is dealt with by the media. It turns out all of this did not pass unnoticed in the free press. There was one mention in a letter to the editor in a newspaper in Raleigh, North Carolina.[10] That is the total coverage of what I have just described.

Now it is not that the facts are unknown. There is no news office in the country that isn't perfectly well aware of these facts.

Anyone who can read Amnesty International reports knows about this. It has been brought specifically to the attention of editors of at least one major U.S. daily, reputed to be the most liberal one, the *Boston Globe*. And there is surely not the slightest doubt in any editorial or news office that it is highly newsworthy. But those who control information evidently do not want to know or to let their readers know. And they have good reasons not to. To provide the population with information about what is being done in their name would open windows that are better left shuttered if you want to carry out effective domestic indoctrination. It simply would not do to publish these reports alongside the occasional mention of U.S. helicopters attacking civilian targets or carrying out targeted political assassinations or reports of stern U.S. admonitions to "all sides" to "refrain from violence."

The continuing provision of attack helicopters by the United States to Israel, with the knowledge that these weapons are being used against the civilian Palestinian population, and the silence of the mainstream U.S. media is just one illustration of many of how we live up to the principle that we do not believe in rewarding violence. Again, it leaves honest citizens with two tasks: the important one, do something about it; and the second one, try to find out why the policies are being pursued.

On that matter, the fundamental reasons are not really controversial, I think. It has long been understood that the gulf region has the major energy resources in the world. It is an incomparable strategic resource and a source of immense wealth. Whatever power controls the region has not only access to enormous wealth but also a very powerful global influence because control of energy resources is an extremely powerful lever in world affairs. Furthermore, the crucial importance of Middle East energy resources is expected to continue and in fact to increase, maybe sharply, in coming years.

The importance of control over oil was understood by about the time of the First World War. At that time, Britain was the major world power and controlled much of the Middle East. Britain, however, did not have the military strength to control the region by direct military occupation after the First World War. So it turned to other means. One was the use of air power and also the use of poison gas, which was considered the ultimate atrocity at that time. The most enthusiastic supporter was Winston Churchill, who called for the use of poison gas against Kurds and Afghans.[11]

Alongside the military component of the control there were also political arrangements, which in some fashion persist. The British Colonial Office during the First World War proposed and then implemented a plan to construct what it called an "Arab facade": weak, pliable states that would administer the local populations, under ultimate British control in case things got out of hand. France at that time was also involved—it was a reasonably major power—and the United States, though not a leading power in world affairs, was powerful enough to demand a piece of the action there. The three countries entered into the Red Line agreement in 1928, which parceled out Middle East oil reserves among them. Notably absent from this process were the people of the region. They were controlled by the facade, with the muscle in the background. That was the basic arrangement.

By the time of the Second World War, the United States had become the overwhelmingly dominant world power and was plainly going to take over Middle East energy resources. France was removed unceremoniously. And Britain reluctantly came to accept its role as a "junior partner," in the rueful words of a Foreign Office official, its role gradually decreasing over time.

The United States took over the British framework, but the basic principle remained. That is, the West (which means primarily the United States) must control events in the Middle East. Furthermore, the wealth of the region must flow primarily to the West, to the United States and Britain; their energy corporations; investors, the U.S. Treasury, which has been heavily dependent on recycled petrodollars; exporters; construction firms, and so on. That is the essential point. The profits have to flow to the West, and the power has to remain in the West, primarily Washington, insofar as possible.

This principle raises all sorts of problems. One problem is that the people of the region have never been able to comprehend the logic of these arrangements or their essential justice. They cannot seem to get it through their heads that the wealth of the region should flow to the West, not to poor and suffering people right there. And it continually takes force to make them understand these simple and obvious principles—a constant problem with backward and uneducated people.

A conservative nationalist government led by Mohammad Mossadegh tried to extricate Iran from this framework in 1953. That attempt was quickly reversed with a military coup sponsored by the United States and Britain that restored the shah. In the course of that coup, the United States largely edged Britain out of control over Iran.

Soon after the coup in Iran, Egypt's Gamal Abdel Nasser became an influential figure and was considered a major threat. He didn't have oil, but he was a symbol of independent nationalism, and that's the threat. He was considered a "virus" that might "infect others." That is conventional terminology and a fundamental feature of international planning—not just in Egypt.

At that point the United States was developing a doctrine that modified and extended the British system of an Arab facade with British force behind it. Namely, it was establishing a cordon of peripheral states that would serve as "local cops on the beat" (in the words of the Nixon administration). Police headquarters are in Washington, but you have local cops on the beat. The two main cops at that time were Turkey, a big military force, and Iran under the shah.

By 1958, the CIA advised that "a logical corollary" of opposition to Arab nationalism "would be to support Israel as the only reliable pro-Western power left in the Middle East."[12] According to this reasoning, Israel could become a major base for U.S. power in the region. That proposal was implemented after 1967. In 1967, Israel performed a major service to the United States— namely, it destroyed Nasser, destroyed the virus of independent nationalism. It also smashed up the Arab armies and left U.S.

power in the ascendant. At this point essentially a tripartite alliance was established among Israel, Iran, and Saudi Arabia.
Saudi Arabia technically was at war with Iran and Israel, but that
made no difference. Saudi Arabia had the oil; Iran under the
shah and Israel were the military force. Pakistan and Turkey were
part of the system too at that time.

That alliance was very clearly recognized both by U.S. intelligence specialists, who wrote about it, and by the leading figures
in planning. So, for example, Henry Jackson, who was the Senate's major specialist on the Middle East and oil, pointed out that
Israel, Iran, and Saudi Arabia "inhibit and contain those irresponsible and radical elements in certain Arab states, who, were
they free to do so, would pose a grave threat indeed to our principal sources of petroleum in the Middle East" (meaning, as he
knew, primarily profit flow and a lever of world control).[13] Saudi
Arabia did its part just by funding and by holding the greatest petroleum reserves by a good measure. Iran and Israel, with the help
of Turkey and Pakistan, provided regional force. They were only
the "local cops on the beat." If something really goes wrong, you
call in the big guys—the United States and Britain.

That's the picture. In 1979, a problem occurred—one of the
pillars collapsed: Iran fell under the grip of independent nationalism. The Carter administration immediately tried to sponsor a
military coup to restore the shah. Carter sent a NATO general,
but that didn't work. He couldn't gain the support of U.S. allies
in the Iranian military.

Immediately afterward, Israel and Saudi Arabia, the remaining
pillars, joined the United States in an effort to bring about a coup
that would restore the old arrangement by the usual means: sending arms. The facts and the purpose were exposed at once, but
quickly suppressed. Bits and pieces reached the public later, when
it became impossible to suppress. It was then called an "arms for
hostage" deal. That has a nice humanitarian sound, even if it was
a "mistake": the Reaganites were seeking a way to release U.S.
hostages taken in Lebanon. What was actually happening was
that the United States was sending arms to Iran—meaning to
specific military groupings in Iran—via Israel, which had close

connections with the Iranian military, funded by Saudi Arabia. It couldn't have been an arms for hostage deal for a rather simple reason: there weren't any hostages. The first hostages in Lebanon were taken later (and they happened to be Iranian). In fact it was just normal operating procedure.

At the same time, the United States was supporting its friend Saddam Hussein in an Iraqi invasion of Iran, again for the same purpose—to try to reverse the disaster of an independent oil-producing state. Saddam's Iraq was also too independent for comfort, but Iran had been one of the firmest pillars of U.S. policy in the region. Independently of that, Iran had committed the grave and unpardonable crime of reversing the U.S.-backed military coup that had blocked the attempt to move toward independence twenty-five years before. That kind of disobedience cannot be tolerated, or U.S. "credibility" will be threatened.

The United States began sending military vessels to patrol the Persian Gulf to ensure that Iran would not be able to block Iraqi oil shipping. That turned out to be a very serious matter. The depth of U.S. commitment to Saddam Hussein at the time is illustrated by the fact that Iraq is the only country apart from Israel that has been granted the right to attack an American ship with complete impunity, as Israel did in 1967 and as Iraq did in 1987, killing thirty-seven sailors.[14]

U.S. involvement went beyond that. The next year, in 1988, a U.S. destroyer, the USS *Vincennes*, shot down an Iranian commercial airliner, Iran Air 655, killing 290 people, in Iranian airspace.[15] In fact the destroyer was in Iranian territorial waters; there is no serious dispute about the basic facts. Iran took the attack extremely seriously. Its leaders concluded that the United States was willing to go to extreme lengths to ensure that Saddam Hussein won the war, and at that point they capitulated. It was not a minor event for them. It is a minor event here because that is just our atrocity, and by definition the powerful have no moral responsibilities and cannot commit crimes.

It is reasonable to assume that Pan Am 103 was blown up in retaliation. The immediate assumption of Western intelligence was that the attack was Iranian retaliation for the shooting down of Iran Air 655. Judging by what has happened since, I think that remains a plausible speculation. The evidence that Libya was responsible remains very shaky. The strange judicial proceedings in The Hague, after the United States and Britain finally agreed to allow the case to proceed (Libya had offered to permit it in a neutral venue years earlier), have only increased doubts among those who have followed the matter closely. But that is not going to be allowed to be discussed. It has, for example, apparently been deemed necessary to suppress entirely the report on the Lockerbie trial in the Netherlands by the international observer nominated by UN Secretary-General Kofi Annan, pursuant to Security Council Resolution 1192 (1998). His report was a sharp condemnation of the proceedings. One may speculate that if he had confirmed the official U.S.–UK position, the report might have received some mention, probably headlines.

Despite all of this, Iraq remained a kind of anomaly. In 1958, Iraq had extricated itself from the U.S.-dominated system in the Middle East. The country was anomalous in another respect too. However horrendous the regime may be, the fact of the matter was that it was using its resources domestically, leading to substantial social and economic development. That is not the way the system is supposed to work; the wealth is supposed to flow to the West. The effect of the war, and particularly the sanctions, however, has been to reverse these departures from good form. By the time Iraq is permitted, as it almost surely will be, to reenter the international system under U.S. control, there will no longer be any serious danger of it using its resources internally. It will be lucky to survive and partially recover. One might argue about whether that is part of the purpose of the sanctions, but it is likely to be the consequence.

All of this raises a question: what about our fabled commitment to human rights? How are human rights assigned to various actors in the Middle East? The answer is simplicity itself: rights are assigned in accord with the contribution to maintaining the system. The United States has rights by definition. Britain has rights as long as it is a loyal attack dog. Members of the Arab facade have rights as long as they manage to control their own populations and ensure that the wealth flows to the West.

What about the Palestinians? They do not have any wealth. They do not have any power. It therefore follows, by the most elementary principles of statecraft, that they do not have any rights. That is like adding two and two and getting four. In fact, they have negative rights. The reason is that their dispossession and their suffering elicit protest and opposition in the rest of the region.

From these considerations, it is pretty straightforward to predict U.S. policy for the last roughly thirty years. Its basic element has been and remains an extreme form of rejectionism, using the term in a nonracist way, to refer to those who reject the national rights of one or the other of the competing forces in the former Palestine. So those who reject the national rights of Palestinians are rejectionists. And the United States has led the rejectionist camp for the last thirty years. The so-called peace process is an extension of this basic framework.

I will end with the comment by one of the leading Israeli doves, Shlomo Ben-Ami, who was the chief negotiator under Ehud Barak and is indeed a Labor dove—pretty much at the extreme. In an academic book written in 1998 in Hebrew, just before he entered the government, Barak pointed out, perfectly accurately, that the goal of the Oslo negotiations is to establish a situation of "permanent neocolonial dependency" for the occupied territories.[16] In Israel, it is commonly described as a Bantustan solution; it is similar in essentials to South African policy.

It is worth noting that among the leading supporters of this solution have been Israeli industrialists. About ten years ago, before the Oslo agreement, they were calling for a Palestinian state of roughly this kind—and for quite good reasons. For them, a permanent neocolonial dependency makes a lot of sense, something like the U.S. relationship to Mexico or El Salvador, with maquiladoras, assembly plants, along the border on the Palestinian side of the border. This offers industrialists very cheap labor and terrible conditions, with no need to worry about environmental concerns or other annoying constraints on profit making.

And the workers do not have to be brought into Israel, which is always dangerous. Not only does this arrangement improve profits, but it is also a useful weapon against the Israeli working class. It offers ways to undermine their wages and benefits. And furthermore it offers means to break strikes, a device commonly used by U.S. manufacturers, who develop excess capacity abroad that can be used to break strikes here. That is a good reason to be in favor of a Palestinian state in a condition of "permanent neocolonial dependency." The story is familiar.

Israel itself is—not surprisingly—becoming very much like the United States. It now has tremendous inequality, very high levels of poverty, stagnating or declining wages, and deteriorating working conditions. As in the United States, the economy is based crucially on the dynamic state sector, sometimes concealed under the rubric of military industry. It is not really surprising that the United States should favor arrangements in its outpost that look pretty much like the United States itself.

Al-Aqsa Intifada

After three weeks of virtual war in the Israeli occupied territories, Prime Minister Ehud Barak announced a new plan to
determine the final status of the region in October 2000.[1] During
these weeks, more than one hundred Palestinians were killed, including twenty-seven children, often by "excessive use of lethal
force in circumstances in which neither the lives of the security
forces nor others were in imminent danger, resulting in unlawful
killings," Amnesty International concluded in a detailed report
that was scarcely mentioned in the United States.[2] The ratio of
Palestinian to Israeli dead was then about 15–1, reflecting the resources of force available.[3]

Barak's plan was not given in detail, but the outlines are familiar: they conformed to the "final status map" presented by
the United States–Israel as the basis for the Camp David negotiations that collapsed in July. This plan, extending U.S.–Israeli
rejectionist proposals of earlier years, called for cantonization of
the territories that Israel had conquered in 1967, with mechanisms to ensure that usable land and resources (primarily water)
remain largely in Israeli hands while the population is administered by a corrupt and brutal Palestinian Authority (PA), playing the role traditionally assigned to indigenous collaborators
under the several varieties of imperial rule: the black leadership
of South Africa's Bantustans, to mention only the most obvious
analogue. In the West Bank, a northern canton is to include
Nablus and other Palestinian cities, a central canton is based in

Ramallah, and a southern canton in Bethlehem; Jericho is to remain isolated. Palestinians would be effectively cut off from Jerusalem, the center of Palestinian life. Similar arrangements are likely in Gaza, with Israel keeping the southern coastal region and a small settlement at Netzarim (the site of many recent atrocities), which is hardly more than an excuse for a large military presence and roads splitting the Gaza Strip below Gaza City. These proposals formalize the vast settlement and construction programs that Israel has been conducting, thanks to munificent U.S. aid, with increasing energy since the United States was able to implement its version of the peace process after the Gulf War.

The goal of the negotiations was to secure official PA adherence to this project. Two months after the peace talks collapsed, the current phase of violence began. Tensions, always high, were raised when the Barak government authorized a visit by Ariel Sharon with one thousand police to the Muslim religious sites (al-Aqsa) on Thursday, September 28. Sharon is the very symbol of Israeli state terror and aggression, with a rich record of atrocities going back to 1953. Sharon's announced purpose was to demonstrate "Jewish sovereignty" over the al-Aqsa compound, but as the veteran correspondent Graham Usher points out, the "al-Aqsa intifada," as Palestinians call it, was not initiated by Sharon's visit, but, rather, by the massive and intimidating police and military presence that Barak introduced the following day, the day of prayers. Predictably, that led to clashes as thousands of people streamed out of the mosque, leaving seven Palestinians dead and more than two hundred wounded. Whatever Barak's purpose, there could hardly have been a more efficient way to set the stage for the shocking atrocities of the following weeks.

The same can be said about the failed negotiations, which focused on Jerusalem, a condition that U.S. commentary strictly observed. Possibly Israeli sociologist Baruch Kimmerling was exaggerating when he wrote in Israel's most prestigious daily,

Ha'aretz, that a solution to this problem "could have been reached in five minutes," but he is right to say that "by any diplomatic logic [it] should have been the easiest issue to solve."[4] It is understandable that President Bill Clinton and Barak should want to suppress what the Israelis and Americans are doing in the occupied territories, which is far more important than the negotiations over Jerusalem. Why did Yasser Arafat agree to do so as well? Perhaps because he recognizes that the leadership of the Arab states regard the Palestinians as a nuisance and have little problem with the Bantustan-style settlement but cannot overlook administration of the religious sites, fearing the reaction of their own populations. Nothing could be better calculated to set off a confrontation with religious overtones, the most ominous kind, as centuries of experience reveal.

The primary innovation of Barak's new plan is that the U.S.–Israeli demands are to be imposed by direct force instead of coercive diplomacy, and in a harsher form, to punish the victims who refused to concede politely. The outlines are in basic accord with policies established informally in 1968 (the Allon Plan) and variants that have been proposed since by both Labor and Likud (the Sharon Plan, the Labor government plans, and others). It is important to recall that the policies have not only been proposed but also implemented with the support of the United States. That support has been decisive since 1971, when Washington abandoned the basic diplomatic framework that it had initiated (UN Security Council Resolution 242), then pursued its unilateral rejection of Palestinian rights in the years that followed, culminating in the "Oslo process." Since all of this has been effectively vetoed from history in the United States, it takes a little work to discover the essential facts. They are not controversial, only evaded.

As noted, Barak's plan is a particularly harsh version of familiar U.S.–Israeli rejectionism. It calls for terminating electricity, water, telecommunications, and other services that are doled out in meager rations to the Palestinian population, who are now under virtual siege. It should be recalled that independent development was ruthlessly barred by the military regime from 1967, leaving the people in destitution and dependency, a process that worsened considerably during the U.S.-run Oslo process. One reason is the "closures" regularly instituted, most brutally by the more dovish Labor-based governments. As discussed by another outstanding journalist, Amira Hass, this policy was initiated by the Rabin government "years before Hamas had planned suicide attacks, [and] has been perfected over the years, especially since the establishment of the Palestinian National Authority."[5] An efficient mechanism of strangulation and control, closure has been accompanied by the importation of an essential commodity to replace the cheap and exploited Palestinian labor on which much of the economy relies: hundreds of thousands of illegal immigrants from around the world, many of them victims of the neoliberal reforms of the recent years of "globalization." Surviving in misery and without rights, they are regularly described as a virtual slave labor force in the Israeli press.

A major barrier to the program is the opposition of the Israeli business community, which relies on a captive Palestinian market for some $2.5 billion in annual exports and has "forged links with Palestinian security officials" and Arafat's "economic adviser, enabling them to carve out monopolies with official PA consent."[6] They have also hoped to set up industrial zones in the territories, transferring pollution and exploiting a cheap labor force in maquiladora-style installations owned by Israeli enterprises and the Palestinian elite, who are enriching themselves in the time-honored fashion.

Barak's proposals, more of a warning than a plan, are a natural extension of what had come before. They extend the project of "invisible transfer" that has been under way for many years, a project that makes more sense than outright "ethnic cleansing" (as we call the process when carried out by official enemies). People compelled to abandon hope and offered no opportunities for meaningful existence will drift elsewhere, if they have any chance to do so. The plans, which have roots in traditional goals of the Zionist movement from its origins (across the ideological spectrum), were articulated in internal discussion by Israeli government Arabists in 1948 while outright ethnic cleansing was under way: their expectation was that the refugees "would be crushed" and "die," while "most of them would turn into human dust and the waste of society, and join the most impoverished classes in the Arab countries."[7] Current plans, whether imposed by coercive diplomacy or outright force, have similar goals. They are not unrealistic if they can rely on the world-dominant power and its intellectual classes.

The situation was described accurately by Amira Hass. Seven years after the Declaration of Principles in September 1993—which foretold this outcome for anyone who chose to see—"Israel has security and administrative control" of most of the West Bank and 20 percent of the Gaza Strip. It has been able

to double the number of settlers in 10 years, to enlarge the settlements, to continue its discriminatory policy of cutting back water quotas for three million Palestinians, to prevent Palestinian development in most of the area of the West Bank, and to seal an entire nation into restricted areas, imprisoned in a network of bypass roads meant for Jews only. During these days of strict internal restriction of movement in the West Bank, one can see how carefully each road was planned: So that 200,000 Jews have freedom of movement, about three million Palestinians are locked into their Bantustans until they submit to Israeli demands. The bloodbath that has been going on for three weeks is the natural outcome of seven years of lying and deception, just as the first Intifada was the natural outcome of direct Israeli occupation.[8]

The settlement and construction programs continue with U.S. support, whoever may be in office. On August 18, 2000,

Ha'aretz noted that two governments, Rabin's and Barak's, had declared that settlement was "frozen," in accord with the dovish image preferred in the United States and by much of the Israeli left. They made use of the "freezing" to intensify settlement, including economic inducements for the secular population, automatic grants for ultrareligious settlers, and other devices, which can be carried out with little protest while the lesser of two evils happens to be making the decisions, a pattern hardly unfamiliar elsewhere. "There is freezing and there is reality," the report in *Ha'aretz* observes caustically.[9] The reality is that settlement in the occupied territories has grown over four times as fast as in Israeli population centers, continuing—perhaps accelerating—under Barak. Settlement brings with it large infrastructure projects designed to integrate much of the region within Israel, while leaving Palestinians isolated, apart from "Palestinian roads" that are traveled at one's peril.

Another journalist with an outstanding record, Danny Rubinstein, points out that

> readers of the Palestinian papers get the impression (and rightly so) that activity in the settlements never stops. Israel is constantly building, expanding and reinforcing the Jewish settlements in the West Bank and Gaza. Israel is always grabbing homes and lands in areas beyond the 1967 lines—and of course, this is all at the expense of the Palestinians, in order to limit them, push them into a corner and then out. In other words, the goal is to eventually dispossess them of their homeland and their capital, Jerusalem.[10]

Readers of the Israeli press, Rubinstein continues, are largely shielded from the unwelcome facts, though not entirely so. In the United States, it is far more important for the population to be kept in ignorance, for obvious reasons: the economic and military programs rely crucially on U.S. support, which is domestically unpopular and would be far more so if its purposes were known.

To illustrate, on October 3, 2000, after a week of bitter fighting and killing, the defense correspondent of *Ha'aretz* reported "the largest purchase of military helicopters by the Israeli Air Force in a decade," an agreement with the United States to provide Israel with thirty-five Blackhawk military helicopters and spare parts at a cost of $525 million, along with jet fuel, following the purchase shortly before of patrol aircraft and Apache attack helicopters. These are "the newest and most advanced multi-mission attack helicopters in the U.S. inventory," the *Jerusalem Post* adds.[11]

The sale of military helicopters was condemned by Amnesty International in an October 19 report, because these "U.S.-supplied helicopters have been used to violate the human rights of Palestinians and Arab Israelis during the recent conflict in the region."[12] Surely that was anticipated, barring advanced cretinism.

Israel has been condemned internationally (the United States abstaining) for "excessive use of force."[13] That includes even rare condemnations by the International Committee of the Red Cross, specifically, for attacks on at least eighteen Red Crescent ambulances.[14] Israel's response is that it is being unfairly singled out for criticism. The response is entirely accurate. Israel is employing official U.S. doctrine, known here as "the Powell doctrine," though it is of far more ancient vintage, tracing back centuries: Use massive force in response to any perceived threat. Official Israeli doctrine allows "the full use of weapons against anyone who endangers lives and especially at anyone who shoots at our forces or at Israelis," according to Israeli military legal adviser Daniel Reisner.[15] Full use of force by a modern army includes tanks, helicopter gunships, sharpshooters aiming at civilians (often children), and so on. U.S. weapons sales "do not carry a stipulation that the weapons can't be used against civilians," a Pentagon official said; he "acknowleged however that anti-tank missiles and attack helicopters are not traditionally considered tools for crowd control"—except by those powerful enough to get away with it, under the protective

wings of the reigning superpower. "We cannot second-guess an
Israeli commander who calls in a Cobra (helicopter) gunship because his troops are under attack," another U.S. official said.[16]
Accordingly, such killing machines must be provided in an un-
ceasing flow.

It is not surprising that a U.S. client state should adopt standard U.S. military doctrine, which has left a toll too awesome
to record, including in very recent years. The United States
and Israel are, of course, not alone in adopting this doctrine,
and it is sometimes even condemned—namely, when adopted
by enemies targeted for destruction. A recent example is the
response of Serbia when its territory (as the United States insists it is) was attacked by Albanian-based guerrillas, killing
Serb police and civilians and abducting civilians (including
Albanians) with the openly announced intent of eliciting a
"disproportionate response" that would arouse Western indig-
nation, then NATO military attack. Very rich documentation
from U.S., NATO, and other Western sources is now available,
most of it produced in an effort to justify the bombing.[17] Assuming these sources to be credible, we find that the Serbian
response—while doubtless disproportionate and criminal, as
alleged—does not compare with the standard resort to the
same doctrine by the United States and its clients, Israel included.

In the mainstream British press, we can at last read that

> if Palestinians were black, Israel would now be a pariah state sub-
> ject to economic sanctions led by the United States [which is not
> accurate, unfortunately]. Its development and settlement of the
> West Bank would be seen as a system of apartheid, in which the in-
> digenous population was allowed to live in a tiny fraction of its own
> country, in self-administered "Bantustans," with "whites" monopo-
> lising the supply of water and electricity. And just as the black pop-
> ulation was allowed into South Africa's white areas in disgracefully
> under-resourced townships, so Israel's treatment of Israeli Arabs—
> flagrantly discriminating against them in housing and education
> spending—would be recognised as scandalous too.[18]

Such conclusions will come as no surprise to those whose vision has not been constrained by the doctrinal blinders imposed for many years. It remains a major task to remove them in the most important country. That is a prerequisite to any constructive reaction to the mounting chaos and destruction, terrible enough before our eyes, and with long-term implications that are not pleasant to contemplate.

United States–Israel–Palestine

In 2001, Hebrew University sociologist Baruch Kimmerling observed that "what we feared has come true." Jews and Palestinians are "in a process of regression to superstitious tribalism. . . . War appears an unavoidable fate," an "evil colonial" war.[1] After Israel's invasion of Palestinian refugee camps in spring 2002, Kimmerling's colleague Ze'ev Sternhell wrote that "in colonial Israel . . . human life is cheap." The leadership is "no longer ashamed to speak of war when what they are really engaged in is colonial policing, which recalls the takeover by the white police of the poor neighborhoods of the blacks in South Africa during the apartheid era."[2] Both stress the obvious: there is no symmetry between the "ethnonational groups" regressing to tribalism. The conflict is centered in territories that have been under harsh military occupation for thirty-five years. The conqueror is a major military power, acting with massive military, economic, and diplomatic support from the global superpower. Its subjects are alone and defenseless, many barely surviving in miserable camps, currently suffering even more brutal terror of a kind familiar in "evil colonial" wars and now carrying out terrible atrocities of their own in revenge.

The Oslo "peace process" changed the modalities of the occupation but not the basic concept. Shortly before joining the Ehud Barak government, historian Shlomo Ben-Ami wrote that "the Oslo agreements were founded on a neo-colonialist basis, on a life of dependence of one on the other forever."[3] He soon became an architect of the U.S.–Israel proposals at Camp David in summer 2000, which kept to this condition of dependence. These proposals were highly praised in U.S. commentary. The Palestinians and their evil leader were blamed for the failure of the talks and the subsequent violence. But that is outright "fraud," as Kimmerling reported, along with all other serious commentators.[4]

True, the Clinton–Barak proposal advanced a few steps toward a Bantustan-style settlement. Just prior to Camp David, West Bank Palestinians were confined to more than two hundred scattered areas, and Clinton–Barak did propose an improvement: consolidation to three cantons, under Israeli control, virtually separated from one another and from the fourth enclave, a small area of East Jerusalem, the center of Palestinian life and of communications in the region. In the fifth canton, Gaza, the outcome was left unclear except that the population was also to remain virtually imprisoned. It is understandable that no maps or details of the proposal are to be found in the U.S. mainstream.

No one can seriously doubt that the U.S. role will continue to be decisive. It is therefore of crucial importance to understand what that role has been and how it is internally perceived. The version of the doves is presented by the editors of the *New York Times*, who praised the president's "path-breaking speech" and the "emerging vision" he articulated. Its first element is "ending Palestinian terrorism," immediately. Sometime later comes "freezing, then rolling back, Jewish settlements and negotiating new borders" to end the occupation and allow the establishment of a Palestinian state. If Palestinian terror ends, Israelis will be encouraged to "take the Arab League's historic offer of full peace and recognition in exchange for an Israeli withdrawal more seriously." But first Palestinian leaders must demonstrate that they are "legitimate diplomatic partners."[5]

The real world has little resemblance to this self-serving portrayal—virtually copied from the 1980s, when the United States and Israel were desperately seeking to evade the Palestine Liberation Organization's (PLO) offers of negotiation and political settlement while keeping to the demand that there will be no negotiations with the PLO, no "additional Palestinian state" (Jordan already being a Palestinian state), and "no change in the status of Judea, Samaria and Gaza other than in accordance with the basic guidelines of the [Israeli] Government."[6] All of this remained unpublished in the U.S. mainstream, as was regularly the case before, while commentary denounced the Palestinians for their single-minded commitment to terror, undermining the humanistic endeavors of the United States and its allies.

In the real world, the primary barrier to the "emerging vision" has been, and remains, unilateral U.S. rejectionism. There is little new in the "historic offer" of March 2002. It repeats the basic terms of a Security Council resolution of January 1976 backed by virtually the entire world, including the leading Arab states, the PLO, Europe, the Soviet bloc—in fact, everyone who mattered. It was opposed by Israel and vetoed by the United States, thereby vetoing it from history. The resolution called for a political settlement on the internationally recognized borders "with appropriate arrangements . . . to guarantee . . . the sovereignty, territorial integrity, and political independence of all states in the area and their right to live in peace within secure and recognized borders"—in effect, a modification of UN Resolution 242 (as officially interpreted by the United States as well), amplified to include a Palestinian state. Similar initiatives from the Arab states, the PLO, and Europe have since been blocked by the United States and mostly suppressed or denied in public commentary.

Not surprisingly, the guiding principle of the occupation has been incessant and degrading humiliation, along with torture, terror, destruction of property, displacement and settlement, and takeover of basic resources, crucially water. That has, of

course, required decisive U.S. support, extending through the
Clinton–Barak years. "The Barak government is leaving
Sharon's government a surprising legacy," the Israeli press reported as the transition took place, "the highest number of
housing starts in the territories since the time when Ariel
Sharon was Minister of Construction and Settlement in 1992
before the Oslo agreements." The funding for these settlements is provided by the American taxpayer, deceived by fan-
ciful tales of the "visions" and "magnanimity" of U.S. leaders,
foiled by terrorists like Arafat who have forfeited "our trust,"
and perhaps also by some Israeli extremists who are overreact-
ing to their crimes.

How Arafat must act to regain our trust is explained succinctly
by Edward Walker, the State Department official responsible for
the region under Clinton. The devious Arafat must announce
without ambiguity that "we put our future and fate in the hands
of the U.S.," which has led the campaign to undermine Palestinian rights for thirty years.[7]

More serious commentary recognized that the "historic offer"
largely reiterated the Saudi Fahd Plan of 1981—undermined, it
was regularly claimed, by Arab refusal to accept the existence of
Israel. The facts are again quite different. The 1981 plan was undermined by an Israeli reaction that even its mainstream press
condemned as "hysterical." Shimon Peres warned that the Fahd
plan "threatened Israel's very existence." President Haim Herzog
charged that the "real author" of the Fahd plan was the PLO, and
that it was even more extreme than the January 1976 Security
Council resolution that was "prepared by" the PLO when he was
Israel's UN ambassador.[8] These claims can hardly be true (though
the PLO publicly backed both plans), but they are an indication
of the desperate fear of a political settlement on the part of Israeli
doves, with the unremitting and decisive support of the United
States.

The basic problem then, as now, traces back to Washington,
which has persistently backed Israel's rejection of a political set-

tlement in terms of the broad international consensus, reiterated in essentials in "the Arab League's historic offer."

Current modifications of U.S. rejectionism are tactical and so far minor. With plans for an attack on Iraq endangered, the United States permitted a UN resolution calling for Israeli withdrawal from the newly invaded territories "without delay"— meaning "as soon as possible," Secretary of State Colin Powell explained at once. Palestinian terror is to end "immediately," but far more extreme Israeli terror, going back thirty-five years, can take its time. Israel at once escalated its attack, leading Powell to say, "I'm pleased to hear that the prime minister says he is expediting his operations."[9] There is much suspicion that Powell's arrival in Israel was delayed so that the operations could be "expedited" further.

The United States also allowed a UN resolution calling for a "vision" of a Palestinian state.[10] This forthcoming gesture, which received much acclaim, does not rise to the level of South Africa forty years ago when the apartheid regime actually implemented its "vision" of black-run states that were at least as viable and legitimate as the neocolonial dependency that the United States and Israel have been planning for the occupied territories.

Meanwhile the United States continues to "enhance terror," to borrow President George W. Bush's words, by providing Israel with the means for terror and destruction, including a new shipment of the most advanced helicopters in the U.S. arsenal.[11]

Washington's commitment to enhancing terror was illustrated again in December 2001, when it vetoed a Security Council resolution calling for implementation of the Mitchell Plan and dispatch of international monitors to oversee reduction of violence, the most effective means as generally recognized but opposed by Israel and regularly blocked by Washington.[12] The veto took place during a twenty-one-day period of "calm"—a period in which only one Israeli soldier was killed, along with twenty-one Palestinians including eleven children, and in which there were sixteen Israeli incursions into areas under Palestinian control.[13] Ten days before the veto, the United States boycotted—and thus undermined—an international conference in Geneva that once again concluded that the Fourth Geneva Convention applies to the occupied territories, so that virtually everything the United States and Israel do there is a "grave breach"— a "war crime" in simple terms. The conference specifically declared the U.S.-funded Israeli settlements to be illegal and condemned the practice of "willful killing, torture, unlawful deportation, willful depriving of the rights of fair and regular trial, extensive destruction and appropriation of property . . . carried out unlawfully and wantonly."[14] As a High Contracting Party, the United States is obligated by solemn treaty to prosecute those responsible for such crimes, including its own leadership. Accordingly, all of this passes in silence.

The United States has not officially withdrawn its recognition of the applicability of the Geneva Conventions to the occupied territories or its censure of Israeli violations as the "occupying power" (affirmed, for example, by George Bush I when he was UN ambassador). In October 2000, the Security Council reaffirmed the consensus on this matter, "call[ing] on Israel, the occupying power, to abide scrupulously by its legal obligations and responsibilities under the Fourth Geneva Convention."[15] The vote was 14–0. Clinton abstained, presumably not wanting to veto one of the core principles of international humanitarian law, particularly in light of the circumstances in which it was enacted: to criminalize formally the atrocities of the Nazis. All of this too was consigned quickly to the memory hole, another contribution to "enhancing terror."

Until such matters are permitted to enter discussion and their implications are understood, it is meaningless to call for "U.S. engagement in the peace process," and prospects for constructive action will remain grim.

III

After 9/11:
The "War on Terror" Redeclared

A Changed World?
Terrorism Reconsidered

The "war on terrorism" declared by the U.S. government on September 11 was actually redeclared. The first such declaration was twenty years earlier, when the Reagan administration came into office, announcing that a war on terrorism would be the core of U.S. foreign policy, particularly state-supported international terrorism, the most virulent form of "the evil scourge of terrorism" (Reagan), a plague spread by "depraved opponents of civilization itself" in "a return to barbarism in the modern age" (Secretary of State George Shultz).[1] Reagan happened to be referring to the Middle East, at a moment (1985) when terrorism in that region was selected by editors as the top story of the year. But Shultz warned that the most "alarming" manifestation was frighteningly close to home: "a cancer, right here on our land mass," a state that was openly renewing the goals of Hitler's *Mein Kampf*, he informed Congress.[2]

We must "cut out" the Nicaraguan "cancer," Shultz warned.[3] And in the light of the immensity of the evil and the threat, we should not be bound by moralistic constraints: "Negotiations are a euphemism for capitulation if the shadow of power is not cast across the bargaining table," he declared, condemning those who advocate "utopian, legalistic means like the United Nations and the World Court, while ignoring the power element of the equation."[4] The United States was exercising "the power element of the equation" with mercenary forces based in Honduras, where John Negroponte was in charge, while blocking efforts by the

World Court and Latin American nations to pursue "utopian, legalistic means."

The military component of the new war on terrorism is led by
Donald Rumsfeld, Reagan's special representative for the Middle
East; the diplomatic efforts at the UN by Negroponte. Other
leading figures of the first war also reappear in a prominent role.
The world has changed little since, and the continuity of leadership also suggests that the first war on terrorism should have instructive lessons.

Before exploring them, some preliminary questions should be
considered: (1) What is terrorism? (2) What is the proper response to it? The answer to the second question should at the
very least satisfy the most elementary of moral truisms: If some
act is wrong for others, it is wrong for us; if it is right for us, it is
right for others.

The first question is held to pose great difficulties, but there
are simple answers that seem adequate, such as the definition
given in U.S. Army manuals published when Reagan and Shultz
were issuing their bitter condemnations: terrorism is "[t]he calculated use of violence or the threat of violence to attain goals
that are political, religious, or ideological in nature . . . through
intimidation, coercion, or instilling fear."[5]

There are many illustrations. September 11 is a particularly
shocking example. Another clear case is the official U.S–UK reaction, announced by Admiral Sir Michael Boyce, chief of the
British Defence Staff, and prominently reported. He informed
Afghans that U.S.–UK attacks will continue "until the people of
the country themselves recognize that this is going to go on until they get the leadership changed," in conformity with the official definition of international terrorism.[6] The actions that he
and his associates in Washington were directing go well beyond
the norm. They were undertaken with the expectation that they
would place huge numbers of civilians at serious risk of starva-
tion; millions, according to unchallenged estimates.

But Boyce's words are familiar: he was closely paraphrasing Israeli statesman Abba Eban, shortly after the first war on terror-

ism was declared. Eban was replying to Prime Minister Menachem Begin's account of atrocities in Lebanon committed under the Labor government in the style "of regimes which neither Mr. Begin nor I would dare to mention by name," acknowledging the accuracy of the account, but adding the standard justification: "there was a rational prospect, ultimately fulfilled, that affected populations would exert pressure for the cessation of hostilities."[7] At the time, with decisive U.S. support, Israel was carrying out military operations in Lebanon in an effort to elicit some pretext for the planned 1982 invasion, carried out, as openly acknowledged, to deter the threat of an unwanted diplomatic settlement along the lines supported by virtually the entire world (apart from the United States and its Israeli client). When provocation failed, Israel invaded anyway with U.S. military and diplomatic support, killing some 18,000 people. It maintained its occupation of much of the country for almost twenty years in violation of Security Council orders, with regular terror. One example is a candidate for the prize of worst terrorist atrocity in the region in the peak year of concern, 1985: the "Iron Fist" operations conducted by Shimon Peres's government, targeting what the high command called "terrorist villagers" opposing the occupation.

Another candidate for the prize was a car-bombing in Beirut at a mosque, timed when people were leaving to inflict maximum casualties: 80 were killed, more than 250 were wounded, mostly women and girls, along with other atrocities described vividly in the national U.S. press. The target was a Muslim cleric, who escaped. The bombing was organized by the CIA with British and Saudi support. The only other plausible candidate for 1985 in the region was Israel's bombing of Tunis, also with no serious pretext, killing 75 Palestinians and Tunisians; the shocking results were graphically reported by the respected journalist Amnon Kapeliouk (in Israel).[8] The United States cooperated by failing to warn its Tunisian ally that the bombers were on the way. Shultz informed Israel that Washington "had considerable sympathy" for the action, but drew back from open approval when the Security Council unanimously denounced the bombing as an "act of armed aggression" (United States abstaining).[9] A few days later Prime Minister Peres arrived in Washington, where he joined President Reagan in denouncing the "evil scourge of terrorism."[10]

None of these examples enter the canon of international terrorism, however, because of a crucial condition: terrorism is terrorism targeting *us*, excluding what we do to *them*. That is standard practice, probably a historical universal. Accordingly, there was no comment when Reagan and Peres issued their denunciations of Middle East terrorism right after having won the prize at the peak moment of concern over the plague, or when the United States and UK frankly described their operations in Afghanistan.

The same convention applies to the operations to "cut out the Nicaraguan cancer," an uncontroversial case, given the judgment by the World Court condemning the United States for the "unlawful use of force" and the supporting Security Council Resolution calling on all states to observe international law (vetoed by the United States, Britain abstaining); uncontroversial, that is, among those with some respect for international law and human rights.[11] The Court ordered the United States to terminate the crime and pay substantial reparations. Washington responded by escalating the war and issuing the first official orders to attack "soft targets"—undefended civilian targets—and to avoid combat with the army. By convention, all of this is excluded from the annals of terrorism, along with the even more barbaric international terrorism then underway in the neighboring countries.[12]

The observation generalizes. Take Cuba, probably the leading target of international terrorism, reaching remarkable levels in Kennedy's Operation Mongoose and continuing to the late 1990s. Cold War pretexts were offered but are known to be false. The terrorist operations and secret decision to overthrow the government preceded any Soviet connection. In secret, the Cuban threat was described as "the spread of the Castro idea of taking matters into one's own hands," which might stimulate the "poor and underprivileged" in other countries, who "are now demanding opportunities for a decent living" (Arthur Schlesinger, reporting the conclusions of JFK's Latin American mission to the incoming president).[13] The Cold War connection was that "the Soviet Union hovers in the wings, flourishing large development loans and presenting itself as the model for achieving modernization in a single generation."[14] The case is by no means unusual. Cuba remains officially a "terrorist state," suspected of supporting international terrorism. But it is not the target of terrorism, thanks to the governing convention.

Though the powerful protect themselves from such unwanted facts, they are of course familiar to the victims. Harsh condemnation of the terrorist atrocities of September 11 was virtually universal but was regularly accompanied by bitter memories. Panamanian journalist Ricardo Stevens, for example, recalled the deaths of perhaps thousands of poor people (Western crimes, therefore unexamined) when George Bush I bombed the barrio Chorrillo in December 1989 in Operation Just Cause, undertaken to kidnap a disobedient thug who was sentenced to life imprisonment in Florida for crimes mostly committed while he was on the CIA payroll.[15] Eduardo Galeano observed that Washington's posture of opposing terrorism is hardly convincing to those who remember well the state terrorism that raged "in Indonesia, in Cambodia, in Iran, in South Africa . . . and in the Latin American countries that lived through the dirty war of the Condor Plan," a small sample.[16] The research journal of the Jesuit university in Managua recognized that the September atrocities might be described as "Armageddon," but added that Nicaragua has "lived its own Armageddon in excruciating slow motion" under U.S. assault "and is now submerged in its dismal aftermath."[17] The record continues to the present: it suffices to compare the list of leading recipients of U.S. arms with human rights reports.

Similar conventions apply to extradition. The United States refused even to consider extradition of the suspected perpetrators of the September 11 crimes, just as it pointedly refused to obtain unambiguous Security Council authorization for its retaliation, as it could easily have done, if not for attractive reasons. The

stance reflects a traditional principle of world order: the powerful must establish that they defer to no authority.

Being small and weak, Nicaragua tried to follow the rules, but
of course failed. Similarly, when Costa Rica requested extradition of a U.S. rancher who turned his lands over to the CIA as
a base for the terrorist attack against Nicaragua, the request was
routinely ignored.[18] One highly relevant current case involves
Emmanuel Constant, the leader of the Haitian paramilitary
forces that were responsible for thousands of brutal killings in
the early 1990s under the military junta, which Washington officially opposed but tacitly supported. Constant was sentenced
in absentia by a Haitian court. Haiti has called on the United
States to extradite him, again on September 30, 2001.[19] The request was again ignored, probably because of concerns about
what he might reveal about ties to the U.S. government during
the period of terror.

President Bush and many others have raised the question "why
do they hate us?" Many sophisticated answers have been proposed, but some simple ones come to mind. It helps to remember
that the question is not new. It was raised in 1958 by President
Eisenhower. Our problem in the Arab world, he informed his
staff, "is that we have a campaign of hatred against us, not by the
governments but by the people," who side with Nasser—a "Communist" (despite firm CIA denials), by virtue of his independent
nationalist stance.[20] One reason for Washington's plight was offered by Secretary of State John Foster Dulles: The "Communists" are able "to get control of mass movements, . . . something
we have no capacity to duplicate. . . . The poor people are the
ones they appeal to and they have always wanted to plunder the
rich."[21] A more formal answer was given by the National Security Council, which concluded that "the majority of Arabs" see
the United States as "opposed to the realization of the goals of
Arab nationalism" and believe that it is "seeking to protect its interest in Near East oil by supporting the status quo and opposing
political or economic progress." The perception is difficult to
counter, the NSC recognized, since it is accurate: "our economic

and cultural interests in the area have led not unnaturally to close U.S. relations with elements in the Arab world whose primary interest lies in the maintenance of relations with the West and the status quo in their countries."[22]

It remains difficult to counter such perceptions. After September 11, the *Wall Street Journal* surveyed opinions of "moneyed Muslims": bankers, professionals, businessmen with close U.S. ties. They expressed dismay about U.S. support for "oppressive regimes" and its opposition to independent development and political democracy, as well as about specific policies, particularly U.S. support for Israel's harsh and brutal military occupation and the sanctions against Iraq that are devastating the population while strengthening its murderous dictator—whom the United States and Britain supported right through his worst atrocities, as they recall, even if the West prefers to forget.[23] The sentiments are broadly shared, and the great mass of the population is not pleased to see the wealth of the region flow to the West and its local clients.

Suppose we depart from convention and adopt the moral truism mentioned at the outset. We can then honestly inquire into the proper response to international crimes. We can, for example, ask whether Haiti has the right to use force to compel Constant's extradition, in accord with Washington's model in Afghanistan (after it had refused to consider extradition). The same question arises about the uncontroversial case of Nicaragua, and many others. Throughout, Admiral Boyce's prescription, which was implemented, is unthinkable, yielding a conclusion too obvious to state.

Other responses to international terrorist crimes have been proposed. One was put forth by the Vatican and spelled out by military historian Michael Howard: "a police operation conducted under the auspices of the United Nations . . . against a criminal conspiracy, whose members should be hunted down and brought before an international court, where they would receive a fair trial and, if found guilty, be awarded an appropriate sentence."[24] Though never contemplated, the proposal seems reasonable. If so, it should apply to even worse terrorist crimes, such as the ones that left tens of thousands dead in Nicaragua and the country devastated perhaps beyond recovery, and more extreme cases close by, and elsewhere. That could never be contemplated.

Honesty would leave us with a dilemma: the easy escape is conventional hypocrisy (as the word is defined in the Gospels). The other option is harder to pursue, but imperative if the world is to be spared still worse disasters.

Notes

Preface

1. See Michel Crozier, Samuel P. Huntington, and Joji Watanuki, *The Crisis of Democracy: Report on the Governability of Democracies to the Trilateral Commission*, New York University Press, New York, 1975.

2. For useful discussion, see Paul Street, "Towards a 'Decent Left'? Liberal–Left Misrepresentation and Selective Targeting of Left Commentary on 9/11," *Z Magazine*, July–Aug. 2002.

3. See Peter J. Katzenstein, "Same War, Different Views: Germany, Japan, and the War on Terrorism," *Current History*, vol. 101, no. 659, Dec. 2002, pp. 427–35.

4. Anatol Lieven, Senior Associate, Carnegie Endowment for International Peace, "The Push for War," *London Review of Books*, Oct. 3, 2002, discussing a very general view in the West. Jane Perlez, "In Search for Democracy, U.S. Is Rejected as a Guide," *New York Times*, Sept. 28, 2002, p. A10, predicting more hatred, more bin Ladens, in a survey of "educated people in the more open Persian Gulf nations" that are generally supportive of U.S. goals and international policies.

5. See, for example, the detailed inquiry of the American Academy of Arts and Sciences, *War with Iraq: Costs, Consequences, and Alternatives*, Carl Kaysen et al., American Academy of Arts and Sciences, Cambridge, 2002, constructing the most sympathetic possible version of the administration's case and dismantling it effectively point by point, on grounds more narrow than many critics would consider appropriate. For a brief but sufficient analysis from a similar viewpoint, see John J. Mearsheimer and Stephen M. Walt, "Iraq: An Unnecessary War," *Foreign Policy*, Jan.–Feb. 2002, pp. 50–59. Academic dean of the Kennedy School of Government at Harvard, Walt speaks for many in the mainstream when he dismisses the contrived arguments for war and attributes the timing of the war plans primarily to domestic politics (David Usborne, "Bush Forced to Play Down

Talk of War," *The Independent* (London), Aug. 11, 2002, p. 15), conclusions that were so strongly supported in the following months that they were discussed widely across the mainstream spectrum.

6. Hussein Agha and Robert Malley, "The Last Negotiation: How to End the Middle East Peace Process," *Foreign Affairs*, vol. 81, no. 3, May–June 2002, pp. 10–18.

7. For details, see chapter 6, this volume.

8. The United States for the first time "voted against a UN decision calling on Israel to repeal the Jerusalem Law" ("US Defies UN Anti-Israel Vote," *Jerusalem Post*, Dec. 4, 2002; see Associated Press and other wire services, Dec. 3). The law, which effectively annexed Jerusalem to Israel, has repeatedly been condemned by the Security Council and the General Assembly (with U.S. support until the Clinton years, when the United States shifted to abstention). In its December 2002 shift, the United States was joined by Israel, Costa Rica, Micronesia, and the Marshall Islands, voting against a near-unanimous General Assembly. The United States also voted the same day against a resolution (passed 160–4: United States, Israel, and the two Pacific island dependencies) calling for concrete steps toward peaceful settlement. As usual, there appears to have been no report in the U.S. media.

9. On the extent of "greater Jerusalem," see the official maps published by B'Tselem (The Israeli Information Center for Human Rights in the Occupied Territories) in the report by Yehezkel Lein and Eyal Weizman, *Gezel Ha-Karka'ot*, Hebrew edition, May 2002, revealing that the boundaries of the "neighborhoods of Jerusalem" extend virtually to Jericho. The English version of this report, translated by Shaul Vardi and Zvi Shulman, *Land Grab: Israel's Settlement Policy in the West Bank*, May 2002, is available with additional maps online at the B'Tselem website (http://www.btselem.org/).

10. See chapter 6, this volume. Agha and Malley do not discuss the matter, but at the Taba negotiations in January 2001 the Palestinian delegation proposed a settlement in these terms, with a 1–1 swap, while Israel's negotiators insisted on a 3–1 swap, crucially leaving in Israeli hands the town of Ma'ale Adumim, which, with its projected borders, effectively bisects the West Bank and was rather clearly constructed for that purpose. See B'Tselem, op. cit., and for background, my introduction to Roane Carey, ed., *The New Intifada*, Verso, New York, 2001. On the Taba negotiations, see the notes by EU representative Miguel Angel Moratinos, with the acquiescence of both sides, published by Israeli diplomatic correspondent Akiva Eldar, *Ha'aretz*, Feb. 18, 2002. The negotiations, though informal, were at a high level, and were clearly making progress. They were called off by Ehud Barak, and the Palestinians failed utterly to capitalize on the opportunity of pursuing them.

Introduction

1. Cited by Jon Kimche, *There Could Have Been Peace*, Dial Press, New York 1973, pp. 223, 226.

2. George F. Kennan, "And Thank You Very Much," *New York Times*, Op-Ed page, Dec. 2, 1973.

3. *Business Week*, Dec. 22, 1973.

4. Harry B. Ellis, business-financial correspondent of the *Christian Science Monitor*, Jan. 29, 1974.

5. *Business Week*, Oct. 20, 1973; Dec. 22, 1973.

6. *Business Week*, Nov. 3, 1973. On tendencies toward state capitalism and nonalignment in Iraq (incidentally, the only oil-producing country where Russian influence is substantial), see the report by Robert Graham of the London *Financial Times* in *Middle East International*, Oct. 1973.

7. Elizabeth Pond, "Japan Gets Blunt Choice on Oil," *Christian Science Monitor*, Jan. 29, 1974, reporting from Tokyo.

8. Elizabeth Pond, *Christian Science Monitor*, Nov. 19, 1973.

9. Elizabeth Pond's paraphrase; cf. note 7.

10. *New York Times*, financial pages, Nov. 14, 1973.

11. Irving Kristol, "Where Have All the Gunboats Gone?" *Wall Street Journal*, Dec. 13, 1973. Neither Kristol's interesting interpretation of recent history nor the moral level of his recommendations should lead the reader to dismiss this article as without significance.

12. Walter Laqueur, "Détente: What's Left of It?" *New York Times Magazine*, Dec. 16, 1973.

13. Laqueur is identified in the *New York Times* as "director of the Institute of Contemporary History in London and chairman of the Research Council of the Center for Strategic and International Studies in Washington," i.e., a neutral expert. The principle of "truth in packaging" might suggest that further information be provided when he writes about Israel and the Middle East.

14. The wording is that of Secretary of State Rogers, Dec. 9, 1969; cited in a discussion of possible United Nations initiatives by John Reddaway, *Middle East International*, Oct. 1973. The Rogers Plan was made public on June 24, 1970, and accepted by Nasser on July 23. Cf. John K. Cooley, *Green March, Black September*, Frank Cass, London, 1973, p. 110. On the Israeli reaction, which was evasive but basically quite negative, see Kimche, op. cit., pp. 286f. The Rogers Plan implied acceptance of the existence of the State of Israel as a sovereign state within recognized borders.

15. A plan to establish a demilitarized belt along both sides of the Suez Canal, so that the canal could be reopened and the cities in the canal zone rebuilt, was suggested to the Israeli cabinet by Moshe Dayan in the fall of 1970, but rejected. Cf. Kimche, op. cit., pp. 294f.

16. Aharon Cohen, *Israel and the Arab World*, Funk & Wagnalls, New York, 1970, pp. 67–9. This valuable work, now available in English, gives a voluminous record of attempts to lay a basis for Arab-Jewish cooperation in Palestine.

17. Ibid., p. 261.

18. Halim I. Barakat, "The Palestinian Refugees: An Uprooted Community Seeking Repatriation," *International Migration Review*, vol. 7, 1973, p. 153, citing estimates by Don Peretz.

19. Barakat, op. cit., citing the detailed analysis by Sabri Jiryis, *The Arabs in Israel*, Institute for Palestine Studies, Beirut, 1969.

20. Cf. General E. L. M. Burns, *Between Arab and Israeli*, Institute for Palestine Studies, Beirut, 1969, p. 93; Kennett Love, *Suez*, McGraw-Hill, New York, 1969, pp. 11, 61–2. Love notes that the "worst single Arab reprisal committed in Israel," the "ambush-massacre" of eleven Israelis on a Negev bus on March 17, 1954, was carried out by members of a Bedouin tribe expelled from the al-Auja region of the Sinai in September 1950. On the interaction of terrorist initiatives, see chapter 1, below. Expulsion of Bedouins continues. See note 72 and chapter 3, section II, below. For some estimates of the scale over the years, see Janet L. Abu-Lughod, "The Demographic Transformation of Palestine," in Ibrahim Abu-Lughod, ed., *The Transformation of Palestine*, Northwestern University Press, Evanston, Ill., 1971, pp. 149, 156, 161.

21. It is widely believed that although "it is unlikely that the Soviet Union wanted a war at that stage," nevertheless "it decisively contributed towards its outbreak through some major errors (at best) of judgment" (Walter Laqueur, *The Struggle for the Middle East*, Macmillan, New York, 1969, p. 78). Jon Kimche argues that military and intelligence relations between the United States and Israel in the years prior to the war were so close as to amount virtually to joint military planning and that a United States–Israeli army understanding of late May in effect "cleared the way for the 5 June initiative" (op. cit., pp. 251–8). For a useful discussion of the military background, see Geoffrey Kemp, "Strategy and Arms Levels," in J. C. Hurewitz, ed., *Soviet–American Rivalry in the Middle East*, Proceedings of the Academy of Political Science, vol. 29, no. 3, 1969. On the backgrounds of the war as seen by the Israeli military command, see below, pp. 22–3; chapter 3, section II, p. 99; chapter 5, pp. 149–50; and references cited there.

22. On earlier Palestinian precedents in the pre–World War II period, see Cooley, op. cit., p. 37; also chapter 1, p. 51, below.

23. According to United States government reports, the United States air force flew 22,300 tons of military equipment, ammunition, spare parts, and medical supplies to Israel from October 13 to November 14, including tanks, helicopters, and heavy artillery. United States intelligence estimates that the Soviet Union carried 200,000 to 225,000 tons of matériel to Syria

and Egypt by sea during a comparable period (Drew Middleton, *New York Times*, Nov. 28, 1973). Total estimates of sea and air transport are conflicting, but there is no doubt that the scale was immense.

24. For details from the Israeli press, see *Viewpoint*, P.O. Box 18042, Jerusalem, Sept. 15, 1973; *Israleft News Service*, P.O. Box 9013, Jerusalem, Sept. 17, Oct. 2, 1973. Cf. chapter 4.

25. Cited in *Viewpoint*, loc. cit.

26. The site of the city has been reported in *Maariv*. According to this report, the town is to be a regional industrial center with a population of several tens of thousands. Cf. *New York Times*, Dec. 10, 1973.

27. *Viewpoint*, loc. cit.

28. For some discussion, see chapters 3 and 4. The former was written on the assumption that these assessments were more or less accurate, so that the military threat to Israel was not immediate, though evidently the long-term threat of destruction remained; it is, plainly, implicit in the policy of repeated confrontation with an enemy that cannot be finally defeated. The immediate threat, under the given assumptions, was that of internal corrosion, as Israel proceeded to incorporate territories with a substantial Arab population that must be deprived of rights, given the ideological commitment to Jewish dominance. The October 1973 events revealed that the assumptions were dubious and that the "long term" may not be too long. After the October war, the Labor Party revised the August electoral program described above. Without explicitly repudiating the Galili Protocols, which laid the basis for annexation of the territories, the new program nevertheless does not reiterate them. Cf. *Davar*, Nov. 29, 1973, reprinted in *Israleft*, Dec. 1, 1973.

29. *Ha'aretz*, Oct. 7, 1973. For extensive quotes, see *Israleft*, Nov. 15, 1973.

30. Cited by Robert Graham, *Middle East International*, July 1973.

31. Kimche, op. cit., p. 338.

32. See chapter 3, below.

33. On these events, see Cooley, op. cit.

34. Kimche, op. cit., pp. 237–8.

35. The expression is that of Gershom Schocken, editor and publisher of *Ha'aretz*, Sept. 30, 1951. For a lengthy excerpt in which this view is developed, see Arie Bober, ed., *The Other Israel*, Doubleday, New York, 1972, pp. 16–17.

36. Cited in Cohen, op. cit., p. 128, from the *Chronicles of the Haganah*. For discussion of the position of the "Zionist extremists" led by Jabotinsky, from the point of view of a Zionist historian, see Ben Halpern, *The Idea of a Jewish State*, 2nd ed., Harvard University Press, Cambridge, Mass., 1969, pp. 32f. See Samuel Katz, *Days of Fire*, Doubleday, Garden City, N.Y., 1968, for defense of Jabotinsky and criticism of the Zionist leadership from his point of view. Katz was a member of the High Command of the Irgun

Zvai Leumi. On the role of the latter organization, see chapter 1, below; and for some of Jabotinsky's views, note 21 of chapter 1.

37. On the gradual emergence of right-wing extremist positions as basic Zionist policy, see chapters 1 and 3. While the causes may be debated, the fact is quite clear.

38. Cf. Saul Friedländer, *Réflexions sur l'avenir d'Israël*, Editions du Seuil, Paris, p. 143. Friedländer is a well-known historian and academic dove, a professor of contemporary history and international relations at the Hebrew University in Jerusalem and the Institut Universitaire des Hautes Etudes Internationales in Geneva.

39. Ibid. Such an arrangement, Friedländer argues, would solve the "demographic problem" from the Israeli point of view. One might recall the status of the Jews in Eastern Europe before World War II. The eminent Israeli historian Jacob Talmon describes it in these terms: "And indeed, knowing themselves to be undesirables, conscious of the determination of the government and majority population to make conditions so unbearable to them that they would be forced to emigrate, with economic opportunities constantly shrinking, with no access to government posts, public works, and services, no wonder the Jewish youth of those countries felt that their existence was unreal, transitional, a kind of preparation for some future reality—redemption through Zion or through the coming World Revolution" (*Israel Among the Nations*, City College Papers, no. 9, New York, 1968). "Flight without ideology," Talmon writes, "would have reduced the Jews of Central and Eastern Europe to a mob of wretched refugees, whereas ideology gave them the dignity of a hard-pressed nation on the march." Similar observations may well apply to the Palestinians. Cf. chapter 1, below.

40. Cf. Friedländer, op. cit., pp. 104f.

41. *Sunday Times*, London, June 15, 1969. A longer excerpt appears in Cooley, op. cit., pp. 196–7. Galili's statement, before a Kibbutz conference in 1969, elicited an important response from Talmon. Cf. Cooley, ibid., pp. 205–7.

42. Cooley, op. cit., p. 197.

43. Cf. chapter 5, p. 138, and the reference of note 23, chapter 5. On the facts of the matter, see also John H. Davis, *The Evasive Peace*, John Murray, London, 1968, ch. 5. (As commissioner general of UNRWA, Davis was in charge of Palestinian refugee programs.)

44. Kimche, op. cit., p. 264.

45. *Yediot Ahronot*, Oct. 17, 1969. Cited in Bober, op. cit., p. 77.

46. Cf. my "Israel and the New Left," in Mordecai S. Chertoff, ed., *The New Left and the Jews*, Pitman, New York, 1971, and chapter 5, below. As discussed there, more was involved than just the affairs of the Middle East. Though small in scale by comparison, the support given by some segments of the left to Palestinian movements has been no less mindless, in my opin-

ion, than the general support for Israeli intransigence. See chapter 2. In this case too, those who advocate that others undertake a suicidal and self-destructive course of action might do well to reflect, quite apart from any judgment as to the rights and wrongs of the case.

47. Reproduced in *Siah*, Nov. 15, 1973, from *Davar*. Characteristically, Sharon speaks only of the problem of settlement with Egypt.

48. Yitzhak Rabin, ibid. General Rabin (former chief of staff and ambassador to the United States) adds that if the Arab states had achieved greater initial success, they would have exploited it for further military goals, and Jordan might have joined seriously in the war.

49. Oil economist Thomas R. Stauffer of the Harvard University Middle East Center, *Christian Science Monitor*, Jan. 10, 1974.

50. Pinhas Sapir, *Maariv*, Nov. 1, 1973.

51. *Ha'aretz*, Nov. 30, Dec. 7, 1973.

52. Yehuda Gotthalf, *Davar*, Oct. 26, 1973; Boaz Evron, *Yediot Ahronot*, Oct. 10, 1973. Translated in *New Outlook*, Oct.–Nov. 1973.

53. Eric Rouleau, *Le Monde*, Jan. 23, 1974; translated in *Le Monde* English section, *Guardian Weekly*, Feb. 2, 1974.

54. Cf. chapter 5. As noted there, these efforts to suppress discussion persist, though with much less success, given the reassessment of United States government policy since October 1973. The examples discussed in chapter 5 may be dismissed as extreme and untypical. Perhaps a personal experience may help convey the mood of these years. In late 1970, I tried to persuade a group of American Jewish professors (liberals and socialists) to sponsor tours in the United States by Israeli doves (writers, professors, journalists) to help make Americans aware of some of the range of opinion in Israel. They refused, though they generally agreed with the views of the Israelis I suggested that they invite. I could only take this to reflect the fear that expression of these views might cause doubt and controversy. To cite one further incident, when Knesset member Uri Avneri visited the United States, a directive was sent to all Hillel foundations on American campuses urging that he not be permitted to speak. (To their credit, several Hillel rabbis disregarded this appeal.) The efforts to limit discussion are wrong in themselves, but also, I believe, harmful to the people of Israel and their security, for reasons I have been discussing.

55. *Maariv*, Dec. 7, 1973, cited in *Viewpoint*, Jan. 1974.

56. *Yediot Ahronot*, Nov. 23, 1973. Translated by *Jewish Liberation Information Service*, Jan. 1974, P.O. Box 7557, Jerusalem. Dr. Bar-Zohar is a well-known political scientist and journalist, very critical of Israeli doves.

57. It is sometimes overlooked that the Syrian shelling followed Israeli encroachments into the demilitarized zones for agricultural development and water-diversion projects. References to the unreliability of a United Nations force commonly overlook the fact that Israel refused appeals to permit the United Nations force to operate on its side of the border, as well

as on the Egyptian side. The situation is complex, considerably more so than the casual reader of the American press might believe. It is also well to bear in mind that Arabs, too, have reason to fear shelling from the Golan Heights. John K. Cooley reports that in the Jordanian city of Irbid, "nearly 100 people have been killed or wounded by Israeli air attacks and artillery shelling from the nearby Golan Heights since the war of 1967" (*Christian Science Monitor*, Jan. 30, 1970).

58. It is less often noted that the Arab states surrounding Israel also have a "security problem," not to speak of the Palestinians. Thus the United States is party to a tripartite agreement guaranteeing that no territories in the region will be taken by force. The value of this guarantee for Egypt, Syria, and Jordan since 1967 is obvious enough, but rarely discussed.

59. For some examples, see the discussion in chapter 5.

60. Cf. the report by Eric Rouleau, *Le Monde*, Nov. 6, 1973. There have been continuing reports since of debate within the leadership of the Palestine Liberation Organization over this matter, but their options seem fairly limited.

61. See below, pp. 28–9.

62. *New York Times*, Dec. 30, 1973.

63. May 21, 1973. The text appears in *War/Peace Report*, July–Aug., 1973.

64. For example, Hans Morgenthau. See chapter 5, note 48.

65. Ibrahim Sus, "L'Offensive diplomatique de l'Arabie Saoudite," *Le Monde diplomatique*, Oct. 1973.

66. It is commonly argued that these vast funds would permit Arab rulers to disrupt the international monetary system and that the funds would be "excessive," considering the domestic needs of the Arab states. On the hypocrisy of these attitudes, see Marwan Iskandar, *The Arab Oil Question*, 2nd ed. Jan. 1974, Middle East Economic Consultants, International Book Services, Inc., Portland, Ore. He points out that the projected oil revenues over the coming thirteen years for 150 million Arabs amount to less than three-fourths of the annual United States national income. One might argue that this income is unlikely to be distributed properly, but then the plea should be for more equitable development, not for reversing the flow of funds to the Western world, where there are also some problems of distribution. Iskandar also points out that during the 1960s the West obtained an implicit subsidy (he estimates $31.5 billion) from the oil producers as a result of its ability then to drive down prices, with no complaints about the unfairness of all of this. Investigation of trade and aid reveals many similar examples. For the justification, we can return to Kristol's insightful distinction between the "significant" and "insignificant" nations.

67. Graham, op. cit. See note 30, above.

68. Drew Middleton, *New York Times*, Nov. 18, 1973. The oil-producing countries already devote 20 to 50 percent of their budgets to military purchases. See Iskandar, op. cit.

69. It is, incidentally, curious to read the denunciations of the European states (France in particular) for attempting to cut into the American arms trade—another example of their irresponsible bilateralism. Cf. pp. 5–7, above.

70. See Sheldon Kirshner, "Report on Israel's Budding Arms Industry," *New Outlook*, Sept. 1973.

71. *Maariv*, Aug. 29, 1973.

72. Amnon Rubinstein, *Ha'aretz*, Aug. 10, 1973, in *New Outlook*, Sept. 1973. To cite another case, the Bedouin tribes evicted by force from the Rafah region in 1972 appealed to the courts that the alleged "security grounds" were fraudulent. The High Court rejected their appeal, on grounds that the courts cannot interfere with such decisions on the part of the military commander. But local Jewish settlements continued to employ Arab workers who had been expelled from their homes. Moshe Dayan warned them to cease this practice, since by doing so they were undermining the plea of the military before the High Court that the Bedouins were evicted for security reasons: "If the settlers continue employing as labourers those same Bedouins that lived on this land and were removed for security reasons, they are just taking away the grounds for our claim and are closing the area for further Jewish settlement" (Ehud ben Ezer, *Ha'aretz*, Aug. 13, 1973). On the court decisions, see articles from the Israeli press translated in *Israleft*, June 21, 1973.

73. "Who Is a Jew?" *Encounter*, May 1965, cited in Georges R. Tamarin, *The Israeli Dilemma*, Rotterdam University Press, Rotterdam, 1973, p. 37. The latter work gives some striking examples of the impact on children's attitudes of life in a "warfare state." On the matter of the religious role in the Israeli state and society, see also Norman L. Zucker, *The Coming Crisis in Israel*, MIT Press, Cambridge, Mass., 1973.

74. Cf. Cooley, op. cit. Also Gérard Chaliand, *La Résistance palestinienne*, Éditions du Seuil, Paris, 1970; trans. *The Palestinian Resistance*, Penguin Books, Baltimore, 1972.

75. Cited in Amos Elon, *The Israelis*, Holt, Rinehart & Winston, New York, 1971, p. 178.

76. Cf. note 39.

77. Cited in Cohen, op. cit., p. 260.

78. Ibid., p. 260.

79. Ibid., pp. 267–9. This detailed plan was presented in a personal note submitted to the Jewish Agency in 1936 and was unknown until reported by Moshe Smilansky in 1953 in his autobiography.

80. Ibid., p. 291.

81. Ibid.
82. Ibid., pp. 285–7.
83. Ibid., p. 258.

Chapter 1

1. See Esco Foundation, *Palestine: A Study of Jewish, Arab and British Policies*, Yale University Press, New Haven, Conn., 1947, vol. 2, pp. 1087, 1100. The 1942 program is generally referred to as the "Biltmore Program."

2. See Christopher Sykes, *Crossroads to Israel*, William Collins, London, 1965, for a description of this occasion.

3. "Meaning of Homeland," *New Outlook*, Dec. 1967.

4. *Le Monde*, weekly selection, July 9–16, 1969.

5. Ibid., July 16, 1969.

6. Zalmen Chen, "A Binational Solution," in *New Outlook*, June 1968. See also the discussion among the editors, March–April 1968. This journal has, for more than ten years, provided sane and highly informative commentary on the Palestine problem.

7. Uri Avneri, *Israel Without Zionists*, Macmillan, New York, 1968.

8. For a preliminary effort in this direction see *Eléments*, journal of the Comité de la Gauche pour la Paix négociée au Moyen-Orient, nos. 2–3, May 1969, 15 rue des Minimes, Paris 3°.

9. Population estimates vary. The Esco Foundation study (op. cit., vol. 1, p. 321) gives these figures: for 1920, 67,000 Jews out of a population of 673,000; for 1930, 164,796 Jews out of a population of 992,559.

10. Quoted in Christopher Sykes, op. cit.

11. The letter appears in *The Middle East Newsletter*, May–June 1969, an anti-Zionist periodical published in Beirut.

12. *Le Monde*, weekly selection, July 10–16, 1969 (Rouleau's paraphrase).

13. See for example the eyewitness report of Amnon Kapeliouk in *New Outlook*, Nov.–Dec. 1968.

14. Ze'ev Schul, *Jerusalem Post Weekly*, reprinted in *Atlas*, Aug. 1969.

15. Shmuel B'ari in *New Outlook*, March–April 1969.

16. See the statement by the Israeli journalist Nissim Rejwan in *New Outlook*, March–April 1968. He writes that: "The official view . . . has been repeatedly explained by the Prime Minister's present Adviser on Arab affairs. It is that one cannot expect loyalty from the Arabs of Israel 'since they belong to another nationality.' As long as such a view prevails we will not in honesty be able to claim that we treat our non-Jewish citizens as equals."

17. *New Outlook*, Feb. 1968.

18. Ibid., March–April 1969.

19. Amos Perlmutter, *Military and Politics in Israel*, Frank Cass, 1969, London, p. 19, a highly expert study by an Israeli scholar. John Marlowe describes the rebellion as "in fact a peasant revolt, drawing its enthusiasm, its heroism, its organisation and its persistence from sources within itself which have never been properly understood and which now will never be known" (Sykes, op. cit.). The Esco Foundation study concluded: "While the bands undoubtedly included genuine sympathizers with the Arab national cause, they also contained many recruits from the lower elements in the towns who were attracted by the pay and the chance of robbery. . . . Acts of terror were committed not only against government officials and Jews, but also against Arabs who did not fall in with the policy of the Mufti party." This is borne out by the casualty figures for 1939: "69 British, 92 Jewish and 486 Arab civilians, besides 1,138 rebels killed" (vol. 2, pp. 876–80). According to figures from official sources cited by Aharon Cohen (*Israel and the Arab World*, Sifriat Poalim, in 1964; Hebrew—translations mine throughout) twice as many Arabs were killed by Arabs as by Jews in the period 1936–1939, "because of friendly relations with Jews (village Mukhtars, Arab guards, Arab workers who worked with Jews, and so on), or because of their political opposition to the Mufti and his associates" (p. 204). (Cohen's book has since been translated; see introduction, note 16.)

20. Perlmutter, op. cit., p. 42. For example, Sykes reports that "in January, 1942, the Sternists murdered two officials of Histadruth, and when they fought the police they concentrated their vengeance on the Jewish personnel." The Esco Foundation study (vol. 2, p. 1040) reports the murder of a member of Hashomer Hatzair by members of Betar who had invaded a meeting in 1944.

21. With justice. It is enough to read the "Ideology of Betar," written by Jabotinsky. Betar is a party "founded upon the principles of discipline. . . . For it is the highest achievement of a mass of free men, if they are capable to act in unison, with the absolute precision of a machine. Only a free, cultured people can do so. . . . Discipline is the subordination of a mass to one leader"—the *Rosh Betar*, Jabotinsky. Continuing: "We have decided that in building a State, we must utilize the means at hand, be they old or new, good or bad, if only we will thus attain a Jewish majority." Among the means was strike-breaking: "An unjust and State-disintegrating strike must be mercilessly broke [sic], as well as any other attempt to damage the Jewish State reconstruction. . . . it is the right and duty of Betar itself to decide as to the justice or injustice of a conflict, help the former, and break up the latter." Revisionist spokesmen in the 1930s expressed their admiration for Mussolini, Franco, and the murderers of Liebknecht and Luxemburg. According to Perlmutter, they also made "attempts to collaborate with the Fascists and Nazis in Eastern Europe, during World War II" (p. 45). He believes that the Irgun "constituted far more of a threat to the Yishuv than . . . toward the Mandatory" (p. 27). As already noted, they were responsible

for attacks on Jews as well as Arabs. (In this respect, they were comparable
to the terrorists of the Arab right.) Their best-known exploit was the Deir
Yassin massacre in 1948 (largely an operation of the Irgun Tsevai Leumi—
the Revisionist paper *HaMashkif*, in August 1948, applauded this "dazzling
display of warfare" because it was a main factor in causing the flight of
Arab refugees). David Ben-Gurion was perceptive when in 1933 he entitled an article "Jabotinsky in the Footsteps of Hitler." The strong antagonism of the Palestinian Jewish settlement to the Revisionists and their various outgrowths is very much to its credit; the relatively good press they
have received in the United States is largely a result of ignorance, I suspect.

22. *This Is Betar*, undated, early 1940s. Betar was a youth group founded
by Vladimir Jabotinsky, the head of the Revisionist wing of the Zionist
movement, which has now become, in effect, the Herut Party in Israel.

23. Vol. 3, no. 12, Dec. 1947. I should emphasize that my own point of
view was heavily influenced by this group and a number of the people associated with it.

24. Cited in Rony Gabbay, *A Political Study of the Arab-Jewish Conflict*,
Librairie E. Droz, Geneva-Paris, 1959. This is an excellent and detailed
study of the period from 1948 to 1958.

25. Nadav Safran, *From War to War*, Pegasus, New York, 1969, pp.
45–6.

26. See particularly the important study of Gérard Chaliand, "La Résistance palestinienne entre Israël et les états arabes," *Le Monde diplomatique*,
March 1969. For a recent journalistic account, see Mervyn Jones in *New
Statesman*, June 13, 1969. He is "wholly convinced" (admittedly, on brief
exposure) that al-Fatah is the "authentic expression" of a new "coherent
and militant nation." Chaliand suggests an analogy to the early Kuomintang, and feels that if it fails, it may be supplanted by a more revolutionary mass movement, as in China or Vietnam. He notes that small
Marxist groups exist which seem to him to share more directly in the daily
life of the refugees (specifically, the PFLP). There is a detailed analysis by
the former Israeli chief of military intelligence, Y. Harkabi: *Fedayeen Action and Arab Strategy*, Adelphi Papers, no. 53, Institute for Strategic Studies, London, Dec. 1968. He is rather disparaging and regards the organization more as a nuisance than a threat. His belief that it has suffered a
serious setback in "its failure to establish bases in the occupied territories"
seems questionable. See note 13.

27. Quoted by Desmond Stewart in *Encounter*, June 1969.

28. Joseph Nasri Nasr, "Palestinians Want a New Elite," *New Outlook*,
Feb. 1969.

29. A spokesman for al-Fatah, quoted by the commentator on Arab affairs for *Davar*, Ehud Yaari, in "Al-Fatah's Political Thinking," *New Outlook*, Nov.–Dec. 1968.

30. Abbas Kelidar, "Shifts and Changes in the Arab World, *The World Today*, Dec. 1969.

31. According to the American political scientist Michael Hudson, in an unpublished paper ("The Palestinian Resistance Exists"), before the Six-Day War "al-Fatah numbered no more than 200–300 men; by the time of the Karamah battle it had increased to around 2,000; but in the three months following the Karamah battle it had burgeoned to 15,000." His account is based on three months of intensive investigation in Israel and the Arab states.

32. *Le Monde*, weekly selection, Feb. 20–26, 1969.

33. In 1965, the first year of intensive bombardment of South Vietnam, local recruitment of the Vietcong tripled, according to American military sources.

34. On these possibilities, see Geoffrey Kemp, *Arms and Security: The Egypt-Israel Case*, Adelphi Papers, no. 52, Institute for Strategic Studies, London, Oct. 1968.

35. Ibid.

36. Esco Foundation study, vol. 1, p. 583. See note 1. The original essay is entitled "The Jewish State and the Jewish Problem," p. 1897.

37. Quoted by Hudson. The spokesman is from the PFLP. See note 26.

38. Quoted in the *Bulletin* of the Council on Jewish-Arab Cooperation, Jan.–Feb. 1946.

39. Unpublished lecture by the Israeli scholar Dan Avni-Segré, Oxford, Jan. 1969.

40. 1925, 1927. Quoted in Cohen's study, pp. 231–2. Some regard such statements as hypocritical, but I think that is an error.

41. Perlmutter, op. cit., p. 28, commenting on the views of Yitzhak Tabenkin, expressed in an article of 1937.

42. George Zaninovich, *Development of Socialist Yugoslavia*, Johns Hopkins Press, Baltimore, 1968, p. 105.

43. See in particular the symposium to which I have already referred in *New Outlook*, March–April 1968.

44. Loutfy Al Khowly, "An International Arab-Jewish Front Against Imperialism and Racism," *Al-Tali'a (The Vanguard)*, April 1969. I am indebted to James Ansara and Dennis Kfoury for bringing this to my attention and providing a rough translation. The translators inform me that the word translated throughout as "racism" refers as well to religious and cultural domination, in a sense which has no exact English equivalent.

45. Yasir Arafat, *Le Monde*, weekly selection, Feb. 20–26, 1969.

46. It might also be argued that the many Fatah statements formulating the goal of a democratic Palestine with equal rights for all citizens are merely intended for propaganda purposes. Harkabi, who has undertaken an exhaustive analysis of Fatah material and whose view, as noted, is highly unsympathetic, concludes that "it should be acknowledged that

there is little difference between what they say for external and what is intended for home consumption."

47. The formulation of Haim Darin-Drabkin in the symposium referred to in note 43.

48. *Jewish Agency Digest*, Aug. 24, 1951. Quoted in John H. Davis, *The Evasive Peace*, John Murray, London, 1968, p. 84.

49. An exception is the Matzpen group, a socialist anti-Zionist party that numbers several hundred members.

50. For an evaluation of the situation, see Curt Casteyger, *Conflict and Tension in the Mediterranean*, Adelphi Papers, no. 51, Institute for Strategic Studies, London, Sept. 1968.

51. Safran, op. cit., p. 119.

52. For discussion of all these events, from 1948 to the present, see Safran and also Maxime Rodinson, *Israel and the Arabs*, Pantheon Books, New York, 1968.

53. For an Arab view, documented largely from Israel sources, see Sabri Jiryis, *The Arabs of Palestine*, The Institute for Palestine Studies, Beirut, 1968. It should be read by those who wish to see "the other side of the coin." An account from a pro-Israeli view is given by Ernest Stock, *From Conflict to Understanding*, Institute of Human Relations Press of the American Jewish Committee, New York, 1968. See also the excellent study by Don Peretz, *Israel and the Palestinian Arabs*, Middle East Institute, Washington, D.C., 1956. The extensive study *Israeli Society* by S. M. Eisenstadt, Basic Books, New York, 1967, devotes 18 out of 424 pages to the Arabs of Israel.

54. Esco Foundation study, vol. 2, p. 1124.

55. Ibid., p. 747.

56. Ibid., pp. 801–2.

57. Ibid., p. 621. The date was 1929.

58. He was murdered in 1933, it is generally assumed, by Revisionist assassins, not long after the conclusion of a conference that he had organized among Jewish and Arab leaders to consider problems of Jewish-Arab cooperation. The conference is discussed by Cohen (op. cit., pp. 235–7), who believes that it "might have opened a new chapter in Arab-Jewish relations in Palestine."

59. The best sources of information are Cohen's detailed and extensive book and the Esco Foundation study, the former considerably more sanguine as to the possibilities for success.

60. Esco Foundation study, vol. 1, pp. 485–6.

61. Cohen, op. cit., p. 351.

62. A contemporary account is given in the *Bulletin* of the Council on Jewish-Arab Cooperation, Nov. 1947.

63. The text is presented in Cohen, op. cit., p. 328. I follow his account.

Chapter 2

1. John Cooley, *Christian Science Monitor*, Oct. 24, 1970.
2. Quoted by Don Peretz, *Mid East*, June 1970.

Chapter 3

1. In *Maariv*, July 7, 1968; cited in a publication of the Israeli Group against Oppression, Jan. 1970.

2. Added, March 1971. John Cooley reports in the *Christian Science Monitor* (March 3, 1971) that thirty-five Syrian villages were "totally demolished by the Israeli Army after its final conquest of the Golan plateau" and that "thousands of new Israeli settlers . . . have moved into the new sites," where Arab villages were formerly located. Three settlements are paramilitary, about fifteen other civilian, he reports. On March 11, Ehud Yonay reports in the *Monitor* that the "master plan" calls for a population of 55,000–60,000 within ten years (including 10,000 Druze), in industrial and agricultural centers including seventeen cooperatives.

3. See E. Luttwak, *New Middle East*, Dec. 1971, for a useful survey.

4. Yigal Laviv, Tel Aviv, April 1972, in *Israel and Palestine*, no. 10, 5-1972, Paris; Peregrine Fellowes, *New Middle East*, May 1972.

5. *The Guardian* (Manchester, London), April 3, 1972.

6. Walter Schwarz, *The Guardian* (London), March 22, 1972.

7. "Truly something terrifying," *Ha'aretz*, March 22, 1972.

8. Jay Bushinsky, *Christian Science Monitor*, Aug. 21, 1971.

9. Michael Bruno, in I. Howe and C. Gershman, eds., *Israel, the Arabs and the Middle East*, Quadrangle-Bantam, New York, 1972.

10. Bushinsky, op. cit.

11. Cited in *The Arabs Under Israeli Occupation*, published by the Institute for Palestine Studies, Beirut, 1970.

12. *Yediot Ahronot*, May 23, 1971; TADMIT Newsletter, June 1, 1971.

13. David Hirst, *Manchester Guardian Weekly*, May 6, 1972.

14. "The claim that Israel was under the threat of destruction—'a bluff,'" *Ha'aretz*, March 13, 1972. General Ezer Weizmann, former heard of the Israeli air force, added his agreement, stating further that the remainder of the Sinai (Port Fuad, specifically) was not conquered only through oversight; *Ha'aretz*, March 20, 1972. For further details, see Amnon Kapeliouk, *Le Monde hebdomadaire*, June 8–14, 1972. He quotes also former army chief of staff Haim Bar-Lev in support of Peled and Weizmann, and states that "no serious argument has been advanced to refute the thesis of the three generals." The American press seems to have ignored this very

important discussion within Israel, apart from a report by John K. Cooley, *Christian Science Monitor*, July 17, 1972.

15. *Yediot Ahronot*, Feb. 2, 1972; TADMIT Newsletter, Feb. 15, 1972.

16. *Ha'aretz*, Dec. 5, 1971.

17. *Ha-Olam Ha-Ze*, in TADMIT Newsletter, March 15, 1972; *Israel and Palestine*, no. 10, 5-1972; "Robbery in Rafiah." *Information Bulletin* of the Israeli Communist Party, April 1972; also same journal, March 1972, citing several Israeli journals; Simha Flapan, *New Outlook*, March–April 1972; Peter Grose, *New York Times*, April 25, 1972.

18. Cited by Amnon Rubinstein, *Ha'aretz*, July 30, 1971; TADMIT Newsletter, Aug. 1, 1971.

19. *Al-Hamishmar*, Jan. 21, 1972; TADMIT Newsletter, Feb. 1, 1972.

20. Cited from the Jewish Telegraphic Agency Daily Bulletin, May 19, 1970, in *The Arabs Under Israeli Occupation*, 1970 (see note 11).

21. *New Outlook*, March–April 1972.

22. *Maariv*, Sept. 1971; TADMIT Newsletter, Oct. 1, 1971.

23. In Howe and Gershman, eds., op. cit.

24. Joachim Prinz, *Wir Juden*, Berlin, 1934, pp. 150–57.

25. See B. Shefi, "Israel: The Jewish Religion Abused," *Middle East International*, Dec. 1971, for some examples cited from judicial opinions and other sources.

26. See, e.g., C. Gershman, *Commentary*, Aug. 1970.

27. From the editors' introduction to Howe and Gershman, op. cit., with "Israel" replaced by "India." The problems involved in "survival of a democratic Israel" are never mentioned. It is merely asserted that "the survival of Israel is a major priority for everyone who cares about democracy." It is tacitly assumed that the only alternatives are the survival of Israel or the destruction of Israel. If correct, then the former would be a major priority for any decent person. But there are other alternatives: namely, the evolution of Israel in a way that will enable it to be a true democracy, hence not (except possibly in symbolic respects alone) a Jewish state, and a variety of possible arrangements, some mentioned earlier, in the former Mandate Palestine.

Chapter 4

1. Anthony McDermott, *Middle East International*, Sept. 1973. United States and Israeli intelligence insisted that there was virtually no chance of an Arab attack, according to Henry Kissinger. Benjamin Welles, *Christian Science Monitor*, Oct. 29, 1973.

2. *Yediot Ahronot*, July 26, 1973.

3. John Cooley, *Christian Science Monitor*, Oct. 27, 1973.

4. David Hirst, *Guardian Weekly* (Manchester, London), Oct. 20, 1973.

5. Joseph Fitchett, *Christian Science Monitor*, Oct. 13, 1973.

6. William Tuohy, *Los Angeles Times–Boston Globe*, Oct. 26, 1973.

7. John Finney, *New York Times*, Oct. 17, 1973; Dana Adams Schmidt, *Christian Science Monitor*, Oct. 26, 1973.

8. Dana Adams Schmidt, *Christian Science Monitor*, Oct. 27, 1973. "Under questioning, Mr. Schlesinger acknowledged that the alert of the Soviet airborne forces had been ordered five or six days ago and was known by United States officials before yesterday's crisis developed" (John Finney, *New York Times*, Oct. 27, 1973).

9. Joseph Fitchett, *Christian Science Monitor*, Oct. 16, 13, 1973.

10. *Ha'aretz*, July 22, 1973.

11. Cf. chapter 3, pp. 91–92, 100; introduction, pp. 15–16.

12. *Ha'aretz*, Sept. 26, 1973. Translated in *Israleft*, no. 25, Oct. 2, 1973. P.O. Box 9013, Jerusalem.

13. Joseph Fitchett, *Christian Science Monitor*, Oct. 16, 1973.

14. Warren Young, *New Outlook*, Jan. 1970.

15. A recent version appeared in the London *Times*, Feb. 3, 1973. The text is reproduced in IDOC, *Controversy in the Middle East*, Sept. 1973. A possible general settlement of this sort is outlined by Michel Tatu, *Le Monde*, Oct. 23, 1973.

16. See the comments by Michael Brecher, Canadian specialist in Israeli foreign policy, in an interview in *New Outlook*, June 1973. He speaks of the "retreat from reason" and the "growing weight being given to mystic identities and irredentist aspirations in government decisions," the "quasi-religious roots" of the new expansionism and the "revival of identification with mystic roots of a regenerated Jewish nation."

17. Drew Middleton, *New York Times*, Oct. 17, 1973.

Chapter 5

1. Papers submitted to, or resulting from, the conference, and some others, appear in Mordecai S. Chertoff, ed., *The New Left and the Jews*, Pitman, New York, 1971. The timing of the conference was appropriate, in that the New Left had no organized existence or expression after this time.

2. Many examples to the contrary are cited in my paper, "Israel and the New Left," in Chertoff, ed., op. cit. Note that what is at issue is Glazer's categorical judgment, not the fact (also illustrated in my review) that there are cases to which his characterization applies. In my review, I barely mentioned "Old Left" groups or "the Black Liberation movement, whose attitudes toward the Middle East must be interpreted in terms of domestic American problems and developments." But I did comment on the zeal with which some American Zionist sociologists seek out statements in obscure periodicals to "prove" that the black groups are anti-Semitic, and I

noted the exaggerated conclusions that are drawn as to the significance of these instances. One might almost think, reading some of these analyses, that American Jews are standing at the gates of the crematoria, barely fending off the Black Panthers. I might add that my personal contacts with black groups that are alleged to be anti-Semitic, while not very extensive, are surely far more extensive than is the case for those who see Nazis around every corner. I have yet to see any instances of anti-Semitism or even antiwhite "reverse racism," even at moments of considerable crisis and tension—for example, at the public funeral of Fred Hampton and Mark Clark. Surely there is nothing that compares with what I experienced personally growing up in a pure white (but non-Jewish) neighborhood in suburban Philadelphia, and nothing that compares with what one would have found at elite universities not too many years ago.

3. Ibid.

4. "The Campus Left and Israel," *New York Times*, Op-Ed page, March 13, 1971. Reprinted in Irving Howe and Carl Gershman, *Israel, the Arabs, and the Middle East*, Bantam Books, New York, 1972.

5. "Thinking the Unthinkable About Israel: A Personal Statement," *New York* Magazine, Dec. 24, 1973.

6. Or in his claim that "self-hatred is becoming a major problem for the American Jewish community." Cf. also note 24. I discuss some of Lipset's examples of "black anti-Semitism" in "Israel and the New Left."

7. People who were active in the New Left in the 1960s will be as interested as Stone himself to learn that he was one of the spokesmen for the New Left.

8. *Boston Globe*, Feb. 12–13, 1970.

9. John Roche, *Baltimore News-American*, Nov. 23, 1973. For some examples of Roche's scholarly analysis of the war in Vietnam, see my *For Reasons of State*, Pantheon Books, New York, 1973, p. 137.

10. Speech delivered July 31, 1972. Reprinted in *Congress Bi-Weekly*, March 30, 1973.

11. Cf. the analyses by Salpeter and Talmon cited in the introduction, pp. 16, 23.

12. The statements by Eban and Meir appear in Pierre Rondot, "Les Palestiniens et la négociation," *Le Monde diplomatique*, Dec. 1973, citing earlier reports in *Le Monde*.

13. What these attitudes actually were I have discussed extensively elsewhere, most recently in *For Reasons of State* and (with Edward S. Herman) *Counterrevolutionary Violence: Bloodbaths in Fact and Propaganda*, Warner Modular, Andover, Mass., 1973. Cf. also note 38.

14. The response to Watergate is unprincipled in many respects. Outrage has been caused more by the choice of enemies than the choice of means. See my articles "The Watergate Illusion," *New York Review*, Sept. 20, 1973; "The President and the Presidency," *Liberation*, Nov. 1973. As an

illustration, consider the following report of a news conference held by Elliot Richardson: "The 'fatal flaw' of the Nixon administration—not yet
corrected—is the proclivity of the White House to perceive critics and opposition as 'enemies' and the willingness to 'adopt tactics used against an
enemy' in handling such criticism" (Guy Halverson, *Christian Science Monitor*, Jan. 23, 1974). It is of little concern to Richardson or the mass media
when these tactics, or worse, are used against legitimate enemies of the
state. Thus, the FBI was recently compelled by court order to release a May
1968 directive by J. Edgar Hoover initiating a program "to expose, disrupt,
and otherwise neutralize the activities of the various New Left organizations, their leadership, and adherents" and to "frustrate every effort of these
groups and individuals to consolidate their forces or to recruit new or
youthful adherents," if necessary "disrupting the organized activity of these
groups" and "capitaliz[ing] upon organizational and personal conflicts of
their leadership." This program represents a use of the political police to
attack dissent that goes well beyond anything exposed in the Watergate
investigations, but one will find virtually no comment in the liberal press.

15. For discussion of what the impact has been in the case of Vietnam,
and for a possible explanation of the specific contributions of the technical intelligentsia, see my *For Reasons of State*, introduction and chapter 1;
also my "Science and Ideology," *Jawaharlal Nehru Memorial Lectures,
1967–1972*, New Delhi, 1973.

16. For some of the remarkable successes of the past, see my *American
Power and the New Mandarins*, Pantheon, New York, 1969, particularly
chapters 1 and 6; also, my *Problems of Knowledge and Freedom*, Pantheon,
New York, 1971, chapter 2; "American Historians as 'Experts in Legitima-
tion,'" *Social Scientist*, New Delhi, Feb. 1973; and the references of note 13.
For some of the contributions of the press as an agency of state propaganda,
see my "Reporting Indochina: The News Media and the Legitimation of
Lies," *Social Policy*, Sept.–Oct., 1973.

17. Later, Stone achieved respectability and even some acclaim. This
was after general opinion had turned against the war as a failed venture
(and also after Stone had suspended regular publication of his *Weekly*).

18. The text appears in *American Report*, Oct. 29, 1973.

19. Virtually unnoticed, to be more precise. A letter in the Marxist-
Leninist *Guardian*, New York, Jan. 30, 1974, by two people who attended
the conference that Berrigan addressed, states that some people in the audience "were at the point of leaving because he attacked the Arabs and
Palestinians too much."

20. The anti-Arab bias of the American press (with rare exceptions—
notably, the *Christian Science Monitor*) is notorious. Arabs are regularly portrayed as sadistic terrorists. Racist caricatures are not uncommon. Furthermore, atrocities committed against them often pass without notice. Thus,
there has been much justifiable outrage over the savage treatment of Israeli

prisoners captured by the Syrians, many of whom are reported to have been tortured or murdered (see, e.g., William Novak, *New York Times*, Op-Ed, Jan. 26, 1974). Less is heard in the United States of the 700 civilians reported killed in the Israeli bombing of Damascus (David Hirst, *Guardian Weekly*, Manchester-London, Jan. 26, 1974), or the blocking by Israeli troops of a Red Cross convoy bringing urgently needed medical supplies to Suez—"20 or 30 men will die tonight [in the Suez hospital] because the Israelis won't let us through," according to the Swiss doctor leading the convoy (UPI, *International Herald Tribune*, Nov. 12, 1973; reprinted in *Middle East International*, Dec. 1973). This is not the first such report. After the Six-Day War, Israel reportedly blocked a Red Cross rescue operation for five days, while thousands of Egyptian soldiers died in the Sinai desert (London *Times*, June 15, 1967; cited in *Who Are the Terrorists?* Institute for Palestine Studies, Beirut, 1972, a detailed factual record reversing the general bias of American reports); also Kennett Love, *Suez*, McGraw-Hill, New York, 1969, p. 689. Bernard Avishai, an Israeli dove, writes in *New York Review* (Jan. 24, 1974) that although the Israeli government now "recognizes that no settlement can be possible without accommodating sensible Palestinian national demands, it understandably cannot contrive the amnesia to overlook Arafat's murderous escapades." Such escapades were real enough, but it is well to recall that the Palestinians also have a slight problem of "contriving amnesia" on this score. See, for example, note 46.

21. *American Report*, Nov. 12, 1973.

22. Henry L. Feingold, *The Politics of Rescue*, Rutgers University Press, New Brunswick, N.J., 1970, pp. 300–1. Further inquiry into this matter indicates that there may be some ugly stories buried here. For one report, see my article "Daniel in the Lion's Den: Berrigan and His Critics," *Liberation*, Feb. 1974, from which much of this discussion of the response to Berrigan's address is taken.

23. See his essay "The Wordless Wish: From Citizens to Refugees," in Ibrahim Abu-Lughod, ed., *The Transformation of Palestine*, Northwestern University Press, Evanston, Ill., 1971.

24. I cited a few examples in my "Israel and the New Left." I also noted that Lipset is wrong in still another of his charges against the New Left, that it has been unaware of the Kibbutz. The charge might be leveled with greater accuracy against Lipset's generation of socialists.

25. Compare the rather similar remarks in Jon Kimche, *There Could Have Been Peace*, Dial Press, New York, 1973, pp. 274–6.

26. *Maariv*, Nov. 26, 1973.

27. See note 5.

28. Cf. chapter 3, pp. 101–2.

29. Sabri Jiryis, *The Arabs in Israel*, The Institute for Palestine Studies, Beirut, 1968, pp. 4, 35. To be accurate, certain provisions of the Emergency Regulations have indeed been repealed, according to Jiryis, whose books

provide a detailed account of these laws and their application in practice: "At the very moment of the establishment of Israel, on the evening of May 14, 1948, after the Declaration of the Establishment of the State had been read, the Provisional Council of State immediately decided to repeal certain articles of the Regulations. These were the articles relative to the Zionist institutions in Palestine, those which dealt with methods of expropriating and confiscating land and those which restricted Jewish immigration into the country. The rest were left unchanged." Sabri Jiryis, *Democratic Freedoms in Israel*, Institute for Palestine Studies, Beirut, 1972, pp. 29–30.

30. Haifa District Court, Criminal Record 64/73, pp. 541–5. Substantial parts of the court record are reprinted in *Mishpatam shel: Rami Livneh, Meli Lerman* (*Siah* publication, Sept. 14, 1973; P.O. Box 8253, Jerusalem). Livneh was sentenced to ten years under a paragraph of the criminal code that states that "anyone who knowingly makes contact with a [foreign] agent without a legitimate explanation may be sentenced to 15 years in prison." The court held that "the contention that the purpose [of the contact] was only exchange of political ideas of the two organizations does not serve as a legitimate explanation" (p. 503; no evidence was presented showing that the contact went beyond exchange of political ideas). This paragraph of the criminal code is a 1967 revision of a 1955 law that related such contact to transfer of official secrets. The logic of the revision is that contact alone is a crime, and the court's decision implies that political discussions with foreign agents are also a crime. Professor Teodor Shanin, testifying for the defense, observed that punishment for expression of revolutionary ideas (as is implicit in the full charge) is unknown outside of such states as Greece, Spain, and Portugal. Perhaps one might argue that under present circumstances Israel must resort to the Draconian measures legitimized by the court decision. I disagree, but that is not the question at issue here. Rather, the point is that this remarkable court decision alone suffices to refute Howe's contention. One might also note that the court decision would appear to rule illegal any contacts between Israelis and Palestinians for the purpose of exchanging ideas on possible resolution of the conflict—in particular, any discussions relating to binational arrangements.

31. Jiryis, *The Arabs in Israel*, p. 134. The two books by Jiryis give a detailed record of these events, and discuss the program of the group.

32. Franz Neumann, *Behemoth*, Victor Gollancz, London, 1943, p. 29.

33. Jiryis, *Democratic Freedoms in Israel*, pp. 58, 94, 95.

34. *Christian Science Monitor*, Dec. 31, 1973. The college was reopened a few weeks later.

35. *Yediot Ahronot*, cited in *Israleft*, Dec. 30, 1973.

36. Cf. chapter 3, section II, for a few examples.

37. The socialist structures of the Yishuv prior to the establishment of the State of Israel were, indeed, remarkable in many respects, and they

have retained their vigor and, in my opinion, their promise. But it is quite untrue that Israel is progressing toward socialism. There has been a relative decline in the importance of the genuine socialist institutions as the state has developed. It may be true that (apart from the fundamental discriminatory system and the theocratic intrusions on personal freedom) Israel provides about as good a model as we have for democratic socialism, but if so, this is, I am afraid, primarily a comment on existing models.

38. *Dissent,* Summer 1964. For discussion, see Bertrand Russell, *War Crimes in Vietnam,* Monthly Review Press, New York, 1967. To the editors of *Dissent,* withdrawal seemed as inhumane as a war of attrition because it would leave the country under communist control "and there would almost certainly follow a slaughter in the South of all those . . . who have fought against the Communists." They seemed oblivious to the likely consequences of a United States–Saigon victory, though the story of Diem's murderous assault on the opposition (with American backing) in the post-1954 period was already well known. See my *For Reasons of State* for some discussion. Particularly striking is the unspoken assumption that the United States has the authority to intervene in Vietnam to impose its concept of "humanity." To support their position in this regard, some democratic socialists have found it necessary to credit American propaganda on policies in North Vietnam even after these had been exposed as fabrications. For a striking example, again from *Dissent,* see *Counterrevolutionary Violence,* note 201.

39. *Yediot Ahronot,* Dec. 26, 1973, cited in *Israleft,* Jan. 15, 1974. Dayan was particularly incensed by Jacob Talmon's articles cited in the introduction, note 51. Shulamit Har-Even retorted aptly: "Professor Jacob Talmon in his famous article in *Ha'aretz* acted as a historian. Not as a battalion commander, not as a political commissar, and not as a defense minister, but as a historian. As such, he is not obliged to find golden rays of light joyfully playing in every act of ministers" (*Ha'aretz,* Dec. 31, 1973, cited in *Israleft,* Jan. 15, 1974).

40. Kimche, op. cit., p. 243.

41. *Ha'aretz,* Nov. 21, 1973, cited in *Jewish Liberation Information Service,* P.O. Box 7557, Jerusalem.

42. Cited in John K. Cooley, *Green March, Black September,* Frank Cass, London, 1973, p. 162, from *Ha'aretz,* March 20, 29; my emphasis. Cooley gives extensive quotes. Cf. Chapter 3, section II, note 14, for further discussion.

43. Often, for expansionism. Cf. the remarks of Peled and Bar-Zohar, cited in the introduction, pp. 23–26.

44. See chapter 3, section II, p. 107.

45. See introduction, p. 19; chapter 3, section I, p. 85; this chapter, p. 132.

46. *Newsletter* of Ha'olam Haze–Koah Hadash (New Force Party), Feb. 8, 1973, represented at the time in the Knesset by Uri Avneri. A detailed account of the incident, with extensive quotes from Israeli court records, appears in Jiryis, *The Arabs in Israel*, ch. 3. The perpetrators of the massacre did not go unpunished. Three soldiers were given prison sentences; a series of pardons reduced the longest to just over a year. The officer in charge was found guilty of a "merely technical" error and fined one Israeli piaster. A few months after his release, Lieutenant Joubrael Dahan, who had been sentenced for the murder of forty-three unarmed Arab men, women, and children, was appointed by the municipality of Ramle as "Officer responsible for Arab affairs in the city." Americans will find all of this rather familiar.

47. El-Aref was a major source for Kimche (op. cit.). His findings are presented in a report by Dr. Israel Shahak. Shahak's courageous work as chairman of the Israeli League for Human and Civil Rights deserves special comment—as does the response to it, both in Israel and here. In November 1972, some two hundred people appeared at a meeting of this small civil rights group, insisted on being registered as members, took over the meeting, and forced out the leadership. The Israeli courts, quite properly, declared the results of the meeting null and void (Judge Lovenberg, Nov. 26, 1972). The Labor Party (Youth Department) then circulated a leaflet headed "internal, not to be published," requesting party members to join the league as a "state duty . . . for the purpose of enabling our party to have a predominant influence in the League . . . ," offering to pay membership dues. There was no mention of civil liberties in this call. Judge Lovenberg ruled (April 8, 1973) that the League must accept mass membership organized in this fashion, while reaffirming his earlier ruling. Obviously, no open organization can survive such tactics on the part of the dominant political party.

On the basis of these events, the New York-based International League for Human Rights, in a most astonishing decision, suspended the Israeli League. In April 1973, Shahak visited the United States. In an interview with the *Boston Globe* (April 18), he identified himself, quite accurately, as chairman of the Israeli League. This interview, dealing with topics rarely discussed here, elicited an abusive response from Harvard law professor Alan Dershowitz, who claimed, among other falsehoods, that Shahak "was overwhelmingly defeated for re-election" as chairman in November 1970 [*sic*] and that the courts had "ruled that the election was legal and that Shahak had been validly defeated" (*Globe*, April 29, May 25; see also my responses, May 17, June 5, citing the court records). The incident illustrates again the lengths to which American Zionists will go in their efforts to silence discussion and discredit political opponents. Dershowitz offered no factual evidence at any point. His assertions are directly refuted by the court records, which are not, of course, normal reading fare here. Still more interesting was Dershowitz's reaction when the Labor Party tactics were brought to his attention. He wrote that he saw nothing wrong with the Labor Party effort to take over the League (May 25). One can imagine his reaction if the Watergate investigations were to reveal a comparable attempt by the Republican Party to take over the ACLU. Dershowitz has done admirable work in defense of civil rights in the United States, but—typically—all standards disappear when the scene shifts to Israel.

48. Hans J. Morgenthau, "The Geopolitics of Israel's Survival," *New Leader*, Dec. 24, 1973. Morgenthau's dire prognosis provides the framework for Howe's "Thinking the Unthinkable About Israel."

49. *Ha'aretz*, Dec. 22, 1967. A lengthy excerpt appears in Arie Bober, ed., *The Other Israel*, Doubleday Anchor Books, New York, 1972, pp. 79–80. Cf. also references of note 42.

50. Reports in the Israeli press suggest that this perception is quite accurate. Thus Yehudit Winkler describes a meeting between a delegation of the APPME and Michael Elitsur, head of the Office of North American Affairs of the Israeli Foreign Office, in which Elitsur explained his views on United States–Soviet détente and the Middle East. Within days, she reports, the APPME published material in the United States reflecting these views (*Ha'aretz*, Dec. 13, 1973). One can have no objection to a group of Americans organizing themselves for one or another purpose, but it is unfortunate—and indicative of the actual situation in the United States—that the one academic group organized to deal with "peace in the Middle East" should serve as a channel for the expression of this particular narrow range of views.

51. As far as I know, Israel is the only country to which American citizens can give tax-free contributions, thus imposing on others a subsidy to Israel, in addition to the direct official aid and loans.

Chapter 6

1. I have written about these matters often since the 1967 war, most recently in *World Orders Old and New*, Columbia University Press, New York, 1994; extended in 1996 with an epilogue carrying the account through Oslo II, the 1996 Israeli attack on Lebanon, and the May 1996 Israeli elections. Where not cited, sources can be found there.

2. In 1995, Venezuela edged out Saudi Arabia for the first time since the 1970s; Allanna Sullivan, *Wall Street Journal*, Jan. 3, 1996. On U.S.-Venezuela relations, which go well beyond oil, see Stephen Rabe, *The Road to OPEC*, University of Texas Press, Austin, 1982.

3. For production data, see David Painter, *Oil and the American Century*, Johns Hopkins University Press, Baltimore, 1986, p. 218. In 1925, the

United States produced over 71 percent of the world's oil, the Caribbean 14 percent. In 1965, the U.S. share was over 27 percent, almost twice that of the next producer (the USSR; Venezuela third).

4. The operative principle was articulated by the State Department in 1944 in a memorandum called "Petroleum Policy of the United States." The United States then dominated Western Hemisphere production, which was to remain the largest in the world for another quarter century. That system must remain closed, the memorandum declared, while the rest of the world must be open. U.S. policy "would involve the preservation of the absolute position presently obtaining, and therefore vigilant protection of existing concessions in United States hands coupled with insistence upon the Open Door principle of equal opportunity for United States companies in new areas." U.S. Department of State, "Petroleum Policy of the United States (1944). Cited by Gabriel Kolko, *Politics of War*, Random House, New York, 1968, pp. 302f.

5. Rabe, op. cit. Lansing-Wilson cited by Gabriel Kolko, *Main Currents in American History*, Pantheon, New York, 1984, p. 47.

6. August, March 1945; William Roger Louis, *The British Empire in the Middle East: 1945–1951*, Oxford University Press, Oxford, 1984, pp. 231, 191. For a recent review of U.S. policies in the region, with special focus on Lebanon (important in large part as a transit point for oil), see Irene Gendzier, *Notes from the Minefield*, Columbia University Press, New York, 1997.

7. David E. Sanger, "U.S. Won't Offer Trade Testimony on Cuba Embargo," *New York Times*, Feb. 21, 1997, p. A1.

8. Roland deLigny, "World Court Denounces U.S. Support for Contras," Associated Press, June 27, 1986.

9. Jules Kagian, *Middle East International*, Oct. 21, 1994.

10. Gerald Haines, *The Americanization of Brazil*, Scholarly Resources, Wilmington, Del., 1989. Gendzier, op. cit., 41, citing treasurer Leo Welch.

11. *Fortune*, Jan. 1948. The specific reference is to the aircraft industry, today the leading "civilian" exporter thanks to massive public subsidy over the years, but it was recognized that this is a model for "the future shape of the U.S. economy" quite generally. For more on the matter, see Chomsky, *World Orders Old and New*, chap. 2.

12. The first extensive work on the topic, still unequaled, is Gabriel Kolko, *Politics of War*. For general review using more recent sources as well, see my *Deterring Democracy*, extended edition, Vintage, Hill & Wang, New York, 1992, chap. 11.

13. See Michael Leffler, *A Preponderance of Power*, Stanford University Press, Stanford, 1992, p. 71; Sallie Pisani, *The CIA and the Marshall Plan*, University Press of Kansas, Lawrence, 1991, pp. 106–7.

14. *Foreign Relations of the United States, 1948*, vol. 3. NSC 1/3, March 8, 1948, pp. 775f.; Kennan, pp. 848f., U.S. Government Printing Office, Washington, D.C.

15. For ample illustration, see Edward Herman, *The Real Terror Network*, South End, Boston, 1982; my *Pirates and Emperors, Old and New: International Terrorism in the Real World*, South End Press, Cambridge, Mass., 2002; Alexander George, ed., *Western State Terrorism*, Polity, London, 1991. On oil companies and Italy, John Blair, *Control of Oil*, Pantheon, New York, 1976, p. 94f.

16. Gendzier, op. cit., 24f. Robert McMahon, *The Cold War on the Periphery*, Columbia University Press, New York, 1994, p. 221.

17. From State Department records, expressing concerns over the "philosophy of the new nationalism" sweeping Latin America, safely interred at a February 1945 hemispheric conference where the United States imposed its Economic Charter of the Americas, which guaranteed an end to economic nationalism "in all its forms." See David Green, *The Containment of Latin America: A History of the Myths and Realities of the Good Neighbor Policy*, Quadrangle, Chicago, 1971, 7: 2. For many examples, including these, see my *Year 501*, South End, Boston, 1993, chaps. 2, 7; and sources cited.

18. *Central America Report* (Guatemala), Feb. 4, 1994. See my *Deterring Democracy*, chaps. 5, 6.

19. In the United States, this is invariably termed "humanitarian aid," another expression of the disdain of the intellectual culture for international law when it interferes with state violence. The explicit determination of the World Court that all such aid was military, not humanitarian, was considered unworthy even of report.

20. The United States has been far in the lead in vetoing Security Council resolutions since the UN fell out of control with decolonization; the UK is second, France a distant third. For fact and propaganda on these matters, see *Deterring Democracy*, chap. 6.5.

21. Peter James Spielmann, "U.S. Says It Acted in Self-Defense in Panama," *Associated Press*, Dec. 20, 1989.

22. Chomsky, *Deterring Democracy*, chaps. 1, 3, 5, 6, afterword.

23. *National Security Strategy of the United States*, the White House, March 1990. See *Deterring Democracy*, chap. 1, for excerpts.

24. For a particularly clear acknowledgment, see Christopher Layne (Cato Institute) and Benjamin Schwarz (Rand), *Foreign Policy*, Fall 1993.

25. Frank Costigliola, in Thomas Paterson, ed., *Kennedy's Quest for Victory*, Oxford University Press, Oxford, 1989; the reference is presumably to Dean Acheson.

26. John Balfour, British Embassy in Washington, to Bevin, Aug. 9, 1945; Bevin, Nov. 8, 1945. Cited by Mark Curtis, *Ambiguities of Power*, Zed, London, 1995, pp. 18, 23.

27. Christopher Thorne, *The Issue of War*, Oxford University Press, Oxford, 1985, pp. 225, 211. On the contempt for England and Europe generally, see Frank Costigliola, "Kennedy and the Failure to Consult," *Political Science Quarterly*, Spring 1995.

28. William Stivers, *Supremacy and Oil*, Cornell University Press, Ithaca, N.Y., 1982, pp. 28, 34; Stivers, *America's Confrontation with Revolutionary Change in the Middle East*, St. Martin's, New York, 1986, pp. 20f. 1946; Louis, op. cit., p. 353.

29. Diane Kunz, *Butter and Guns: America's Cold War Economic Diplomacy*, Free Press, New York, 1997, pp. 226, 88. Nadav Safran, *Israel: The Embattled Ally*, Harvard University Press, Cambridge, 1978, pp. 576, 110. Under Carter, U.S. aid to Israel rose to about half of total aid. Increasingly over the years, the official figures are greatly underestimated because of failure to include prepayment, forgiven loans, and other devices.

30. See my article in *Le Monde diplomatique*, April 1977; reprinted in *Towards a New Cold War*, Pantheon, New York, 1982, chap. 11.

31. Keegan quoted by Richard Hudson, *Wall Street Journal*, Feb. 5, 1991; Lloyd George by V.G. Kiernan, *European Empires from Conquest to Collapse*, Fontana, London, 1982, p. 200. On Churchill's enthusiasm for the use of "poisoned gas against uncivilised tribes" (specifically Kurds and Afghans, but "recalcitrant Arabs" generally), see Andy Thomas, *Effects of Chemical Warfare*, Stockholm International Peace Research Institute (SIPRI), Taylor & Francis, London, 1985, chap. 2. For quotes, see my *Turning the Tide*, South End, Boston, 1985, p. 126; *Deterring Democracy*, chap. 6.1.

32. Irving Kristol, *Wall Street Journal*, Dec. 13, 1973.

33. Walter Laqueur, *New York Times Magazine*, Dec. 16, 1973.

34. Emma Rothschild, "Is It Time to End Food for Peace?" *New York Times Magazine*, March 13, 1977.

35. Ruth Wisse, *Commentary*, May 1988; Janet Tassel, "Mame-Loshn at Harvard," *Harvard Magazine*, July/Aug. 1997. Martin Peretz, interview in *Ha'aretz*, June 4, 1982.

36. For a broader sample, see my *Necessary Illusions*, South End, Boston, 1989, pp. 315f.; *Towards a New Cold War*, chap. 8.

37. Daniel B. Schirmer, *Fidel Ramos: The Pentagon's Philippine Friend 1992–1997*, Friends of the Filipino People, Cambridge, Mass., 1997.

38. Komer cited by Melvyn Leffler, *Diplomatic History*, vol. 7, 1983, pp. 245f. Dulles/Eisenhower cited by Irwin Wall, *Diplomatic History*, Fall 1994, from the Eisenhower library. *Foreign Relations of the United States, 1958–1960*, vol. 27, *Indonesia*, U.S. Government Printing Office, Washington, D.C., 1994, April 8 and Aug. 12, 1958; quotes are from U.S. Jakarta embassy cables, reporting Indonesian government conclusions, endorsed by the Joint Chiefs of Staff the same day. On Indonesia, see my *Powers and Prospects: Reflections on Human Nature and the Social Order*, South End, Boston, 1996, chap. 7, and sources cited; and on the reaction to the slaughter, *Year 501*, chap. 5. North African policy, *Foreign Relations of the United States, 1947*, vol. 5, p. 688, cited by Curtis, op. cit., p. 21. On the Middle East at the time, see particularly Gendzier, op. cit.

39. Kunz, op. cit., p. 237.

40. Albert Cavallo, "What Price Oil?" *Proceedings*, 17th Annual Wind Energy Conference, July 1995, Mechanical Engineering Publications, London, 1995.

41. Wilbur Edel, "Diplomatic History—State Department Style," *Political Science Quarterly* 106, no. 4 (1991/2).

42. For further elaboration, quotes, and sources on what follows, see Chomsky, *Deterring Democracy*, chap. 6. See also my *World Orders Old and New*, chap. 3; Gendzier, op. cit.

43. For sources and background discussion, see Chomsky, *World Orders Old and New*, pp. 79, 201ff.

44. Telegram no. 1979, July 19, 1958, to Prime Minister from Secretary of State, from Washington; File FO 371/132 779. "Future Policy in the Persian Gulf," Jan. 15, 1958, FO 371/132 778.

45. Undated sections of NSC 5801/1, "Current Policy Issues" on relations to Nasser-led Arab Nationalism, apparently mid-1958; NSC 5820/1, Nov. 4, 1958. See also Chomsky, *Deterring Democracy*, pp. 53ff; Chomsky, *Fateful Triangle: The United States, Israel, and the Palestinians*, updated ed., South End Press, Cambridge, Mass., 1999, chapter 2. See also Kirsten Cale, "'Ruthlessly to Intervene,'" *Living Marxism* (London), Nov. 1990; Irene Gendzier, "The Way They Saw It Then," ms., Nov. 1990.

46. National Security Council Memorandum 5801/1, "Statement by the National Security Council of Long-Range U.S. Policy toward the Near East," January 24, 1958, *Foreign Relations of the United States, 1958–1960*, vol. 12 (*Near East Region; Iraq; Iran; Arabian Peninsula*), U.S. Government Printing Office, Washington, D.C., 1993, pp. 17–32. See also "Issues Arising out of the Situation in the Near East," July 29, 1958, *Foreign Relations of the United States, 1958–1960*, pp. 114–24.

47. On Southeast Asia, see my *For Reasons of State*, Pantheon, New York, 1973, chap. 1; *Rethinking Camelot*, South End, Boston, 1993. For Latin America the point is obvious. Britain's analysis was much the same throughout the Third World. See Curtis, op. cit.

48. The statement continues: "the demise of the Soviet Union left the United States as the single power broker in the region and as such interested in its stability and prosperity." The United States is indeed interested in the "stability" of the region, in the technical sense of the term (meaning subordination to U.S. power) but is no more interested in its "prosperity" than its European predecessors, as policy demonstrates beyond serious doubt. Boas Evron, introduction to *Jewish State or Israeli Nation?* Indiana University Press, Bloomington, 1995.

49. Shlomo Gazit, *Yediot Ahronot*, April 27, 1992, cited and translated by Israel Shahak, *Middle East International*, March 19, 1993.

50. For some discussion, see my *Fateful Triangle*.

51. For references and further details, see Chomsky, *Towards a New Cold War*, chapter 7, and Chomsky, *Fateful Triangle*, chapter 2.

52. *Fateful Triangle*, pp. 457f. On the aftermath, see John Marshall, Peter Dale Scott, and Jane Hunter, *The Iran–Contra Connection*, South End, Boston, 1987; and my *Culture of Terrorism*, South End, Boston, 1988. Note that there were no hostages when the arms sales to Iran via Israel began, so it cannot have been an "arms for hostage" deal, as the affair is conventionally interpreted, picking it up at a later stage. Arming the military is a standard device for overthrowing a government, often successful, as in Sukarno's Indonesia and Allende's Chile, to mention two cases that might have been models for the Iran operation.

53. See testimony of Assistant Secretary of Defense Edward Gnehm, March 1, 1989, to House Subcommittee on Europe and the Middle East; Dore Gold, press briefing, Jerusalem, March 9, 1989; Dore Gold, *America, the Gulf, and Israel*, Westview, Boulder, Colo., 1988. Reported in Media Analysis Center *Backgrounder* no. 255, Jerusalem, March 1989. Gnehm testified that over half of the U.S. Foreign Weapons Evaluation budget was devoted to Israeli products, designed and developed in cooperation with the U.S. military industry.

54. For specific details and references, see sources already cited; see also Naseer Aruri, *The Obstruction of Peace*, Common Courage, Monroe, Maine, 1995; Norman Finkelstein, *Image and Reality in the Israel-Palestine Conflict*, Verso, London, 1995; Donald Neff, *Fallen Pillars*, Institute for Palestine Studies, Washington, 1995, among others.

55. See William B. Quandt, *Peace Process: American Diplomacy and the Arab–Israeli Conflict Since 1967*, rev. ed., University of California Press, Berkeley, 2001, appendix B: Joint U.S.–USSR Working Paper, Fundamental Principles (The Rogers Plan), October 28, 1969.

56. John Norton Moore, ed., *The Arab–Israeli Conflict*, Princeton University Press, Princeton, N.J., 1974, 3: 1103–11.

57. Yitzhak Rabin, *The Rabin Memoirs*, expanded ed., University of California Press, Berkleley, 1996, pp. 192f.

58. Yossi Beilin, *Mehiro shel Ihud*, Revivim, 1985, pp. 118f., 155.

59. *Ha'aretz*, March 29, 1972, cited by John Cooley, *Green March, Black September*, Frank Cass, London, 1973, p. 162.

60. Haim Bar-Lev, *Ot*, March 9, 1972, cited by Amnon Kapeliouk, *Le Monde diplomatique*, Oct. 1977. Amos Elon, *Ha'aretz*, Nov. 13, 1981; the occasion was the "emotional and angry" reaction of the government to the Saudi peace plan of 1981, which "threatened Israel's very existence," Labor Party chairman Shimon Peres wrote (*Ha'aretz*, Aug. 10, 1981)—by calling for diplomatic settlement. In the *New York Times* today, criticizing Arab intellectuals for lack of support for the peace process, Elon writes that Sadat "was not yet ready to make peace" with Israel in 1972 and attacked

the "defeatists" who called for a settlement; *New York Times Magazine*, May 11, 1997.

61. See my *Fateful Triangle* and *Pirates and Emperors*; Finkelstein, op. cit. For a brief review, see *World Orders Old and New*, chap. 2.

62. For a rare discussion, see my review of his memoirs, reprinted in *Towards a New Cold War*; see also David Korn, *Stalemate*, Westview, Boulder, Colo., 1992.

63. The PLO representative at the UN condemned the United States for blocking this two-state plan. See *Towards a New Cold War*, p. 430. Haim Herzog, *Jerusalem Post*, Nov. 13, 1981. The PLO gives the impression that it is unaware of its public support for the resolution. Spokespersons give various versions of PLO positions over the years, many not very credible.

64. *Towards a New Cold War*, chap. 12; *Fateful Triangle*, chap. 3, esp. nn. 88, 111; *Necessary Illusions*, app. 5.4; *Powers and Prospects*, chap. 7.

65. Rami Tal, "Moshe Dayan: Heshbon Nefesh," *Yediot Ahronot*, April 27, 1997, interview of Nov. 22, 1976. See also n. 60. Dayan, Kapeliouk, op. cit., pp. 29, 279; Beilin, op. cit.

66. Along with other analysts, Dayan recognized that Sadat's intentions in the 1973 war were far more limited, but seemed not to see the implications: that Sadat's actions were an attempt to initiate the diplomatic track that the United States and Israel had blocked.

67. Ariel Sharon, *Yediot Ahronot*, July 26, 1973; radio, Joseph Fitchett, *Christian Science Monitor*, Oct. 27, 1973. "Arabs' game," Amnon Kapeliouk, *Israel: La Fin des mythes*, Albin Michel, Paris, 1975, pp. 200f., 281, a conception he attributes to the "General-Professor Yehoshaphat Harkabi," a Hebrew University Arabist and former head of military intelligence, later a leading dove. Kapeliouk gives many similar quotes from high-ranking military officers and political leaders. See also chapter 4 of this volume.

68. Avner Yaniv, *Dilemmas of Security: Politics, Strategy, and the Israeli Experience in Lebanon*, Oxford University Press, New York, 1987, p. 70.

69. *Jerusalem Post*, Aug. 16, 1981.

70. Cited by William B. Quandt, op. cit., p. 576.

71. Ya'acov Lamdan, "What the PLO and Americans Told One Another," *Jerusalem Post*, Jan. 6, 1989.

72. Meeting with Jewish leaders, released under the Freedom of Information Act. *MERIP Reports*, May 1981; *Journal of Palestine Studies* (Spring 1981). See my *Towards a New Cold War*, 457.

73. UN press release GA/7603, Dec. 7, 1987 (42/159); see my "International Terrorism: Image and Reality," in *Western State Terrorism*, ed. Alexander George; Assistant Secretary of State for Human Rights John Shattuck, cited by Joseph Wronka, *American Society of International Law: Interest Group of the U.N. Decade of International Law*, Feb. 1997, no. 13.

74. Nahum Barnea, *Yediot Ahronot*, Feb. 24, 1989.

75. Israeli Government Election Plan, Jerusalem, May 14, 1989, Embassy of Israel.

76. Military correspondents Michael Gordon and Gen. (ret.) Bernard Trainor, USMC, *New York Times*, Oct. 23, 1994, excerpt from their book *The Generals' War: The Inside Story of the Conflict in the Gulf*, Little, Brown, Boston, 1995.

77. See Chomsky, *Deterring Democracy*, chap. 6, afterword; Hamid Mowlana, George Gerbner, and Herbert Schiller, *Triumph of the Image*, Westview, Boulder, Colo., 1992; Curtis, op. cit. The best general study is Dilip Hiro, *Desert Shield to Desert Storm*, HarperCollins, New York, 1992. Another is Lawrence Freedman and Efraim Karsh, *The Gulf Conflict 1990–1991*, Princeton University Press, Princeton, N.J., 1992. The authors praise themselves for "the scope and originality of our analysis," which uses "evidence from *all* available sources," contrasting their achievement with mere journalism. In reality, they ignore entirely or omit basic sources on major issues (e.g., prewar diplomatic interactions, which, furthermore, they misrepresent in their scanty comments; the views of Iraqi democrats and the population of the region generally; the illuminating record of U.S. and British documents). Even their efforts to present the U.S.–UK effort in the most favorable light conclude that Saddam's goal was not annexation or "a permanent military presence" but "to establish hegemony over Kuwait, ensuring its complete financial, political and strategic subservience to his wishes," much as intended by the United States in Panama and Israel in Lebanon (and achieved, in the former case). Saddam's scheme "turned sour," they say, because of the international reaction; to translate, because of the differential U.S. reaction. The authors seem not to realize that their conclusions undercut the central thesis of their book about the nobility of the U.S.–UK leadership.

78. Rick Atkinson, Ann Debroy, and *Washington Post* staff writers, "Bush: Iraq Won't Decide Timing of Ground War," *Washington Post*, Feb. 2, 1991, p. A1.

79. Thomas L. Friedman, "The World: A Rising Sense That Iraq's Hussein Must Go," *New York Times*, July 7, 1991, sec. 4, p. 1.

80. Quoted by John Pienaar, "Crisis in the Gulf: Arm Rebels, Senior Tory Urges," *The Independent* (London), April 6, 1991, p. 1.

81. For review and sources, see my *Deterring Democracy*, chap. 6 and afterword; *World Orders*, chap. 1; *Powers and Prospects*, chap. 7.

82. David Bar-Illan, director of communications and policy planning in the office of the prime minister, interview with Victor Cygielman, *Palestine–Israel Journal* (Summer/Autumn 1996). Among his other noteworthy observations is that Lebanon "has been able to attack us and make our lives intolerable for more than 15 years," a statement that might not be easy to match in the annals of apologetics for state terrorism.

83. Bill Freund, *The Making of Contemporary Africa*, University of Indiana Press, Bloomington, 1984, p. 270.

84. Asher Davidi, *Davar*, Feb. 17, 1993, trans. Zachary Lockman, *Middle East Report*, Sept.–Oct. 1993.

85. Michael Yudelman, "Labor Government Ready to Take On Labor Unions," *Jerusalem Post*, Nov. 26, 1993. Ya'akov Yona, "The Peace Process as an Obstacle to Employment," *Ma'ariv*, Jan. 19, 1996. On the use of transfer threats to undermine labor organizing, accelerating since the NAFTA agreement with Mexico (illegal, but "tolerated" by the administrations from Reagan through Clinton), see Cornell University labor economist Kate Bronfenbrenner, "We'll Close," *Multinational Monitor*, March 1997, based on the study she directed: "Final Report: The Effects of Plant Closing or Threat of Plant Closing on the Right of Workers to Organize." The study, conducted under NAFTA rules in response to labor complaints of violations (upheld after a long delay but with trivial penalties, as is the norm), was authorized for release by Canada and Mexico but has so far been blocked by Clinton's Labor Department.

86. See Ronen Bergman and David Ratner, "The Man Who Swallowed Gaza," *Ha'aretz Supplement*, April 4, 1997; David Hirst, "Shameless in Gaza," *The Guardian* (London), April 21, 1997; Judy Dempsey, "Poor Pickings in Gaza for Palestinian Entrepreneurs," *Financial Times* (London), May 3/4, 1997, reviewing also Israeli economic sabotage; "The Netanyahu Government Will Pay the PLO about [$1.5 billion] a Year," *Nekuda*, April 1997. David Bedein, "So Much for Promises," *Jerusalem Post*, Feb. 4, 1996.

87. David Gardner, "Gloom over Palestinian Economy: IMF Says Joblessness Has Soared and Per Capita Income Has Fallen since Oslo Accords," *Financial Times* (London), March 7, 1997, p. 4.

88. United Nations Relief and Works Agency (UNRWA), Reuters, *New York Times*, May 27, 1997. Peter Kiernan, *Middle East International*, June 27, 1997.

89. Dayan, Herzog, quoted from internal discussion in Beilin, op. cit., pp. 42, 147.

90. See epilogue, *World Orders Old and New*, citing *Report on Israeli Settlement*, March 1996; Chronology, *Palestine-Israel Journal*, Summer/Autumn 1996. Nadav Shragai, *Ha'aretz*, March 3, 1997. Beilin, quoted by Tikva Honig-Parnass, *News from Within*, April 1997.

91. See epilogue, *World Orders Old and New*.

92. Aluf Ben, *Ha'aretz*, Feb. 7, 1995. For information and background, see Israel Shahak, *Ideology as a Central Factor in Israeli Policies* (in Hebrew), May–June 1995.

93. Farouk Kaddoumi, interview, *Frontline* (India), May 30, 1997, at the Non-Aligned Foreign Ministers Conference in New Delhi. El-Abayad, Embassy of Egypt in Washington, letter, *National Interest*, Summer 1997.

94. Yossi Melman, "Dunam after Dunam Amounts to a Billion," *Yom Rishon*, April 20, 1997.
95. Avi Shlaim, *Collusion across the Jordan*, Columbia University Press, New York, 1988, p. 491, citing Israeli state archives.

Chapter 7

1. Carol Christian, "Sanctions against Iraq Killing Thousands, ex-U.N. Official Says; Protest Tour Stops at Houston Church," *Houston Chronicle*, Feb. 24, 1999, p. A25.
2. *60 Minutes*, May 12, 1996.
3. General Lee Butler, "The Risks of Deterrence: From Superpowers to Rogue Leaders," remarks at the National Press Club, Feb. 2, 1998 (see http://www.cdi.org/issues/armscontrol/butler.html).
4. "Essentials of Post–Cold War Deterrence," 1995. For excerpts, see my *New Military Humanism*, Common Courage Press, Monroe, Maine, 1999, chap. 6.
5. Yoev Appel, "Indyk Expresses US Condemnation of Attack," *Jerusalem Post*, March 5, 2001.
6. For figures, see the tables compiled by B'Tselem (http://www.btselem.org/English/Statistics/Al_Aqsa_Fatalities_Tables.asp) and the Palestinian Red Crescent (http://www.palestinercs.org/crisistables/oct_2002_table.htm).
7. Dave McIntyre, "U.S. Walks Fine Line of Neutrality in Mideast Crisis," *Deutsche Presse-Agentur*, Oct. 3, 2000.
8. See the Amnesty International website, http://www.amnesty.org.
9. Associated Press, "Israel Orders Nine Apache Longbow Helicopters for $500 Million," Feb. 20, 2001. "Israel to Buy Boeing Helicopters," *Wall Street Journal*, Feb. 20, 2001, p. B10. See additional references in my introduction to Roane Carey, ed., *The New Intifada*, Verso, New York, 2001, p. 21n10. Reprinted in Chomsky, *Pirates and Emperors, Old and New: International Terrorism in the Real World*, South End Press, Cambridge, Mass., 2002.
10. Ann Thompson, "Arming Israel . . . ," *News and Observer* (Raleigh, N.C.), Oct. 12, 2000, p. A19.
11. See my *Deterring Democracy*, extended edition, Vintage, Hill & Wang, New York, 1992, pp. 181–82.
12. "Issues Arising out of the Situation in the Near East" July 29, 1958, *Foreign Relations of the United States, 1958–1960*, vol. 12 (*Near East Region; Iraq; Iran; Arabian Peninsula*), U.S. Government Printing Office, Washington, D.C., 1993, pp. 114–24.
13. For references and further details, see my *Towards a New Cold War*, Pantheon, New York, 1982, chap. 7, and *Fateful Triangle: The United States, Israel, and the Palestinians*, updated ed., South End Press, Cambridge, Mass., 1999, chap. 2.

14. David Hoffman, "President Gives Eulogy for 37 Killed in Attack on U.S. Ship; Men Hailed for 'Extraordinary' Acts," *Washington Post,* May 23, 1987, p. A1.

15. Molly Moore and George Wilson, "Captain Saw 'Definite Threat'; Firing at Plane Called Defensive, 'a Burden I Will Carry'," *Washington Post,* July 5, 1988, p. A1.

16. Shlomo Ben-Ami, *Makom Lekulam* [A Place for All], Hakibbutz Hameuchad, Jerusalem, 1987. Cited in Efraim Davidi, "Globalization and Economy in the Middle East—A Peace of Markets or a Peace of Flags?" *Palestine–Israel Journal,* vol. 7, no. 1–2, 2000.

Chapter 8

1. Judy Dempsey, "Barak Warned That Cutting Off Palestinians Could Backfire," *Financial Times* (London), Oct. 21, 2000. Also, Deborah Sontag, "Israel Weighs Plan to Create Borders if Talks Fail," *New York Times,* Oct. 22, 2000, section 1, p. 1.

2. For more on the negotiations and their background, see my "'Peace Process' Prospects," ZNet Commentary, July 27, 2000, online at http://www.zmag.org/chompeacepro.htm; and for further background, see Alex R. Shalom and Stephen R. Shalom, "Turmoil in Palestine: The Basic Context," ZNet Commentary, Oct. 10, 2000, online at http://www.zmag.org/turmoil_in_palestine.htm.

3. See the tables compiled by B'Tselem (http://www.btselem.org/English/Statistics/Al_Aqsa_Fatalities_Tables.asp) and the Palestinian Red Crescent (http://www.palestinercs.org/crisistables/oct_2002_table.htm).

4. Baruch Kimmerling, *Ha'aretz,* Oct. 4, 2000.

5. Amira Hass, "Beaten and Betrayed: Israel Has Reneged on the Oslo Accords with Arafat's Collusion; Palestinians Have Had Enough," *The Guardian* (London), Oct. 3, 2000, p. 21.

6. Dempsey, op. cit.

7. Avi Shlaim, *Collusion across the Jordan: King Abdullah, the Zionist Movement, and the Partition of Palestine,* Columbia University Press, New York, 1988, p. 491, citing the Israeli state archives. For references and further details, see my *Towards a New Cold War,* Pantheon, New York, 1982, chap. 7; *Fateful Triangle: The United States, Israel, and the Palestinians,* updated ed., South End Press, Cambridge, Mass., 1999, chap. 2; and chap. 7, this volume.

8. Amira Hass, *Ha'aretz,* Oct. 18, 2000.

9. Shlomo Tzezna, "The Construction in the Territories Was Frozen, and It Continues," *Ha'aretz,* Aug. 18, 2000.

10. Danny Rubinstein, *Ha'aretz,* Oct. 23, 2000.

11. Amnon Barzilai, *Ha'aretz,* Oct. 3, 2000; Avi Hoffman, "The Colossus of Seattle," *Jerusalem Post,* Oct. 8, 2000.

12. See "Israel and the Occupied Territories," http://www.amnestyusa. org/news/2000/israel10192000_2.html.

13. Associated Press, "U.S. Abstains in Resolution Condemning Use of Force," *New York Times*, Oct. 8, 2000, section 1, p. 10.

14. William A. Orme Jr., "Israelis Criticized for Using Deadly Force Too Readily," *New York Times*, Oct. 4, 2000, p. A20.

15. Quoted by Judy Dempsey, "Palestinians Count Human Cost of the Violence," *Financial Times* (London), Oct. 6, 2000.

16. Quoted in Dave McIntyre, "U.S. Walks Fine Line of Neutrality in Mideast Crisis," *Deutsche Presse-Agentur*, Oct. 3, 2000.

17. See Noam Chomsky, *A New Generation Draws the Line: Kosovo, East Timor and the Standards of the West*, Verso, New York, 2000.

18. "Israel Must End the Hatred Now: A True Palestinian State is Essential," *Observer* (London), Oct. 15, 2000, p. 28.

Chapter 9

1. Baruch Kimmerling, "Preparing for the War of His Choosing," *Ha'aretz*, July 12, 2001. Available online at http://www.palestinemonitor. org/israelipoli/preparing_for_the_war_of_his_cho.htm.

2. Ze'ev Sternhell, "Balata Has Fallen," *Ha'aretz*, March 7, 2002.

3. Shlomo Ben-Ami, *Makom Lekulam* [A Place for All], Hakibbutz Hameuchad, Jerusalem, 1987. Cited in Efraim Davidi, "Globalization and Economy in the Middle East—A Peace of Markets or a Peace of Flags?" *Palestine–Israel Journal*, vol. 7, nos. 1–2 (2002).

4. Kimmerling, op. cit.

5. "Moving Past War in the Middle East," *New York Times*, April 7, 2002.

6. Text of a peace initiative authorized by the government of Israel on 15 May 1989 (the Peres–Shamir coalition plan, endorsed by the first President Bush in the Baker plan of December 1989). See my *World Orders Old and New*, Columbia University Press, New York, 1999, pp. 231–2 for an informal translation of this peace initiative; see also http://domino.un.org/ UNISPAL.NSF/bdd57d15a29f428d85256c3800701fc4/2fa32a5884d90dc9 85256282007942fa!OpenDocument.

7. John Donnelly and Charles A. Radin, "Powell's Trip Is Called a Way to Buy Time for Sharon Sweep," *Boston Globe*, April 9, 2002, p. A1.

8. See my *Fateful Triangle: The United States, Israel, and the Palestinians*, updated ed., South End Press, Cambridge, Mass., 1999, p. 75.

9. Patrick E. Tyler, "Arab Ministers Announce Support for Arafat," *New York Times*, April 7, 2002, section 1, p. 17; Agence France-Presse, "Israeli Troops Keep Up Offensive as Powell Starts Regional Tour," April 8, 2002; Toby Harnden, "It Is When, Not If, the Withdrawal Will Start,"

Daily Telegraph (London), April 8, 2002; Robert Fisk, "Mr. Powell Must See for Himself What Israel Inflicted on Jenin," *The Independent* (London), April 14, 2002, p. 25.

10. Melissa Radler, "UN Security Council Endorses Vision of Palestinian State," *Jerusalem Post*, March 14, 2002.

11. See chap. 8 and, for more details, my introduction to Roane Carey, ed., *The New Intifada*, Verso, New York, 2001. Reprinted in Chomsky, *Pirates and Emperors, Old and New: International Terrorism in the Real World*, South End Press, Cambridge, Mass., 2002.

12. Fiona Fleck, "114 States Condemn Israelis," *Daily Telegraph* (London), Dec. 6, 2001; Herb Keinon, "Geneva Parley Delegates Blast Israel," *Jerusalem Post*, Dec. 6, 2001.

13. Graham Usher, "Ending the Phony Cease-Fire," *Middle East International*, Jan. 25, 2002, p. 4.

14. Geoffrey Aronson, ed., *Report on Israeli Settlements in the Occupied Territories* (Foundation for Middle East Peace), vol. 12, no. 1, Jan.–Feb. 2002; Ian Williams, *Middle East International*, Dec. 21, 2001; Judy Dempsey and Frances Williams, "EU Seeks to Reassert Mideast Influence," *Financial Times* (London), Dec. 6, 2001, p. 7.

15. Francis A. Boyle, "Law and Disorder in the Middle East," *The Link* (Americans for Middle East Understanding), vol. 35, no. 1, Jan.–March 2002, pp. 1–13. (Full text available online at http://www.ameu.org/uploads/vol35_issue1_2002.pdf.)

Chapter 10

1. Associated Press, Oct. 17, 1985 (Reagan); Associated Press, Oct. 25, 1984 (Shultz). See also Shultz, U.S. Dept. of State, *Current Policy*, no. 589, June 24, 1984; Shultz, U.S. Dept. of State, *Current Policy*, no. 629, Oct. 25, 1984.

2. David K. Shipler, "Shultz Assails Nicaragua in Asking Aid for Rebels," *New York Times*, Feb. 28, 1986, p. A6. Testimony to the Senate Foreign Relations Committee, Feb. 27, 1986.

3. "Shultz Denounces Nicaragua and Says It Endangers U.S.," *New York Times*, Aug. 5, 1988, p. A5, drawing on Associated Press reports from Aug. 4, 1988.

4. John Hanna, "Shultz Blasts Critics, Calls Nicaragua a 'Cancer,'" Associated Press, April 14, 1986. See also United Press International, Report of Shultz's April 14, 1986, speech at Kansas State University. See also Shultz, "Moral Principles and Strategic Interests," U.S. Dept. of State, *Current Policy*, no. 8201, April 14, 1986. On Shultz's congressional testimony, see Jack Spence's chapter in *Reagan versus the Sandinistas*, ed. Thomas Walker, Westview Press, Boulder, 1987.

5. *U.S. Army Operational Concept for Terrorism Counteraction*, TRADOC Pamphlet no. 525–37, 1984.

6. Michael R. Gordon, "Allies Preparing for a Long Fight as Taliban Dig In," *New York Times*, Oct. 28, 2001, section 1A, p. 1.

7. *Jerusalem Post*, Aug. 16, 1981; see also Chomsky, *Fateful Triangle: The United States, Israel, and the Palestinians*, updated ed., South End Press, Cambridge, Mass., 1999, chap. 5, sections 1, 3, 4, for further quotes, background, and description.

8. See Chomsky, *Pirates and Emperors, Old and New: International Terrorism in the Real World*, South End Press, Cambridge, Mass., 2002, pp. 39–40.

9. Bernard Gwertzman, "U.S. Defends Action in U.N. on Raid," *New York Times*, Oct. 7, 1985, p. A3; Elaine Sciolino, "U.N. Body Assails Israeli Air Strike," *New York Times*, Oct. 5, 1985, p. 1.

10. Bernard Weinraub, "Israeli Extends 'Hand of Peace' to Jordanians," *New York Times*, Oct. 18, 1985, p. A1.

11. Roland de Ligny, "World Court Denounces U.S. Support for Contras," Associated Press, June 27, 1986.

12. See Chomsky, *Deterring Democracy*, extended edition, Vintage, Hill & Wang, New York, 1992, pp. 315–16.

13. "Report to the President on Latin American Mission," March 10, 1961, *Foreign Relations of the United States, 1961–1963*, vol. 12 (*The American Republics*), U.S. Government Printing Office, Washington, D.C., 1996, Record No. 7, p. 13; "United States Policy Toward Latin America," July 3, 1961, *Foreign Relations of the United States, 1961–1963*, vol. 12 (*The American Republics*), U.S. Government Printing Office, Washington, D.C., 1996, Record No. 15, p. 33.

14. "Report to the President on Latin American Mission," March 10, 1961, p. 13.

15. Ricardo Stevens on Radio La Voz del Trópico (Panama), Oct. 19, 2001. Reprinted in "The Americas React to Terror," NACLA *Report on the Americas*, vol. 35, no. 3 (Nov.–Dec. 2001).

16. Eduardo Galeano, in *La Jornada* (Mexico), quoted in Alain Frachon, "America Unloved," *World Press Review*, vol. 48, no. 12, Dec. 2001, and Alain Frachon, *Le Monde*, Nov. 24, 2001.

17. *Envío*, Universidad Centroamericana, Managua, Nicaragua, Oct. 2001.

18. Richard Cole, "Costa Rica Asks U.S. to Extradite Iran-Contra Figure in Bombing Deaths," Associated Press, April 26, 1991.

19. Associated Press, "Aristide, in 3rd Term, Marks 1991 Ouster," *New York Times*, Oct. 1, 2001, p. A10.

20. For sources and background discussion, see Chomsky, *World Orders Old and New*, updated ed., Columbia University Press, New York, 1996 pp. 79, 201ff.

21. For sources and background discussion, see Chomsky, *Year 501*, South End, Boston, 1993, p. 39.

22. National Security Council Memorandum 5801/1, "Statement by the National Security Council of Long-Range U.S. Policy toward the Near East," Jan. 24, 1958, *Foreign Relations of the United States, 1958–1960*, vol. 12 (*Near East Region; Iraq; Iran; Arabian Peninsula*), U.S. Government Printing Office, Washington, D.C., 1993, pp. 17–32.

23. Peter Waldman et al., "The Moneyed Muslims Behind the Terror," *Wall Street Journal*, Sept. 14, 2001, p. A6; Peter Waldman and Hugh Pope, "Worlds Apart: Some Muslims Fear War on Terrorism Is Really a War on Them," *Wall Street Journal*, Sept. 21, 2001, p. A1.

24. Michael Howard, "Mistake to Declare this a 'War,'" *The London Evening Standard* (online edition), Oct. 31, 2001 (http://www.fpp.co.uk/online/01/11/WTC_MichaelHoward.html).

Index

About the Author

Noam Chomsky, Professor in the Department of Linguistics and Philosophy at MIT, is a world-renowned linguist, philosopher, and political analyst. He writes extensively and lectures around the world on international affairs, U.S. foreign policy, and human rights.

Chomsky's 1957 book *Syntactic Structures* is widely credited with having revolutionized the field of modern linguistics. Chomsky is the author of numerous best-selling political works. His latest books are *9–11* (Seven Stories Press), *Rogue States* (South End Press), *Understanding Power* (New Press), *The Minimalist Program* (MIT), and *New Horizons in the Study of Language and Mind* (Cambridge University Press). The *New York Times* has called Chomsky "an exploder of received truths."

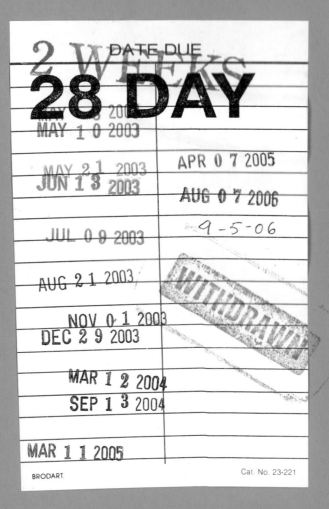